Who
Needs
A Road?

who needs a road?

The Story of the Trans World
Record Expedition by Harold Stephens
and Albert Podell

with maps by Van Beverly

THE BOBBS-MERRILL COMPANY, INC.
A Subsidiary of Howard W. Sams & Co., Inc., Publishers
Indianapolis • Kansas City • New York

To Lord Jim
and
to Sandy Krinski—
and
to all the Lord Jim's
and
all the Sandy Krinski's
of the world.

All the events in this book actually took place, and all the people are real people, though several names have been changed. The book is narrated in the voice of Mr. Stephens, but both authors shared equally in its writing.

Contents:

Illustrations

Maps drawn by Van Beverly

Photographs taken by the authors during the expedition will be found in four sections following pages 152, 216, 280, and 296.

Material in this book has previously appeared in the New York Times, Bangkok World, Washington Post, U.S. Camera, the Khyber Mail, Camping Journal, Bow and Arrow, and Public Relations Quarterly and is reprinted here with their permission. All photos are by Albert Podell unless otherwise credited.

Chapter 1
The End

We are in a cellar in Dacca. We know no one; we are strangers in the city. Air-raid sirens are howling. The skies echo with the drumming of approaching warplanes, and we listen for the bombs to fall. Outside, vigilantes are marching through the streets with sticks, beating on the gates. They have armed themselves to defend their sacred Pakistan, which has just gone to war with India. There is hysteria throughout the city. The people race through the streets, destroying alien property, pulling foreigners from their cars. A woman is dragged from her car and beaten. The USIS library is smashed.

We have entered the cellar by a narrow stairway from the house. Other steps lead to a door outside, but it is boarded up now and only admits the sounds from the street: "Americans are no longer our friends." "You have armed India against us." The walls are moist, and when we lean against them our clothes stick to the bricks. There are benches against the walls, and we sit on them, tense and disillusioned. The only light comes from a gas lantern hung from the rafters.

The cellar has become our refuge—and our prison. We cannot leave, for they know that we have come from their enemy, India. And they have seen us taking pictures inside their Defense Ministry. We have been interrogated twice already, and threatened. A car from the Pakistan secret police follows us wherever we go.

But even if we could leave, there is no place to go, for Dacca is cut off from the rest of East Pakistan, and East Pakistan is cut off from the world. No planes are flying—only warplanes—and the harbors are all blockaded. We have a car, a car that we have driven half-way around the world to Dacca, but the roads are flooded by the monsoon rains. There are no bridges across the swollen rivers of East

1

Pakistan, only ferries, and the Army has confiscated them all. So even if we did escape the cellar and the city, we could not drive more than ten miles before being blocked by an uncrossable river. We have tried and we know. And if we could cross? There is still no escape, still no place to go, no near safe haven. To the east there is Burma, whose borders have been sealed for years. Foreigners are forbidden to enter. To the south there is only the Bay of Bengal, blockaded. To the north, Red China, and Indian Assam where the border has become a battle-field. And to the west there is invading India, from which we have just come, but to which we cannot return. We can only listen to her bombers overhead as the air-raid sirens wail.

Is this, we wonder, the finish for us and our expedition that set out to challenge the world? Is this, after all the revolutions and robberies survived, all the sicknesses and delays overcome, all the breakdowns and near-disasters weathered, is this the end of the road?

Was our friend Lord Jim wrong when he said, "Who needs a road?" Was Krinski right, Krinski and the others who said it was impossible, a long time before, back when it all began . . .

Chapter 2

The Beginning

It began on a gray December day in New York. I was sitting in the offices of *Argosy,* overlooking the dismal winter scene twenty floors below. The magazine was publishing the story of my trip across Russia, and Al Podell, the picture editor, had just finished going over the layout with me.

Al asked what I planned next.

"Another auto trip," I said. "This time completely around the world."

I saw him looking at me strangely.

"After Europe," I remember explaining, "I'll cut across the top of Africa, camp in the desert, share meals with roving bands of nomads. Then Cairo. I'll pitch camp in the shadow of the Pyramids, cooled by the evening breeze off the Nile . . . the Great Salt Desert of Persia . . . mosques and minarets . . . Baghdad . . . wilds of Afghanistan . . . the twists and bends of the Khyber Pass where the Mongols and British fought and where fierce Pathan warriors still roam unchallenged . . . two weeks later bathe in the Ganges . . . two more weeks and I'll be climbing the Himalayas . . . then the jungles of Thailand, camp at the edge of a forest pool where elephants and tigers drink together . . ."

I rambled on about Tangier and Tahiti, Calcutta and Kathmandu, Bangkok and Singapore, sights that I had seen and others that I longed to see. A faraway look came into Al's eyes, a look I had seen many times on the faces of those to whom I spoke of my adventures. The words that followed were also familiar.

"I wish I could go with you."

People had often asked if they could accompany me. There's something magic about the name Tahiti or the vision of a white sail upon

3

the sea. Call it romance or a dream, or anything you like, but it awakens in every man at the wail of a train in the night or the blast of an ocean liner leaving port. Somewhere beyond the horizon lies romance, and every heart yearns to find it.

The world opened to me when I was a young boy on a farm in Pennsylvania. It opened with books of adventure and travel, for those were the golden days when a young reporter named Lowell Thomas wrote about exotic places like Timbuktu and Kathmandu, and Richard Halliburton crossed the Alps on an elephant and swam the Bosporus. To me, these places and the lives these men led spelled romance. But when the real world came leaping at me, it was like the earth coming up to meet a skydiver. There was no casual introduction; it came up suddenly—with World War II.

I left high school to enlist in the Marines, and at seventeen sailed west to find romance. My ocean liner was a troop ship and my Shangri-La was the shell-torn island of Okinawa. When the fighting ended, the Marines sent me to Peking, and I discovered the cruel world that was post-war China. But somehow I couldn't accept the idea that romance was dead. I went to Paris with the U.S. naval attaché and there decided upon a diplomatic career. I went to Washington, took my discharge, was graduated from Georgetown University, and spent the next few years in government service. But the dreams that colored my childhood could not be forgotten, and armed with nothing but the wish to discover the world's ends, I set forth.

During the next decade the world became my backyard. When I had to, I taught school, but I much preferred other kinds of work——surveying the Choco Jungles of Colombia, culling the deer herd in the Ureweras of New Zealand, crewing on copra schooners across the Pacific. I crossed Afghanistan by camel caravan and hunted kangaroo for their hides in Australia. In a very deep sense, I got to know and love the world.

After circling the globe four times, I realized that no matter how I had traveled, whether by ship or bus or train or plane, there was always something lacking. I concluded that there was only one way to see the world, and that was to drive, to be free from flight schedules and familiar routes. I wanted to get to the world's heart, far off the tourist track, to the untouched villages, the nomad camps, the jungle ruins. I wanted to really get to know it, and if this meant following caravan routes long forgotten, traversing trackless deserts, crossing lofty mountain passes and fording unbridged rivers——I wanted to try it.

After driving a Jeep 18,000 miles across Europe and the Soviet Union, I knew I was right. I decided to drive completely around the world. The only thing standing in my way, as I was explaining to Al Podell, was $20,000.

"Twenty thousand dollars! Where you going to get it?" Al asked.

"You're buying the story, aren't you?"

"What about the other $19,000?"

"I'll try to work something out," I said.

"I know some people who might be interested in helping you. I'll call them and let you know."

Al didn't mention again that he wanted to go with me, and I once more realized it is not within the realm of possibility for all men to cast off their jobs and homes and fortunes-to-be-made and turn to adventure and the unknown, except in dreams. But dreams are what men are made of. Two weeks later in California I had a long distance call from New York. When I heard Al's voice over the wire I knew he had passed beyond dreaming. "Steve, listen. I want to go with you."

Now I hoped he hadn't passed too far. I emphasized that the trip would have hardships as well as grandeur, that a breakdown in the desert could mean disaster, that bandits still roamed the mountain passes in Afghanistan, that there would be thirst and hunger and the possibility of epidemic and disease in India and the Far East. Al listened quietly, and after I finished, he said he still wanted to go. "You know, I've been at *Argosy* four years," he said, "and I've met just about every adventurer in the business. They all come to me with their stories and plans. Guys want to go by bicycle from Capetown to Cairo, to dog-sled across America, to go pogo-sticking up the Amazon, even to drive around the world. But I've never been tempted to go with any of them."

In a sense I could understand why he never had been tempted. Al was the youngest picture editor of any major magazine in America, and ran several prosperous trade newspapers in his spare time. His apartment on East 55th Street was a luxurious four-room bachelor's layout with palm trees and oil paintings and colored lights where he entertained some of the prettiest models and actresses in New York. You might say that Al had everything a young man could want, so why should he be tempted when I talked about the blazing heat of the Great Syrian Desert?

"It's your enthusiasm, Steve. It's contagious. You make the world sound more exciting than anyone I've ever met. You've convinced me that I've got to see what it's really like. I want to go with you."

"Well, I hope you like to drive."

"Drive is right," Al said. "Did you know your route would be the longest automobile trip ever made around the earth?"

Later, back in New York, I studied the accounts that Al had gathered of past trans-world expeditions. He noted that they had traveled between 19,000 and 21,000 miles by land, and all had gone by one of two routes. The expeditions in the early part of the century, including the great race of 1908, had all crossed the width of the United States and driven through Manchuria, China and Russia to France. After World War II and the descent of the Iron and Bamboo Curtains, this route became impossible. In the twenty years since then, only two expeditions had been able to drive completely around the world: the Oxford-Cambridge group in 1955, and Peter Townsend the year after. They had angled down from France through Greece and Turkey, driven on to India and Southeast Asia, and from there shipped directly to the United States. In all cases, the non-repetitive mileage (eliminating sidetrips, backtracking, indirect routing and city travel) never exceeded 21,000. The route I had chosen would, Al pointed out, better all past marks by 3,000 miles and set a record for the longest non-repetitive automobile trip ever made around the earth.

My proposed route would abandon the tourist shortcut through Greece and Turkey. Instead we would drive across all of North Africa from Tangier to Cairo, through the Sinai Peninsula into the Middle

East and India, all the way to Singapore. Then, instead of shipping to
California as previous expeditions had done, we would continue our
drive. We would cross Indonesia, hopefully as far as Bali, next ship to
Australia and drive across it, then ship to Panama and from there drive
back to New York through Central America. Our non-repetitive mileage would be approximately 24,000 miles, a new, clear, and unbreakable record. Optimistically, we decided to call ourselves the Trans
World Record Expedition.

The opportunity to set a record particularly pleased Al, who, as an
editor, was friendly with most of the major public relations agencies
and was certain they'd be willing to help us if we had a good peg—as
he told me they say on Madison Avenue—to hang the trip on. An
attempt to set a record for the longest auto journey around the world
was ideal. All I could do was hope that he was right and cross my
fingers, for we still needed a new car and a ton of equipment and
thousands of dollars to make the trip.

The biggest problem was an automobile. I had an old Jeep in Spain,
but there was only a slim chance that it would make it around the
world without breaking down. Nor could we rely on any standard
automobile or truck. Because of the extremely rough terrain we
planned to cross, we had to have a rugged four-wheel drive vehicle.
From experience I preferred the Toyota Land Cruiser. As it turned out,
Al had worked on several projects with Chief Samuelson, Toyota's
public relations man, and was certain he'd lend us a receptive ear if
anyone would. Al wrote Samuelson and offered to test one of his Land
Cruisers on the world's roughest roads on the world's longest auto trip,
and to furnish him with performance reports and pictures that he
could use in his publicity and advertising campaigns.

Samuelson bought our idea. It fitted perfectly with Toyota's slogan
that the Land Cruiser could "Go Anywhere." Not only did his client
agree to give us a new Land Cruiser and complete spare parts, but
they also promised to ship us several thousand dollars' worth of color
movie film to record the trip.

In the meantime, I had approached Carl Dretzke, an old friend and
president of Trade Wind Campers, a large camper-trailer manufacturer in Manawa, Wisconsin. A camper-trailer is a big box on wheels

hauled behind a car. It can carry and store a thousand pounds of gear, and can be opened up in five minutes into a canvas house that sleeps about six. When I told Dretzke that we planned to circle the globe with a camper, something no one had ever done, he immediately agreed to give us one. I flew to the Trade Winds factory, where, with half of Manawa (pop. 1037) in attendance, Dretzke presented me with his biggest model right off the assembly line; then Manawa's mayor, George Jensen, gave me a three-foot long, gold-painted plywood key to the city (which came in handy on a cold night in the Himalayas).

Once we had our car and trailer set, the rest of the sponsors came quickly. After writing 300 letters, making 500 phone calls, and planting several articles in industry trade papers, Al had 25 sponsors, all of whom gave us equipment we needed and publicity fees which ranged from a few hundred to a few thousand dollars.

Nearly all our requirements were filled: the Firestone Tire and Rubber Company offered to equip our Land Cruiser with a set of high-flotation tires especially designed for use in mud, snow, and on rough roads. The Thermos Division of King-Seeley loaded us up with picnic chests, gasoline stoves, lanterns, vacuum bottles and two fast-erecting Poptents. The Creslan Division of American Cyanamid agreed to outfit us with raincoats, jackets, sports shirts, knit shirts, insulated underwear, regular underwear, socks, gloves and trousers. Sandy Teller, the PR man for The Hat Corporation of America, insisted we take cowboy hats and tropical hats, safari hats and rain hats, cold weather hats and desert hats, even a top hat. The PR man for Thom McAn gave us 44 pairs of shoes, "everything but the brake shoes," he joked.

Elgin weighed in with a dozen wrist watches, two auto clocks and a shortwave radio. Union Carbide supplied four cartons of Eveready batteries, seven flashlights and lanterns, eight cases of Glad Wrap, and 100 aerosol cans of everything from shave cream to dog repellent to an insultingly large supply of deodorant. The Ben Pearson Company sent five hunting bows and 100 arrows, plus quivers, repair kits, and a big straw target. Johnson's Wax sent twenty cases of insect repellent, insecticide, disinfectant, car wax, and shoe polish.

Sea and Ski provided sunglasses and suntan oils; Lampette sent portable high-intensity lamps that worked from the auto cigarette lighter socket; Dow Chemical filled our Land Cruiser's radiator with anti-freeze and desert coolant; Dow-Corning gave special chemicals to keep the car engine dry and functioning in the monsoon climates; Globe Rubber furnished floor mats and mudguards; and Macmillan Ring-Free Oil undercoated the car and agreed to supply us with motor oil, grease, and conditioners around the world; Niagara Company sent a portable automobile massager that could relax the driver or keep him awake, and Honeywell added three Pentax cameras. And there was more: a complete set of pots and pans, a year's supply of paper cups and plates, four Scotchply fishing rods, six Zebco reels, an assortment of tapes from recording to electrical, and even cigarette lighters that worked from solar energy.

We had sponsors for almost everything we needed, although a few companies turned us down. The toilet tissue manufacturers, for example, rejected our proposal when Al was unable to come up with an acceptable shooting script for the pictures and movies we offered to take of their products being used in a variety of exotic locations.

In the end, we had more than $10,000 worth of equipment and supplies, and $15,000 in cash from 25 sponsors, all in exchange for publicity rights to our names, pictures, and testimonials.

Several companies, declining sponsorship, still sent samples of their products. Upjohn, figuring that we wouldn't be eating too well, sent three thousand vitamin pills. Johnson & Johnson, knowing we'd be doing some hard traveling, sent a first aid pouch and a snake-bite kit, and a note expressing the hope that we didn't have to use either. Allied Chemical showed both its charity and pessimism with a set of inflatable splints. And Travelers Insurance Company, after rejecting our application for a policy, sent us a half dozen of their famous red umbrellas. God knows what they thought.

Between the corporate givings and misgivings, we were fully equipped and bankrolled. In fact, I'm sure that few private expeditions in history have been so completely outfitted.

After carefully studying the seasons and weather conditions along our route, I determined that we should sail before the end of March. I booked us on the *Queen Elizabeth*, which sailed for Cherbourg on March 24th. That left us less than a month to prepare.

While Al worked with the sponsors, I attended to the dozens of details necessary for getting a trans-world expedition on the road. On the front of the Land Cruiser, I installed a powerful Ramsey winch in case we had to haul ourselves out of a ditch or up a cliff. I put locks on the hood and gas tank to prevent pilferage, and welded a ball hitch to the rear of the vehicle for connecting the camper. Bill Mitchell of Toyota helped me install Warn Hubs on the front wheels, special devices which would enable us to disengage the front axle on smooth roads to conserve gasoline. I then drove the Land Cruiser to Washington to break it in, and there attended to two important matters. At the American Automobile Association, after putting up a $2,000 bond, I was issued a *carnet du passage,* a document without which international automobile travel is almost impossible; it guarantees to foreign countries that the owner of the automobile entering that country will not attempt to sell this car there in violation of their import taxes.

The other matter was Burma, the big question mark on our trip. Since its takeover by General Ne Win, Burma has severed her connections with the rest of the world, but so quietly that few are aware of it—the few who try to get in. She has forbidden travel and thwarted tourists, and she has not allowed anyone to drive across her in years. I applied for permission at the Burmese Embassy and was told they would process my request and give me an answer in New Delhi.

By the time I returned to New York, Al's apartment looked like a warehouse. Where the thick carpets had been and where the colored lights once glowed, now crates and cartons and boxes were piled to the ceiling. Where the palm trees once stood, now fishing poles and archery bows and my three-foot key to Manawa leaned against the walls. A striped awning stretched between the couch and the loaded rocking chair. There wasn't a seat in the place left for sitting, and when I went to hang my coat in the jam-packed closet I got hit with 44 pairs of Thom McAn's—maybe even the brake shoes.

Al was busy in his living room testing out the Poptent and repacking the first aid kit. Thermos bottles floated in the bathtub beside the neglected palm trees. Lampettes were plugged into all the light sockets, and the shortwave set was picking up belly dance music from Baghdad. When I asked Al for a cup of coffee, he told me to use the gasoline stove he was testing in the bedroom. "Then come back here when you're finished," he said. "I want to try these inflatable splints on you."

All through this the doorbell and phone never stopped ringing—sponsors, press agents, newspapermen, and people who wanted to join the expedition.

The building superintendent barged in without knocking and bore down on me. "You've blocked the entrance with that Jeep and that damn big whatever it is," he said.

"Yes, yes, I was just going to move it."

"And tell Mr. Podell that he's blocked the incinerator chute again."

When I got back from moving the car and camper, Sandy Krinski was climbing over a mound of boxes into the apartment. Krinski is a comedy writer and old friend of Al's, and when Al told him he was planning to drive around the world he said it was the funniest joke he'd heard all year. He had rushed over to talk him out of it.

"Tell me," he asked, "is Al really serious about this trip?"

"Why shouldn't he be?"

"But you can't go around the world."

"Magellan did it 400 years ago."

"Yeah, and he died, didn't he? Besides, look at this ridiculous itinerary of yours. How are you going to cross all those deserts? You'll fry up. And what about the monsoons and snowstorms?"

I explained to Krinski that we'd taken all that into consideration, that by sailing at the end of March we should be through the Pyrenees as soon as the snows melted in the mountain passes, and across the deserts of Africa in early May before they got too hot, and through India just before the monsoon hit in June.

But Krinski was not convinced. "Listen, Al," he said, "I've known you since we were kids. Don't do it. You can't drive around the world these days. Come on, it's a gag, isn't it?"

"I'm not the gag man, Sandy, and we are driving around the world."

"But it's impossible. I'll bet you never make it."

"How about two steak dinners?" Al asked.

"OK. But if you guys try this, I'll never collect."

"I know you won't," Al said. "We will."

Two busy days passed before we saw Krinski again. He came into the apartment waving a sheet of paper and beaming victoriously. "Ah ha!" he said, pointing to the bows in the corner. "A lot of good those will do you. You'll need machine guns. A company of Marines! The whole U.S. Army! Just listen to this news."

He tossed his coat over a carton of bug spray and unfolded his paper. "Yesterday there were big riots in Morocco, 25 killed and hundreds injured. Algeria has begun a new propaganda campaign against the United States. The rest of the Arab world is the worst since the Suez crisis. Why? Germany has announced plans to recognize Israel and everybody's in an uproar. There were riots in Damascus, Yemen, Cairo, all over. Farther east, Pakistan's president—remember, our old ally?—is now in Peking, making some sort of deal with the Reds. And Vietnam—shall I take the dinner now or go on?"

"Go on," we said.

"Okay. Vietnam. We've already got 23,000 military advisers there. Another 3,000 shipping out this month. And there's talk it may become a full-scale war. A lot of good your bow and arrows will do you. And Indonesia. Forget about wearing those straw hats on Bali—did you know that yesterday mobs in Jakarta sacked our embassy and broke into our ambassador's house? And they burned the USIS library. At the same time Sukarno stepped up his campaign against Malaysia. You're supposed to drive from Bangkok to Singapore? Well, Sukarno's got guerrillas all over that road, blowing up bridges and shooting up cars.

"One of the papers totaled it all up. There's open warfare in 35 countries in the world right now and 38 million men under arms. And, what's more important, *there are major disturbances in 29 of the 34 countries along your route.* I'd like my steaks well-done."

"And we'll take ours rare, Sandy, because we're going to make it."

Sandy Krinski wasn't the only one who thought we'd never make it. When Al approached the photographers who worked for him at *Argosy*, looking for someone to join the expedition to take photos for our sponsors and magazine articles, none of them were willing to leave security for the uncertainty of the open road.

We could be our own photographers, but to capture the real essence of the expedition, we needed someone whose only function would be to take pictures. On my trip across Russia, I'd picked up an energetic Swiss photographer, Willy Mettler. I knew Willy was now footloose in Madrid, and I knew he'd be interested in our expedition, so I cabled him. Three days later he accepted.

We had two weeks left. It was time to attend to one of the most important items on our list, and one we had deliberately left for last, obtaining visas. With the exception of the European countries, nearly every nation on our route required visas. Most of them have expiration dates, so if one gets them too far in advance they can expire before he ever reaches his destination. On the other hand, I knew that it was risky to wait until we were next to a country before applying, because neighboring nations were often enemies, and there might be no visa office in the country in which we found ourselves that represented the one to which we wanted to go.

Al, who is Jewish, was worried about getting visas for the Arab nations since the more fanatic ones absolutely forbid Jews to enter. He applied to the Arab consulates on Ash Wednesday, a smudge of charcoal prominent on his forehead. Not only did he get all his visas, but later that evening I found him at his apartment cuddled on the couch with the receptionist from the Jordanian legation.

The phone was ringing as I entered. It was Woodrow Keck, a reporter at a small Mid-Western paper. Two weeks before he'd driven through a snowstorm from Illinois to Washington to ask me if he could join the expedition. I'd told him then I didn't really think we needed an extra man. He persisted. Though he didn't look like the adventurous type, he was so sincere and eager that I'd agreed to let him call me later in New York to see if we had any openings. I hadn't quite forgotten about him, for I had come to realize that with another person to handle the minor details we would have more freedom for our own duties. Despite a few misgivings, when I saw that he was still eager, I told him he could join the expedition.

"I only hope you know what you're getting into," I said. He assured me he did, and agreed to join us in New York the day before departure.

The week before we left, Al dragged me around to picture agents who wanted to market our photos, magazine editors who wanted to buy our stories, and sponsors who wanted to discuss our assignments. Most of the sponsors were reasonable, but a few of them came up with some weird projects. The public relations man on the Sea and Ski account shoved 500 mimeographed questionnaires into my hand and told me to "make a survey of what the natives use for suntan oil along your route. Also what brand of sunglasses they wear."

The press agent for Creslan fibres asked us to take pictures (to illustrate the wash-and-wearability of the clothes she had given us) whenever we came to a photogenic waterhole. "Especially the ones with crocodiles and elephants and interesting things like that," she added.

But perhaps the wildest ideas of all came from Jane Kohler, the cute young publicity director of the Elgin National Watch Company. Jane wanted us to submerge our hands in snow to show how well her watches resisted the cold, and later reach into our campfire to show how well they resisted the heat. Then she wanted us to get ourselves lost "in the middle of some big desert" and find our way out with an Elgin wrist watch as a compass, using a Girl Scout technique she said she'd show us.

Her last idea was for some photos of us in New Guinea (which wasn't even on our route), getting some shrunken heads (which they don't have there) from some savage natives (which they certainly *do* have there), in exchange for one of her watches. "Those savage tribesmen are fascinated by little mechanical things," she assured us with the authority of a *National Geographic* regular. "We'd like some good meaty pictures and movies of them threatening you with their spears until you make friends by giving them your wrist watches and one of our nice dashboard alarm clocks. Then ask the savages to give you a shrunken head in return. And then ship the head back to us. It will make a real eye-catching display."

"That's ridiculous," I said to Al when Jane had left the room for a minute. "We can't go through with that contract."

"It does have weak points, doesn't it?" he admitted. "I'm worried about that shrunken head bit. How do we figure out its declared value for import duties?"

"Shrunken heads, suntan surveys, crocodile holes . . ." I muttered.

"Bourbon," Al said.

"Bourbon?" I said, forgetting the head hunters.

"That's right. We have an appointment over at the Bourbon Institute. "I've arranged for them to ship cases to us all around the world."

Jim Beam in Paris . . . Old Granddad in Madrid . . . I.W. Harper in Singapore . . . What a life!

The three days before departure were the most frantic, and no matter how thoroughly we thought we had planned, there remained things to be done: cables to be answered, addresses to be changed, bank accounts to be closed, bank accounts to be opened, more vaccinations, shipping forms filled out, tickets picked up, traveler's checks bought, equipment boxed, forwarding addresses distributed, and, of course, sponsors to be humored. The hours were not long enough, and Al and I worked through the nights. On the morning of the day before our departure I'd barely gotten to sleep when the phone rang. I fumbled for the receiver.

"Schistosomiasis," the voice on the phone shouted at me.

"You must have the wrong number," I answered, and was about to hang up.

"No, no. Schistosomiasis. It's me, Krinski."

"Krinski? Good God, man, it's six o'clock in the morning."

"I know. I know. But I had to read this to you. I wrote the AMA and told them about your trip and they sent me a list of all the diseases you and Al can get. Just listen to this: schistosomiasis, trachoma, typhoid fever, malaria, phlebotomus fever, amabiasis, filariasis, fasciolopsiasis, encephalitis, smallpox, yellow fever, clonorchiasis——"

I hung up. I was asleep less than an hour when the door bell rang. I stumbled to it and a Western Union boy shoved a yellow envelope in my hand. It was a cable from Madrid:

MEET YOU IN CHERBOURG. BON VOYAGE. WILLY.

I was happy Willy Mettler had gotten my letter about our arrival date and could meet us, but I was even happier to get back to bed. I'd been there only a few minutes when Al came dashing in waving a special delivery letter.

"It came. It came," he shouted. "Operation Termite is on the move."

It was the first I'd heard of Operation Termite, Al's plan for getting us into Burma. It seems Al had convinced a curator at the American Museum of Natural History that he was a proficient, although amateur, entomologist. The letter was from the curator, authorizing us to collect termites on our expedition around the world, and especially in Burma, where the museum's collection was weak. In truth, Al didn't know a termite from a piece of fried zucchini, and I hoped the Burmese didn't either.

I also hoped I could get some sleep, but in ten minutes Al was poking me awake. He told me to have the car polished and to meet him in front of the main library on Fifth Avenue at exactly 10:30.

"Be sure to wear one of those Creslan sheepskin jackets," he said, "and your Dobbs safari hat."

As I was leaving to get the car waxed, I heard him on the phone with Bob Levy, a publicity man at Ruder and Finn: "What's that, Bob, another sponsor? Manischevitz . . . Matzos? . . . pictures with Arabs in front of the pyramids . . . gefilte fish . . . right!"

I thought back to December and my wish for the unencumbered freedom of the open road—and headed for the library.

At 10:25 I turned down Fifth Avenue from 50th Street. A block from the library I spotted an enormous traffic jam ahead and I pulled to the curb rather than get hopelessly entangled. Before I could turn the key off two men came running up, followed by half a dozen others, all waving their hands frantically, shouting, "This way. This way. Over here!"

People crowded the front steps of the library. The street was jammed with trucks and station wagons from radio and TV stations and newspapers. The sidewalk was packed with news photographers. Radio interviewers shoved mikes through the window, reporters jumped on the running boards, newsreel cameramen shouted for me to move forward, and there, in the middle of everything, jumping up and down, directing the whole operation, was Al decked out in a Mexican serape.

What was the purpose of our trip? one reporter asked. How many countries would we visit? asked another. What did we carry? How would we cross the oceans? How long would the trip take? What languages did we speak? Was I married? Did I think this would be my toughest trip? How much would it cost? Was it true I was collecting termites? Would I mind holding my head up for a picture?

That afternoon, after Woodrow had flown in from Illinois, the three of us drove the Land Cruiser and camper to the Cunard pier and photographed them as they were put aboard the *Queen Elizabeth.* We'd packed everything we could into the camper, but we still had 47 boxes and cartons of equipment at Al's apartment which we'd have to take to the ship by taxi caravan the next day.

The next day was March 24th, our sailing date, and the New York newspapers carried the story of our trip. But they also carried another story. On the front page was the headline: WILDCAT TAXI STRIKE HITS CITY. There wasn't a taxi on the streets, nor could we rent a car at any price, and our ship sailed in a few hours. It looked for a while as if the Trans World Record Expedition would be stuck in the middle of Manhattan, a notably inauspicious beginning for a trans-world record expedition.

Unless . . .

This time it was *I* who awoke Krinski. "Schistosomiasis," I shouted. "You can't win your bet if we never get out of New York. You have to drive us to the ship!" And so he did.

After the hectic sailing party, Woodrow and Al and I walked up on deck. I leaned against the rail and watched the massive towers of Manhattan slip by. How long before we'd see them again? We were bound for strange lands and exotic places. What adventures lay in store for us?

I waved a last, long farewell to grand old Lady Liberty as we headed toward the Atlantic.

I turned to look at Al, and he was talking to a young blonde oil heiress from Texas.

I looked at Woodrow, and he was seasick.

I looked at the deck steward, and he handed me a radiogram:

DON'T DRINK THE WATER—KRINSKI

The Trans World Record Expedition had begun.

Chapter 3
Our Moveable Feast

The French customs officer in Cherbourg smiled in welcome as we heaved our suitcases on the quayside counter.

Fifteen minutes later, though we could barely see his head behind our mound of dufflebags and cartons and luggage, we could tell he was no longer smiling. And thirty minutes after that, by which time we'd unloaded the last of our gear from the *Queen Elizabeth* onto the counter, making a small mountain braced by an intertangle of hunting bows and fishing rods, and capped by a big, round archery target, the officer was yelling for his chief.

The chief looked at our six cases of insect repellent, our seven flashlights, and our eight dozen arrows and asked, "Perhaps messieurs plan to open a sport shop in Boulevard des Capucines?"

When Willy Mettler met us outside the customs shed and saw the pile of equipment, he looked even more distressed than the customs man.

"It won't work," he exclaimed.

"Don't worry, Willy, we'll manage," I assured him. "We can throw most of the stuff in the camper and the Land Cruiser, and we can put the rest in your car until we get to Paris and get squared away."

"No, it just won't work," he muttered, kicking the straw target. "This spare tire will never hold up."

Unable to reach Paris that first night, we had to camp in dark chaos in a field off the highway. Disorder reigned. When I groped for a flashlight I got a handful of shoe polish, and when I wearily crept into my sleeping bag it turned out to be Al's laundry sack. It was a rough night. I woke up with a bottle of borscht under my neck; Woodrow had slept on and crushed a month's supply of paper cups; Al smelled like gefilte fish.

18

We stretched, rubbed our aches, and opened the camper door to savor the first of what we hoped would be several hundred glorious mornings on the road. We were camped in a manure pit and were the objects of the rapt attention of some sixty cows who'd come to make their morning's contributions, and two puzzled farm hands who'd come to supervise. We moved out for Paris.

April in Paris was for us a quiet campsite by the edge of the Seine in the Bois de Boulogne. Mornings we'd emerge from our camper and stop to watch the coal-laden river barges come 'round the bend through the mist, while farther down the river, almost lost in the haze, the haunting outline of the Eiffel Tower challenged the lightening Paris sky. Through the stillness of the park came the sound of polo ponies warming up on the green at Longchamps, and the air carried the moist caress of warming earth. In the evenings, with the campfire thwarting the not wholly vanquished chill of winter and its ally breeze off the Seine, we watched the sunset and ate from plates heaped with fresh mushroom omelette and great hunks of soft crusted French bread, which we washed down with glass after glass of warming red wine. Other campers wandered over to say hello, compare equipment, and share a glass of wine or offer a wedge of cheese. There was a family of eight in a Microbus from Munich, a bearded Australian with only a sleeping bag, two newlyweds from Holland in a too-small puptent, four college students from Copenhagen, a British professor and his wife. As night falls, Paris elsewhere becomes the City of Light, but in the Bois she remained calm and dark, and we'd sit around the fire, passing the good red wine around, telling tales—haltingly—in a mixture of each other's tongues, and singing the universal drinking songs. Such was the Trans World Record Expedition's home in Paris.

We spent five days in Paris, buying auto insurance for Europe, taking photos for the sponsors, beginning the movie of our trip, getting Algerian visas, repacking our equipment, and holding a press conference under the auspices of the French National Tourist Association. The start of our trip was so deceptively peaceful that when a wire service reporter asked if I expected any trouble, I answered, "Maybe a flat tire or two or a case of dysentery, but that's about it. We should be able to handle any difficulty that comes up." I'd have to eat those words in a few days.

It was the 5th of April when we dismantled our camp in the Bois, said good-bye to our friends, and headed south. We moved through a green, green land along a road lined to the horizon with stately trees, and the country passed in a charming blur of cobbled medieval towns, of great cathedral towers in the grayish distance, of Chartres, Orleans, Blois, Tours, Chateauroux, Limoges, Loches, Toulouse. The pace was unhurried, the living easy, the meals simple—dairy-fresh cheese, farm-fresh eggs, bakery-fresh bread, fish we caught in the misty Loire at morning, and lots of thick red wine. I drove, Woodrow slept, Al read from our guidebook about the famous cathedrals and the wars, sieges, and intrigues they had once looked upon.

Today they look down on prosperous farms, growing towns, elegant chateaux and, sadly, here and there, a monstrosity of paint and chrome exhorting the driver to METTEZ UN TIGRE DANS VOTRE MOTEUR. There are few changes in the French countryside as obvious as those in Paris, and the gas station was the worst offender. These glaring bastions stand out in harsh contrast to the sculptured beauty of the chateau-studded countryside, though we had to accept them as a necessary evil in a country whose traditional bicycles have succumbed to the Citroen and the 4CV. The thing we refused to accept as necessary, albeit an evil, was the price of gasoline—90 cents a gallon—most of it for De Gaulle's taxes.

We were gradually working into our camping routine, slowly getting organized. Willy had driven ahead with our load of extra equipment to Spain, where we planned to resurrect my old Jeep to serve as a storage vehicle. No more borscht for pillows, and no more manure pits. We stopped at the registered campsites along the road. They were clean, and guarded, and had the last hot showers we'd see for weeks. There would be regular campsites down through Spain and into Morocco, but after that we'd be strictly on our own. That's the way we'd planned it: a month of easy camping to get ourselves in shape before plunging into the rough going east of Algiers.

One day south of Carcassone, passing through rising land toward Ax-les-Thermes in the foothills of the Pyrenees, we celebrated our first thousand miles by land, the first of 42,000, and the easiest. We were now well on our way to Spain and the gateway to Africa, far away from the traditional, easy motor route to the Orient that ran from Paris through Italy on to Istanbul.

At the gas station in Quillan before the long haul into the mountains, we *mettezed un tigre* in our tank with the last of our French francs. Woodrow asked the attendant about the road ahead, particularly the pass at Port d'Envalira which, since Paris, we'd been warned might still be closed with snow.

"Non, messieurs, c'est impossible," he replied, explaining that it was too early in the tricky spring season. The 8,000-foot pass had been open for a week, it was true, but had been blocked again by a storm two days before, and more snow was forecast for the evening. He suggested we detour east by way of Perpignan and Barcelona on the Mediterranean, skirting the Pyrenees. But that would have meant bypassing Andorra, and Andorra was a must. It was still just about, as my idol Halliburton had found it 40 years before, "the oldest, the smallest, the highest, the quaintest, the most isolated republic on earth," and I was determined to see it. It was too early in the trip to skip a country, too insignificant an obstacle. We headed into the Pyrenees.

We first met fog, then rain, then fog and rain again. The snow coated the ground at the 5,000-foot level, with spruce and pine standing in dark contrast against it. At 6,000 feet it was snowing hard and fogging thick. We had to get out to read the signposts. The narrow road was a winding blur, with a 600-foot drop off its side.

At 6,500 feet the road was deep with snow, the retaining fences were almost covered, and day had darkened into night. The pass was 1,000 or 2,000 feet higher, ten miles up ahead. We hadn't seen another car all afternoon. Perhaps the pass was blocked? If we turned back it might be a week before it was open. If we pushed on we might spend the week stuck in a snowbank. We pushed on.

It was impossible to see. The thick screen of snow reflected our lights. The road and the ground were of one grayness, and the sheer drop filled with fog was only a shade away. The road snaked and twisted up toward the pass, and I could no longer guess which way it was going. Al got out with a lantern to lead us, but the howling storm drove him back. There were five inches on the asphalt now and it was hard to hold the road. I regretted that we had had our special tires shipped directly to Spain.

Then it happened. I had turned slightly to the right, and the wheel clawed at space. It was over the edge. Before I could react, the car was going off the road, down the mountain slope, down toward certain destruction in the gorge 2,000 feet below. Now both front wheels were over the edge. The brakes locked. The rear wheels slid. The fog opened to bid us welcome.

It was the longest foot I ever fell. That's all it was, though it seemed to take forever. Our bumper lodged fast against a big spruce just down the slope. Below that tree, nothing.

We winched our way back onto the road, and two hours later plowed through the pass in four-wheel drive, up to the hubcaps in snow. There was not another tire track to be seen. An hour more and we had dropped 1,500 feet, below the danger zone. Ahead a faint light glimmered from a house half-buried in the snow. Our pounding was answered by a robust Andorran in a heavy sweater who explained that the building was his home, but also a restaurant where he served meals to skiers. We weren't skiers, but we were famished, so we trooped in. The meal was delicious. His wife served, and their round-cheeked daughter flirted with us from the corner. The owner sat with us and shared the wine. There was a problem with payment: we were out of French francs and hadn't had a chance to buy any Spanish pesetas, either of which are acceptable in Andorra. We had traveler's checks, but the owner had never seen them and wouldn't accept them, all American Express advertisements to the contrary. After some friendly mutual embarrassment Al paid for our meals with a pair of ski boots from our 44-pair collection and a couple of rolls of Glad Wrap.

I explained to the owner that we needed a place to camp for the night, and he suggested we drive on to Andorra la Vella down in the valley. But we'd had enough of night driving in the snow. There was a flat spot off the other side of the road, a large ledge with a small wood tool shed on one edge, so we decided to make camp there. The man was nervous about it, but the ledge was flat enough to take the camper and wide enough so we wouldn't be blown off the mountain.

The night was incredibly cold. The wind tore down from the mountain pass and rattled the camper. The ledge beneath us creaked and groaned. Tired as we were, it was several hours before the storm abated enough to let us sleep, and it was only a short while later that I awoke with a start on hearing someone or something walking in the snow around the camper. The steps circled us three times, stopping, listening.

I threw open the camper door and jumped out with my flashlight. No one was there, just two fresh sets of bootprints. What were people doing prowling around us high on a mountain miles from the nearest town in the dead of night?

The morning broke clear and crisp, the sky a bluest blue, the snow a startling white, the dark fir trees a forest of exclamation points.

Woodrow couldn't be roused, so Al and I dressed and headed to the house hoping for some hot coffee and perhaps an explanation of our nocturnal visitors. I got there first, Al having lagged behind to take some pictures of our campsite, and the owner greeted me nervously, giving me the feeling he wished we'd taken off. I moved into the restaurant room where two strangers stood beside a potbellied stove that had obviously been burning much of the night. I was not introduced.

"My camp is on the ledge and I heard noises in the night. Could that have been you and your friend?" I asked one of them, first in French, then in broken Spanish when I got no answer. He saw me looking at his boots.

"Perhaps. We might have walked by your camp on the way up here to go skiing."

When Al came in with his camera the two strangers jerked away as if they'd seen a snake, and when he started taking pictures of the innkeeper's family they walked outside. I let it pass, but later, when we stood outside admiring the sparkling day, Al took out the camera to put on a filter and the two men vanished back into the house.

What was going on? What were they afraid of? I had a theory: smuggling was still an important though illegal activity in Andorra, and one in which our two rough-looking characters could easily have been engaged. Or was I letting my imagination get the best of me? Here we were, barely a week on the road, and I was seeing smugglers popping up all over the place. In any case, we'd never know, for we had to push on.

But we couldn't. Our wheels had sunken in deep during the night, and a coating of ice held them fast. We unhitched the trailer and threw the Land Cruiser into four-wheel drive, but the tires spun hopelessly. We shoveled away with our entrenching tools, but the wheels only dug in deeper.

We'd have to try to winch our way out, but there was nothing to anchor the winch wire to, except the little tool shed, about thirty yards from us. It was old and rickety, and I didn't know if it would take the tremendous strain. Yet there was no alternative. It was either that or spend Easter in Andorra.

Al turned on the motor and released the winch lock while I grabbed the hook and cable and pulled them around the shed. As I knelt on the far side of the shed to fasten the hook, I saw something green through a hole in the wall. I looked closer: it was two huge backpacks partly covered by paper and loose boards. Now all my questions were answered.

Except one: how did we get out? If we pulled the shed down and exposed their hideout, who knew what the smugglers would do to us on that lonely mountain? But there was no other way out. I decided to take the chance and signaled Al to start winding in on the winch. The shed creaked and groaned as the cable went taut, but the car was still stuck fast. I looked back toward the house and saw the strangers running at me with a pick and shovel in their hands, obviously upset. Al revved up the winch again, the cable shuddered, the shed trembled, and the car seemed to pull forward a fraction. The two men were up to me now, one of them stopping close beside me with an ugly pick in his hand and the other trying to undo the winch hook. But it was too late for that. With a painful rumble, the winch drum heaved in on the cable again. A board popped loose and the flimsy shed started to tilt and seemed about to collapse—when the car leaped forward, free.

As we drove away Al turned to me. "You know, Steve," he said, "it just goes to show how wrong a person can be. I really misjudged those guys. Wasn't it nice of them to come out with tools to help you?"

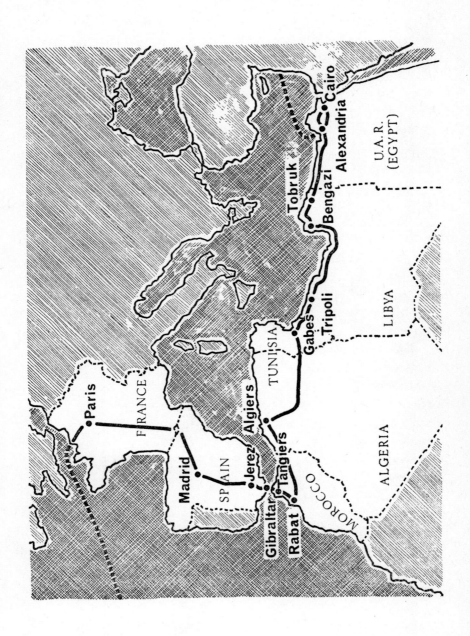

Chapter 4

The Reins in Spain

The ride down the Pyrenees was lovely, a panorama of green-on-white peaks gleaming in the spring sun, a serenade of gurgling streams and thunder in the gorge from the melting snows. By afternoon we were in Spain.

We were almost out of gas when we reached the outskirts of the big city of Lerida, so Woodrow pulled into a service station. A few miles farther, in the heart of town, in the center of traffic, after a piston-shaking struggle, the engine stopped dead. The policeman directing traffic whistled and waved frantically. Cars and carts piled up behind us. A motorcycle trooper screeched to a stop beside us, shouting and waving. Limited though my Spanish is, I knew that he wasn't inviting us to dinner. But the engine would only sputter.

A passerby concluded we'd mistakenly bought diesel fuel instead of gasoline. To get diesel oil you ask for "gas," as indeed Woodrow had; to get gas you ask for "benzene." Our Land Cruiser must have looked like a small truck to the attendant, so he'd put in diesel.

The next morning we were on the road early, driving through castle country where, on small arid hills above the winding road, mementoes of the ancient glory and grandeur of Spain watched over the countryside. The land, though dry, was heavily farmed; olive and fig trees sent their roots deep in search of moisture, and shady cork oaks husbanded their water behind thick insulating bark; grape vines followed the laboriously terraced contour of the slopes. Here and there we saw dams and bridges being built, the only hints that Spain acknowledged the 20th century, that a country whose inhospitable climate and schismatic topography had long been its formidable enemies was at last beginning to fight back, that a few inches less rain would no longer

27

mean ruin for the farmers, and that people who had long thought of themselves as Andalusians and Catalonians, Basques and Castilians, Asturians and Galicians were at last beginning to be united into a nation of Spaniards.

We camped at Osona, 20 minutes east of the heart of Madrid. And what a heart! *Tapas* and *copas*. The Echegaray and the caves in *Madrid Viejo*. What better treat after a lonely week on the road? What better send off for a journey across Africa!

The Echegaray is a street near the Puerta del Sol where every night is Mardi Gras, where the rich and poor alike go arm in arm from bar to bar sampling *tapas* and *copas*. *Tapa* and *copa* are a must in Spanish; in fact, it's said a visitor can survive in Spain knowing no other words. A *tapa* is an appetizer, a tasty anything from fish to nuts and, to the Spanish mind, a good excuse for another *copa*. The Spaniards are masters at preparing *tapas* in unending varieties, each one an adventure in tastes. During the summer the accent is on barnacles, baby shrimp, mussels, crayfish, oysters, and prawns; in winter it's sliced beef, chicken breasts, kidneys cooked in sherry, pickled eggs. You're stuffed to contentment for less than what a ham sandwhich costs back home.

Then it's over to the caves of Old Madrid. There, centuries before, notorious figures of the underworld hid out in the subterranean caverns, linked by a network of tunnels to other parts of the city. Where once the caves rang with pistol shots, today they rock to the sound of a *buleria;* everybody is high and happy and clapping in time to guitars and castanets. The best cognac is fifteen cents, and you warm it in your hands as you lean against moist brick walls deeply carved with names and dates. The tables and benches are dark wood, also carved and nicked. There are alcoves and balconies, all underground, all crammed with people. When you order a drink you can also order a guitar. You strum, and soon everyone joins in, the cave resounding with singing and clapping until the din reaches so feverish a pitch that men jump on the tables and stomp their heels in spirited flamencos.

Over the Saturday night roar of the cave of Luis Candela, Willy introduced us to Manu—Manu Angel Leguineche Bolar—a young Spanish journalist who wanted to join our expedition. As we approached his table he was deftly pouring wine down his throat from a *bota*, a Spanish flask held suspended over the head. The distance from which a man can pour wine into his mouth without spilling it is a mark of status in Spain. Six inches is considered good; Manu was doing eighteen, and I noticed his expensive London suit was spotless. A beautiful girl was clinging to his free arm as though it were already understood he was leaving soon for distant lands.

Manu leaped to his feet and embraced us, almost knocking over the table. He summoned the waiter with a clap of his hands and ordered *sangría* for everyone. He was of medium height and somewhat on the chubby side, and he was so good natured, with a deep laugh and infectious smile, that we liked him the minute we saw him.

After some casual conversation, which was conducted mostly in French since Manu spoke little English and we spoke little Spanish, I asked him bluntly why he wanted to join the expedition. He explained that he wanted to see the world, and that the publisher of his magazine had agreed to pay his expenses.

"Have you spent much time outdoors?" I asked him.

"My father has an estate in the Basque country. You must meet my father. He is an excellent hunter. Doves, pheasants, everything. We Spanish from the Basque country all like outdoors."

"How about mechanics, Manu, and automobiles, driving——"

"I am Spanish from the Basque," he stopped me with a wave of his hand. "We can do anything."

We found him quick-witted and quite knowledgeable about world affairs. His warm sense of humor broke through the language barrier, and his resounding voice set the tables aroar. Even as we walked back to our car through the silent streets of Madrid he occasionally broke into song.

"Africa," he said, "I know it very good. They speak Spanish there."

We agreed to take him.

He would meet us in Jerez in southern Spain as soon as he completed arrangements with his publisher and wound up his personal affairs, he said, winking at the girl still clutching his arm.

I was anxious to move on to Jerez where my old Jeep was stored, but we had to stay in Madrid over the weekend to claim the equipment our sponsors had air-freighted to us at Barajas Airport.

On Monday the bad news broke. Al returned from the airport to report that the Spanish customs agents wanted close to a thousand dollars to release our equipment.

In most European countries, when a tourist has something sent to him which he plans to take out of the country at the end of his visit, the customs officials will waive all duties and tariffs. But not the Spaniards. Spain is notorious for her huge import duties—often as high as 200 per cent, often twice the cost of the item—which she uses to curtail imports and conserve foreign exchange. Al had tried to explain that we were on an expedition around the world, that we were just using Spain as a transshipment point, that we'd be taking everything out of the country with us, that we should not have to pay any customs duty. It was too much for the bureaucrats, who couldn't imagine anyone driving around the world. They were sure we planned to sell the shortwave radio, the expensive watches, the cases of condensed milk, and the camera lenses, and they were taxing us as if we were in the import business.

Al felt that if we could convince the customs agents that we were really on an expedition around the world, they might give us our stuff without duty; so we held a press conference that evening. Willy, with the help of some friends in the publicity business, had 40 journalists there, and the next morning all the wire services, every paper in Madrid, and half the papers in Spain carried our pictures and the story of our trip.

That afternoon, loaded with news clippings, Al left for the Barajas customs house; he returned three hours later, with neither clippings nor equipment. "They liked the stories, all right. Passed them all around. Said it sounded like a hell of a good trip. Even wished us luck. But they still wanted a thousand dollars."

I appealed to the American Embassy; Willy pleaded with the Spanish Tourist Ministry; Al petitioned the American Chamber of Commerce; Manu tried his magazine.

We rendezvoused that afternoon at the American Express office, all with the same report: nobody could do anything. Yet we had to do something. We had to get to Jerez to put the Jeep in shape for the trip, and we had to get moving toward Africa before the deserts were blazing. The next day we hired a Madrid customs clearance agent—a

strikingly attractive, tall, blonde Finnish girl who spoke six languages
—to work on our problem while we moved on to Jerez to work on the
equipment.

The Spaniards are a very proud people. They have lost the great
wealth and empire they had in the days when they were masters of the
New World and its riches, and they've fallen so far behind under their
Fascist regime that theirs is one of the most backward countries in
Europe. But will the Spaniards admit they're behind the times?
Hardly! Look at their road maps, for example; that's just what we made
the mistake of doing. On these maps you will find, radiating from
Madrid like beams from a star, six roads labeled "first-class highway,"
and, crossing them, several dozen others labeled "second-class roads."
If the Spaniards were less proud or more honest they might admit
that the only classification system in which their roads could be considered "first" would be an anthropological one, for they are aged,
weathered, worn, and pocked. And those holey horrors they rate "second class" would make our most wretched farm tracks look like
turnpikes.

Leaving Madrid we decided to take a scenic second-class road that
wandered down to Jerez by way of the historic cities of Toledo, Cordoba, and Seville. When we reached Toledo we drove through the gate
into the city which so charmed us with its undisturbed medievality,
looking much today as it did when El Cid trod its cobbled streets, that
we forgot that in those days two donkeys passing abreast would have
constituted a traffic jam. We were inspired by Toledo's churches, awed
by its paintings, impressed by its craftsmen, and mauled to pieces by
its streets.

Constructed in the days before sidewalks were the fashion, the
streets of Toledo are so closely walled in by ancient stone houses that a
Middle Ages housewife could easily have borrowed a cup of gruel from
the lady across the street without leaving her pantry. The deeper we
drove into the city the narrower its streets became, but we were past
the point of no return. We could only move forward and hope. Our
hope and our forward progress ran out the same time our clearance
did. We were stuck, wedged between the walls, with a raucous chorus

of screaming school kids, braying donkeys, and clucking old crones jammed up behind us.

We had the choice of either trying to back up or pitching a permanent camp in the middle of one of the main alleys of Toledo. Even backing out was impossible with the trailer, and we scratched it so badly we were forced to unhitch it and, with the help of a dozen laughing Toledoanos, push it by hand all the way back to the town gate.

Near Ciudad Real we saw a sign indicating the road to Cordoba that seemed, however, to point farther west than the route indicated on our map. We asked two local people, and they assured us it was the road to Cordoba. As we drove along it, at ever decreasing speeds, the road, if such it could be called, deteriorated from new asphalt to old asphalt, to old asphalt full of cracks and holes, to gravel, to dirt, and finally and principally, to dirt riddled with deep holes, layered with large rocks, covered with dust and twisted into washboard corrugations.

We found a farmer, and asked the way to Cordoba. He pointed us down the road. It had been our experience when asking for directions, that the average Spaniard just would not know, usually because he'd never been out of his own village; but being a proud Spaniard, he would never confess his ignorance, especially if some of his friends were near. His momentary look of mystification would quickly yield to a smile of enthusiastic knowledgeability, whereupon he would point us down the road, inevitably in the direction we were already headed. You can ask a Spaniard the way to Cordoba or Casablanca or Canarsie and he'll nod and smile and point you down the road.

After having covered only 35 miles in three hours, we reached a sign, one of those interesting Spanish road signs so far off the side of the road and so faded and weathered you never know if it's currently applicable. This particular sign informed us that this particular road to Cordoba was "not recommended." What was recommended was that we retrace our route all the way back to Ciudad Real and start over again on another road.

Since the sign was so weathered, we hoped that it might be out of date, and since we couldn't conceive of any European road getting worse than the one we'd come on, we decided to push ahead. As a safety check, for we still hadn't learned our lesson completely, we asked the first peasants we saw if many other cars used this road to Cordoba and if there were many gasoline stations on it. They proudly assured us that this road on which they lived was quite important, that there were many gas stations on it, and that at least 50 cars a day passed this way.

Three terrible hours later we were still far from Cordoba, had not seen a single gas station, and had met only one other car, a Microbus driven by a Dutch tourist who was also obviously lost, having taken his instruction from some proud citizens on the other end of the line.

After ten hours, during which we covered 130 miles, we finally reached Cordoba, though not without penalty, for our camper was listing heavily to one side where the rough road had cracked the undercarriage in four places. The damage could not be repaired because it was Holy Week; so we pushed on for Seville where we planned to see the processions on Good Friday and Holy Saturday, the highlights of *Semana Santa* in Spain.

Some travelers will tell you that the Sevillianos are coarse and rude, but we found them a delight. They are intense, energetic people who enjoy life to the fullest. They drink hard, dance hard, drive hard, play hard, sing loud, and eat like there's no tomorrow. They live life to the hilt, perpetually in voice or motion, so much so that anyone with a spark of spirit is irresistibly swept along with them. With regard to its citizens as well as its architecture, it is well said that "He who has not visited Seville has not seen a marvel."

The processions were also a marvel. For hours they flowed by: awesome religious floats of candle-lit saints carried by hundreds of sweating penitents; priests bearing huge gleaming crucifixes; Christ on the Cross, his crown of thorns half-hidden in the darkness; hundreds of hooded marchers, some in black, others in white, holding stately candles.

An old man explained the reason for the hoods: When the Moors were expelled from Spain in the 1490's, after having held the country for 600 years, the devout Catholics, who had been practicing their faith in secret in cellars and caves, brought their religious symbols and services back to the churches; but many of them, fearful that the Saracen blade might strike again or that Moorish spies would report them, wore hoods and robes to conceal their identities. The custom survived the generations and is honored each year at *Semana Santa*.

But not everything has survived the generations unchanged; for it seemed to us that Catholicism, the official state religion, powerful as it still is in Spain, was losing its hold on the younger people, especially the college students. Spain's Catholicism has been, with Italy's, the most conservative in the Old World, stiff and unchanging for centuries, even opposed to the much-needed reforms of Vatican II, and we saw signs everywhere that the young people were determined to live in the 20th century even if their clerics weren't. Even Holy Week is not so holy any more, having become as much a festival as a reverent or penitential occasion. The people underneath the pointed hoods are often not the ones who should be doing penance; they have paid gypsies to take their places so they can slip out of their duties undetected, to go carousing and drinking in the cafes. Young girls, who all year long are under watchful eyes in the closely chaperoned society, are at liberty for *Semana Santa,* and they meet boys, stay out late, and get into trouble. There's a saying among the young Spaniards that *Semana Santa* is when the virgins lose their virginity, but this didn't quite correlate with the findings of our own independent research.

As part of our adjustment to life on the road, we began to fall into distinct personal habits. Woodrow's habit was sleep. We were getting seven hours a night at this stage of the trip, but it wasn't enough for Woodrow, who'd grumble when we'd wake him, take forever to get dressed, and fall asleep in the car soon after breakfast. Willy's fault was taking pictures to excess, shooting every bird or bush or cloud that caught his fancy, wasting time and film, taking pictures even as he was talking or eating or driving. My fault was daydreaming. The slightest thing would set me off and I'd be centuries away—marching beside El Cid as he drove out the Moors; kneeling with Columbus as he petitioned Queen Isabella for ships with which to sail to India; trudging the dusty roads behind Don Quixote's faithful steed, Rosinante—only to snap back to the present and find out I'd nearly run over somebody's ass.

But Al's habit was the worst: he couldn't sit still. When he wasn't driving, he'd fidget and fuss, check the cameras, wipe the lenses, count the filters, reorganize our glove box, and exhaust the guidebooks. His favorite diversion was poring over the maps and mileage charts and our daily log, during which he'd infallibly rouse Woodrow from his slumber and me from my reverie to involve us in his endless calculations. "How many miles were we when we left Seville this morning?" he'd begin, nudging me to check the speedometer. "Now let's see," he'd go on, "if gas here is nine and a half pesetas a litre and if there are sixty pesetas in a dollar—what was the last rate of exchange we got? Fifty-nine?—and 3.875 litres in a gallon, and we're getting 14.7 miles to a gallon, that means . . . "

We set up our tents and limping trailer at Camp Pinar, south of Jerez. Thick rows of man-high flowering cactus ran the boundary, a cool breeze swept in from the Gulf of Cadiz, and a grove of tall pines gave the camp shade and its name. The location was ideal: we were close to Cadiz where our sponsors had shipped the rest of our heavy equipment by boat from New York, close to the welding shops at Puerto where we could work on our shattered camper, close to Jerez de la Frontera, the wine capital of Spain, where my old Jeep was stored and where we could eat, drink, and make merry before moving on to the deprivations of Africa. And close to Arcos de Frontera where we went for the running of the bulls.

Easter Sunday dawned in glory, sunny but cool, as we headed north toward Arcos for the once-a-year-day when the Spanish aficionado can demonstrate his own manliness and courage. Great puffs of cloud rolled over the land of Don Quixote in a blue, blue sky, each cloud its separate shape, but all of them heading for the hill of Arcos. Nor did they lack for company, for the road was filled with cars, bikes, scooters, carts, and pedestrians.

Arcos grabs your breath at first sight. It clings to a cliff high above a sleepy river that winds through an otherwise flat and repetitious countryside. A medieval castle and a spiring church look down upon the whitewashed houses that clutch the thousand-foot cliff. Hundreds of birds, who nest in the cliff face, form a living halo about the town.

The first bull was scheduled to be turned loose at 11:00, but it was nearly noon before we heard the shouting down below. We had found ourselves a perch out of harm's way, atop a wall bordering the main street, and I was still undecided whether to join or just watch until a quick review of the other wallflowers made my decision for me: they were all women, children, and very old men, and even the last seemed to long to run again before the bull. That did it! I'd be damned if I'd sit and watch with the women and children. I didn't know the twists and turns of Arcos, and I didn't even know the Spanish word for HELP, but I was going to join the running of the bulls.

The noise from below grew louder and closer until a surging mob of shouting, sweating, happy, hysterical, frightened men charged past, with a black bull snorting in hot pursuit. From the broad main street they turned down a side street too narrow to hold them all. Jammed against the walls, squeezed against the houses, pushed and elbowed against each other, some were bound to get caught. It was a young boy, about twenty, in the back of the pack, scrambling madly to get through the human impasse, who got it. I could hear him scream in agony as the bull dug a horn in his thigh, then flung him high overhead like a broken old doll. He crashed to the cobblestones and lay crumpled there, blood spreading around him, while the bull mercifully forgot him and took off after the running crowd, with the sweet smell of flesh in his nostrils, and a fresh crimson banner on his horns.

I leaped from the wall, ran past the bleeding boy, and took off in pursuit of the bull. I wasn't sure what I was doing, but I was doing it. I thought I'd come just to watch these crazy people, but I found myself running along with the craziest of them, swept along with the infectious spirit of the mob, ducking down side streets, climbing over walls, racing through alleys.

As I mused on this, the bull turned, and the crowd with him. I was caught unaware. A frenzied fat man crashed into me and I tripped over a boy's foot, taking three Spaniards down with me.

When I looked up it was into the face of the biggest, maddest, meanest, horniest bull I'd ever seen in my life. The four of us were so inextricably jumbled together on the ground that the bull had time to pick his victim; I just hoped he had no preference for *Americanos*. I was wrong: his decision made, he lowered his head toward mine. His horns caught the gleam of the high noon sun and I felt his hot, stinking breath inches from my face. What kind of way was this to go, this ignoble finish, my guts gored out by a bull while playing a stupid game with a bunch of half-stewed village idiots?

As a final act of defiance, I spit at the bull, a rather feeble salvo of saliva, my throat was so dry, but as satisfactory a final comment as I could think of at the moment. And the bull turned away. *Ole!* It was neither the spit nor a magic charm so much as a drunken teenager who had seized the chance to show his bravery by yanking *el toro's* tail. The bull snorted off after the upstart, and my companions of the cobblestones and I stumbled to our feet, the cheers of the crowd ringing in our ears. *Ole! Ole!* A shopkeeper ran out with a bottle of good *aguardiente* that I held to my lips and gulped until my throat burned and tears came to my eyes. *Ole!*

The taste of the bull and near disaster was still strong in my mouth as we left Arcos for Jerez to check on my Jeep which, after my Russian trip, I'd left with Blackie McManus, a big ex-Marine fighter pilot, expatriate and old friend. He and his wife and five children live on the outskirts of Jerez in an old Spanish house. The walls are cracked, the plaster is peeling, the roof leaks. Everything smells of a glorious past and an uncertain future.

Blackie had promised to treat my equipment as if it were his own. He meant it literally, and judging by the condition of his house and grounds, I had cause for concern. When I didn't see the Jeep I hesitantly asked Blackie where it was. "It's in the shop at Puerto. I took it there after I got your telegram last Wednesday. Nothing much wrong. I heard a slight knock in the engine and turned it in." A slight knock, I thought, and went to use the bathroom where none of the plumbing worked.

The next morning Al and Woodrow went to Cadiz to claim our shipment, Willy and I to Puerto to weld the camper and pick up the Jeep. When we met back at camp that evening, Al reported that our equipment, including our vital tires and engine oil, were all safe in the Cadiz customs shed and we could get them whenever we wanted—after we paid $750 customs duty. It was Madrid all over again. My day was no less discouraging. I'd had the camper welded, but the breaks were severe, the cost high, and there was no guarantee the welds would hold. The Jeep looked terrible when I found it behind the big workshop in Puerto, covered with dust and dirt, the spare wheel missing, the tires worn, the engine in pieces on the floor. During the four days of *Semana Santa*, no work had been done at the shop, whose normal work day resembled a six-hour siesta sandwiched between two hours of desultory labor at a pace which, with the Jeep's crankshaft scored, pistons pitted, a rod broken, and spare parts needed from Seville, meant it might be weeks before the job was *terminado*. The date was April 19th, and the deserts of North Africa were getting hotter every day.

We were a dispirited group at the camp that night, faces long, tempers short. A few of us were even beginning to believe that our globe-girdling expedition was going to end then and there, at Camp Pinar, Spain, with all the world still to see.

A miracle dispelled the gloom, a warm and friendly miracle. As we prepared to bed down for the night, a pretty blonde head poked through the front camper flap, followed by a body that was suntanned and solid, dressed in short shorts, and curved in all the right places. "Say there, chaps," she said in a fetching British accent, "thought you might be Yanks. We heard you clear across the camp. Just got here, we did. Hitched all the way from Seville. Wonder if it would inconvenience you chaps if we laid out our sleeping bags near you. It's rather dark and spooky out there and my friends would feel safer with some Yanks around." The friends were two: one tall, genteel, poised, the fashion-model type; the other, short, freckled, red-haired, cute, vivacious. Something for everybody! Welcome travelers! Good-bye gripes! *Ole!*

The girls looked as good by dawn's early light as they had by lantern. The coffee they woke us with was as heavenly as the breakfast in bed that followed it——our first of the trip. After introductions, we learned that Elizabeth, Barbara and Mira were all nurses, born in New Zealand, trained in London, hitching through Spain and France before going to work. Little did they or we know then that they'd come half way across Africa with us and almost end up in some Arab's harem.

The girls took over our shopping, cooking, cleaning, and pot-washing. Never was a trans-world expedition so pampered. Our camping in Europe was supposed to condition us for the rigors of Africa; but it was more like being prepared for a sojourn in a seraglio. It was surely, as are all honeymoons, doomed to end, but for the moment, we made the most of it.

The nurses had caused us to forget our beautiful customs clearance girl in Madrid until her cable arrived. The Spanish customs officials, she said, had agreed to release our equipment, duty-free, if we posted a $1,000 bond which would be returned to us, they promised, when we left Spain, provided we took all the equipment out with us. Al left for Madrid to seal the deal while the rest of us decided to put the delay to good use and take advantage of our location and company. If you have to be stuck somewhere with somebody at sometime, you couldn't ask for more than springtime in Jerez with three adventurous Kiwi nurses.

Jerez, more formally, Jerez de la Frontera, is a most remarkable town: in no place on earth is drinking so important. In Jerez it is refined; in Jerez it is an art; in Jerez it is everything. If Bacchus were looking for a ball, if Dionysus wanted a drink, they'd head for Jerez; its cup runneth over.

Four days after he'd left for Madrid we received a telegram from Al: he'd gotten our equipment out of customs and would be arriving in Jerez that night with it and Manu. Since the Jeep repairs were also finished, it looked as if we'd be ready to leave Spain at last. I spent the morning convincing the girls to come with us to Africa, as far as Tunis where they could catch a ferry to France, and the afternoon at Blackie's, discussing the trip with his friends and saying good-bye. As we were leaving. Blackie gave me something he said we might need——a .38 pistol.

On the way back from Blackie's the Jeep began to knock and stall so badly that we just made it to the shop at Puerto. There a German mechanic whom we called in for consultation found that three of the rods were worn. They should have been replaced, he said, when the engine was dismantled during the original repair, but the workers were probably too lazy. Parts would again have to be ordered from Seville, the engine taken apart once more, and our expedition set back another week.

I broke the bad news to Al when he pulled in from Madrid that

night with Manu and our equipment, but he didn't seem to mind the
delay—nor did Leila, the customs clearance agent, whom he'd brought
back with him, and who looked devastating in tight stretch pants and
high leather boots as she explained shyly, "I had a few days' vacation
coming, and I've always wanted to go camping." From the way she
clung to Al, I suspected she'd just as readily have spent them climbing
the Matterhorn or exploring the Arctic Circle if he had happened to be
heading in those directions.

Even after Al had explained that Leila had offered to help us with
our customs problems in Cadiz, Barbara and Mira were still so jealous
they didn't speak to him, except to let him know he could expect no
special favors from them when Leila had gone. "But what the hell,"
as Al said, "isn't a bird in the hand worth two in the (African) bush?"

Our problems in Cadiz were not easily settled, even with Leila's
assistance in pleading, translating, cajoling, explaining, promising, and
threatening. Aside from the complications involved in arranging to post
bond for our equipment, we were anchored by a shipping agent who
discovered a slight mistake on the invoice attached to our oil. It was a
simple oversight that consigned that shipment to The Trans World
Record Expedition rather than to a particular one of us, but one that
his worship of petty regulations wouldn't allow him to ignore and
whose rectifications required a cable from us to Macmillan Oil in New
York, a cable from Macmillan back to us in Cadiz, followed by letters
from us to the shipping company, the shipping company to the customs
clearance agent, the customs clearance agent to the shipping company,
the shipping company to us, us to the customs clearance agent, the
customs clearance agent to us, us to the assistant chief of customs, the
assistant chief of customs to the chief of customs, and the chief of customs back to us, the last granting us permission to claim our equipment
—as soon as the initial bonding arrangement had been effectuated. A
sharp clerk in the States would have taken it on himself to settle the
whole mess in a minute, but in Spain there is no premium on initiative,
no reward for innovation, no bonus for speed, for what's the use of
hurrying when tomorrow is sure to be the same as yesterday.

It was the same everywhere in Spain: slow and sloppy. For instance, when we went back to the shop to pick up the Jeep, we got no farther than Blackie's house (where we'd gone to say good-bye again) when the engine conked out. Blackie towed us back to Puerto where we complained and raged; but they still wouldn't look at it until *mañana*.

When we had first arrived in Jerez, in mid-April, people had asked if we were planning to stay for the famous spring fair which would begin May 7th.

"No," I'd always answered, "I'm afraid we'll have to miss it. We'd love to see it, but we only plan to be around Jerez a few days. By the 7th of May we'll be crossing Egypt."

Well, May 7th came, and the only thing we'd been crossing was the stretch of asphalt between the auto shop at Puerto and the customs shed at Cadiz. Two thousand miles we'd put on the Land Cruiser— and moved not an inch on the map. But that morning we were ready at last. The equipment was out of customs, the Jeep was out of the shop, and we were ready to roll. We closed down the camper and loaded up the cars, taking hours to find space for the recently added passengers and equipment. The canvas sides of the Jeep were strained to bursting, the top of the camper was covered with new tires, and six sloshing four-gallon jugs of Jerez wine hung from the Land Cruiser's back bumper. An English tourist waited for an hour with movie camera in hand to record our departure. The camp manager wept to see us leave. The German mechanic wished us luck. Blackie and his family waved good-bye for the third time.

Fourteen miles out of Camp Pinar, on the road to Gibraltar, the Jeep broke down again.

There were some surprised people at the spring fair in Jerez that night.

By the third day of the fair our Jeep was in far better shape then we, though we somehow managed to pack everything again and get moving toward Gibraltar, the fourth country on our itinerary and our last in Europe.

As we drove, the shortwave set—which had been released from Spanish customs—brought us up to date on the world we had left a month before and heard little from since.

A fanatic terrorist group, El Fatah, organized by Syria, had attacked Israel through Jordanian territory, and Israel had vowed reprisals, inflaming the Middle East.

In the Rann of Kutch, a miserable salt marsh on the sub-continent, India and Pakistan were shooting over a disputed boundary line, throwing tanks and planes into the worst flareup since partition.

Prince Sihanouk of Cambodia had broken relations with the United States, claiming we had armed his enemies in Thailand and had helped the South Vietnamese raid his territory.

In Vietnam itself, American Marines had moved out from Danang to fight their first ground battle of the war against the Vietcong.

The world was heating up all over our route, but in wondering how these wars and feuds would affect our trip, we looked too far ahead. One of our worst problems was coming up just around the bend: the Spanish blockade of Gibraltar.

Chapter 5

The Rock on the Road

The Rock of Gibraltar:

To the geologist, a faulted, 1,400-foot mountain of porous Lower Jurassic Age limestone rising abruptly from the easternmost extremity of the Mediterranean Basin. To the geographer, two and one-quarter miles of inhospitable rock near the southernmost tip of the Iberian Peninsula. To the poet, a metaphor for might, a simile for strength. To the inhabitants of the ancient world, one of the twin Pillars of Hercules that marked the boundary beyond which no man dared to sail for fear he'd fall off the edge of the sea. To the historian, the site and scene of sixteen of mankind's longest sieges and bloodiest battles. To the military strategist, a once indispensable bastion, the impregnable, invincible Lion of the Rock, crouched in dominance astride the shipping lifeline to Suez——strategically still important, even in an era of jumbo jets and superbombs.

To me, a place I'd always wanted to visit, a soaring stone peak forever imprinted in my childhood dreams. To our expedition, the shipping point to Africa, and, even more important, the only free port in Europe and the place we had to go to buy the $2,000 worth of film and equipment we still needed, a purchase that would have cost us twice as much anywhere else in Europe.

But to the British and Spanish, a still formidable symbol: to the former, a treasured vestige of a glorious empire on which the sun still never sets; to the latter, an irritating reminder of destiny's desertion, of a dead Empire on which the sun no longer shines; to the two, a bone of contention for almost 300 years.

As we drove along the coastal road from Cadiz, Manu gave us the whole story. After the war of the Spanish Succession in 1704, Spain had been forced to cede Gibraltar to Great Britain. The deed rankled. Gibraltar was no unseen and quickly forgotten overseas island, but a part of the Spanish mainland itself, and Spain wanted her back. Three times she tried to blast out the British garrison, and three times she was thrown back. By 1830 Britain had made Gibraltar a Crown Colony, the status it holds today. With the opening of the Suez Canal, in 1869, Gibraltar's importance expanded a thousandfold, placing Britain astride both outlets of the Mediterranean. The Rock became a symbol of British power and Spanish impotence.

The situation was relatively quiet until the spring of 1954 when Queen Elizabeth II paid an official state visit to Gibraltar, re-emphasizing British sovereignty over it and touching off in Spain vigorous demands that the Rock be returned or else. Six months before we arrived the "or else" became an economic embargo.

Gibraltar is a rock in more ways than one: it grows nothing, produces little. Its livelihood depends on tourists and their purchase of cameras, liquor, film, perfume, cigarettes, binoculars and a thousand other items which are cheaper in Gibraltar's duty-free shops than anywhere else in Europe. It was this tourist trade Spain decided to choke, and to do so she put prohibitive taxes on items being brought by tourists into Spain from Gibraltar. She later decided to slash the flow of traffic *into* Gibraltar, something she was ideally situated to do since the only road onto the Rock passes through the Spanish border post at La Linea de la Conception. In order not to insult Britain overtly, she operated under the guise of requiring time to search vehicles for smuggled goods, wasting a full hour on each car so that only ten a day got in, instead of hundreds as before.

As we brooded over this, we rounded a turn on the coastal road, and suddenly—there was Africa, looming up out of the mists in the distance, far across the sparkling Straits of Gibraltar. We stopped the cars and stared across the continents. Africa. The cloud-capped mountains of Morocco beyond the distant water's edge rose alluring and beckoning. *Africa.* Home of the Sahara and the Sudan, land of the Niger and the Nile, Cairo and Khartoum, Kilimanjaro and the Mountains of the Moon. AFRICA. Still the living land of adventure.

We reached La Linea slightly after noon to find ten cars ahead of us in line, which meant that if this policy of one car an hour were true we'd never get through that day. And we didn't. When six o'clock came the border closed with four cars still ahead of us. Neither flattery nor intimidation ameliorated the situation. Even the bribe, a time-honored custom in Spain, bore no results in this case, as two unhappy men in the Renault ahead of us learned. There was no nonsense, no leniency, and no more than one car an hour on the road to Gibraltar.

We pitched our camper at the border. Two cars had pulled out of line, so with luck we'd be through by ten the next morning. Despite the delay, we were all, save Woodrow, in good spirits, for we had wine, food, friendly companions, and an interesting story to tell our friends about the time we had to wait overnight to get into Gibraltar. Poor Woodrow was in the middle of a diarrhea siege, his third or fourth on the trip, and he was forced to spend most of the night visiting various shrub-hidden sites off the road near the heavily patrolled border. Near midnight he had an armed escort back to our camper. His last latrine, it seemed, had been somebody's foxhole.

The border opened at eight, and by ten we led the line, all anxious to push through. But the Spaniards were pushing also—backwards. If we wanted to go to Gibraltar, they told us, we'd have to go in an empty auto because the embargo rules wouldn't abide our heavily loaded cars and camper. They also told us that we couldn't get our bond refunded if we left Spain by way of Gibraltar. We'd have to ship our equipment directly from Spain to Africa if we wanted our $1,750 back. Manu, they also pointed out, was a Spaniard—something he hardly let us forget—and as a Spaniard he was forbidden to go to Gibraltar for any reason—something he'd neglected to mention.

We left the border and drove to the bustling ferry and fishing port of Algeciras and camped to ponder our problems. We had to get to Gibraltar to buy our film and other important equipment. We had to find some way of getting that material to Africa. And we had to find some way of getting back our customs bond and getting to Africa ourselves.

There was only one way, complicated and extremely inconvenient: we would leave the Jeep, the camper, and all our equipment in Algeciras with Manu so that the rest of us would be free to drive to

Gibraltar to make our purchases; and while Willy and Woodrow took them by ferry from Gibraltar to Tangier, Al and I and the girls would return to Algeciras to meet Manu, pick up our equipment, claim our customs bond, and sail to Ceuta, the Spanish port in Morocco, and from there drive the difficult mountain road to Tangier to pick up Willy and Woodrow and the rest of the equipment. It was about as convenient as going from Brooklyn to the Bronx by way of Cucamonga but there was no other way.

Early the next morning, with Manu soundly guarding the camp in his sleep, the seven of us set out for the Rock, reaching La Linea at eight only to find thirteen cars already in line. That meant we couldn't get in until the morning after, but our ferry sailed that next day at noon.

We went to work on the line. The thirteenth, twelfth, and eleventh cars were easy enough to get rid of by simply explaining the arithmetical facts of life.

I told the occupants of the tenth car, five American sailors from the naval base at Rota, that there was absolutely nothing for them to do in Gibraltar, that the women were all married, the goods overpriced, the beaches overcrowded, the casino crooked, and the sightseeing attractions closed until summer; and that they'd be much better heading for the action up around Torremolinos. Hadn't they heard about the bikini contest there?

Now we were sure of getting in, but why stop there? Willy and Al slipped out of the Land Cruiser and walked around the long way to the front of the line where they befriended the driver of the third car and made themselves so much at home that, after half an hour, everyone else in line assumed it was their car. Then they could operate; surely no one would suspect deviousness from someone at the head of the line.

Walking back to the ninth car in line, a German family of six crammed in a VW, Willy introduced himself as a fellow Deutschlander. After a while he said, "By the way, why do you wait in line? You won't be able to get in today."

"No, you are wrong," the German answered. "I have it carefully computed. I will be the last car in, just when they close the frontier at six o'clock."

"Oh, haven't you heard?" asked Willy, looking genuinely upset. "They've changed the system in the past few days. Now they close the border at five o'clock."

"But when I was in Algeciras this morning I was told six."

Willy thought for a moment, then asked, "Do you speak Spanish? —No—only the numbers—well, let's go ask the guard."

So Willy, with the distraught German following, went over to the guard, whom he asked in his speediest Spanish what time it would be one hour before the border closed.

The guard looked puzzled. Willy repeated his question. The guard thought for a minute and answered, "*A las cinco.*"

An angry beetle buzzed out of line.

"I say there," I yelled at Willy, pretending not to know him, and making sure that the car ahead of us could hear, "why did that Volkswagen leave?"

Willy, going along with the ruse, and making sure his reply wasn't lost on the car ahead of me, answered, "The guard told him they close the border at four o'clock today because of a holiday."

"What did you say?" our victim responded.

"I said the guard said they close the border at four today. That's why the Volkswagen left. You'll just miss getting in."

A couple of curses, a turn of a key, and we were up another hour.

Al and Willy walked back to their adopted car—by now second—to chat awhile and re-establish their credentials and their unselfish motives. Then they started out again, with Willy after another German and Al onto another American. Soon I heard Al say, "I wonder if it's really worth visiting really—I mean what with the epidemic and all."

"Epidemic? What epidemic?" the man asked.

"Oh haven't you heard? Nothing too serious, I guess—just some schistosomiasis. But they say it's all right as long as you have a schistosomiasis vaccination."

"I have cholera and smallpox, that's all the travel agent said I'd need."

"Probably didn't know about this—came up pretty quick—43 cases in the past three days."

"I've waited this long I'm not going back. I don't think I'll catch anything in one day."

"Probably not, but you know the Gibraltarians aren't letting people in unless they have schistosomiasis shots."

"You sure?"

"Why should I lie?"

Their last intended victim, an American lawyer, was a toughie. He understood Spanish, insisted he had all his vaccinations, and his wife vetoed the bikini contest. When I heard him mention that it was the next to last day of his vacation I decided to have a go at him.

"I suppose you've heard about the bloody queue on the other side?" I asked, affecting my most British manner and my best colonial accent.

"No, what do you mean?"

"Well, it's even worse getting out of Gibraltar, you know. These Spainies only let one car an hour out. Why, the last time I went in it took me five days to get out."

"I find that hard to believe. I never heard about any trouble getting out. If it's so bad how come you're going back?" the lawyer asked.

"I wish I weren't, but I have to. Own a shop there. Going back to try to sell it, I am. The bloody blockade has ruined the business. Nobody wants to go in when they know they may be trapped for days."

"You sure?"

"Sure as I live there," I answered, moving up to the head of the line.

Once in Gibraltar we headed for the shops on Main Street. They're run by the wiliest collection of merchants west of Baghdad—British, Maltese, Gibraltarians, Sephardics, Greeks, Indians, Chinese—men who pace their store fronts shouting in a cacophony of accents that they have lower prices and better merchandise than the crook next door. Fortunately, we had the pick of the place, because the Spanish embargo had slashed the 850,000 tourists who visited Gibraltar in 1964 to 200,000 in 1965.

We split up to do our shopping. Willy went to buy our 500 rolls of film and some extra filters. I went to look for a small storage trailer to pull behind the Jeep, because the load on our cars and camper was still much too heavy. Woodrow, whom we had appointed treasurer, sought out a bank to buy Moroccan money, sold in Gibraltar for almost half what it costs in Africa. And Al, our self-appointed medic, wandered off in search of "a few things for the first aid kit."

We rendezvoused two hours later, Willy with the film, I with the trailer, Woodrow with the Moroccan *dirhams*, and Al up to his ears with bags and boxes.

"What the hell do you have there?" I asked.

"Just a few things we need to round out the first aid kit. I mentioned it before," he answered, hoping to let it go at that.

I pointed out that it looked more like a year's supplies for a traveling hospital and that we already had space problems.

"Right, Steve, that's why I only got the essentials."

"Like what?" asked Woodrow.

"Like these pills for your diarrhea. See, 500 tablets."

"I guess we do need something like that——"

"I don't want any of these," Willy cut in. "Everybody should buy their own. He'll use up more than all of us. I never need them."

"And what about these salt tablets?" I asked Al.

"You know, they prevent heatstroke in the desert. Help retain moisture, metabolize protein. Good stuff to have," Al explained.

"Yes, but 3,000 of them?"

"They were on sale."

"Was this terramycin also on sale? You aren't supposed to use that without a prescription," I pointed out.

"You're right, Steve, but you never know when we might need a powerful antibiotic, like if we're hundreds of miles from another doctor."

"*Another* doctor?"

"Well, you know what I mean, Steve."

"I'm afraid I do. And what the hell is this stuff—this Darvon 65?"

"Well, I thought we should be prepared for any emergency, so I bought that. It's an anesthetic."

"What in the world do we need an anesthetic for?"

"We probably don't—but just in case. Somebody might break an arm, for instance, or you might get appendicitis, and I'd have to operate. With this stuff you won't feel a thing."

I was sure of that. "Al, be serious, how can you operate on anybody? You don't know the first thing about——"

"I bought this book, too. It's called *Understanding Surgery,* and I'm sure I——"

As we were driving along Main Street toward the ferry, a cute girl waved at Al and shouted a spirited "Cheerio."

"Who was that?" I asked him.

"Who was who?"

"You know who I mean—the girl in front of that drugstore."

"Oh, her? Well, uh—that's Muriel. She works there . . . you see it was like this . . ."

After dropping Woodrow, Willy, and the stuff at the ferry, and promising to meet them in Tangier the next afternoon, we headed back to Spain. But the road out of Gibraltar was blocked. The policeman manning the barricade could have passed for a London bobby, except for his suntan, as he walked up to us and asked, "Heading back to Spain, chaps? Afraid you won't be able to make it tonight."

"Why not?" I asked. "It's only five-thirty and we've still got half an hour until the border closes."

"Sorry, lads, last car's gone through. The Spanish only let one an hour out, you know," the policeman said.

"You must be kidding. I told that to somebody this morning for a joke."

"It's no joke. They wouldn't be lettin' you through 'til tomorrow, now, and there're four cars queued up ahead of you already."

Al turned to me: "That means we can't get out until twelve."

"That's no good," I explained to the policeman. "We have to catch the ferry for Cueta at noon. Isn't there any way to get out earlier?"

"Well, now, lads, you can walk across the border and catch the bus to Algeciras, but no more cars 'til tomorrow."

I noticed that Al had his right elbow cradled in the palm of his left hand, his right hand on his chin, the way he does when he's cooking up some scheme.

"What's the fastest you could drive to Algeciras?" he asked me.

"About twenty minutes."

"Make it fifteen."

"What's the difference? The ferry sails at noon."

"Don't worry. Just be there," he said, grabbing the girls and starting to walk toward Spain.

"What about packing our equipment and getting the Jeep and collecting the bond?" I shouted after him.

"Don't worry. Just be at the pier at twelve-fifteen."

After a sleepless night in the Land Cruiser, I was first in line at the Spanish customs shed by eleven. For an hour I waited impatiently while the guard wasted time, pretending to search the empty car. At the stroke of noon he lifted the barrier. I shot through the gate and roared along the road toward the city. In twelve minutes I was on the outskirts of Algeciras and could plainly see the harbor——and our ferry steaming toward Africa. It was the first time Al had let me down. I'd be stuck in Spain for three or four days until the next ferry. Dejected, I drove to the pier to get the exact schedule.

A smart white ship was tied up to the pier, moored by one line, waiting to cast off. It was a ferry. It was our ferry! A crowd was gathered near the vehicle ramp, and I drove straight for it, blowing my horn. When the crowd parted I saw our Jeep and camper stuck halfway up the ramp and Al beside them turning his pockets inside out. The captain was shouting frantically to a dozen sailors and wharf laborers pushing and pulling at the Jeep.

Al leaped down from the ramp and came running up to me with the ship's angry first mate right beside him.

"I lost the key as we drove on," he winked. "Let me have your spare."

After I'd given it to him he turned to the officer and said, "You see, I told you our *jefe* had an extra key. Tell the captain we can sail now. All right, *jefe*, welcome aboard."

Later, on deck, before I'd quite caught my breath, Al handed me a big paper bag.

"What's this?" I asked. "Tranquilizers?"

"On the contrary, very untranquilizing. Open it."

I did. It was filled with money, Spanish money. The customs officials had refunded our $1,750 in Spanish pesetas—which were about as useful as subway tokens in Alaska.

"What can we do with this junk?" I asked.

"Well, I've been checking around," Al answered, "and if there's one thing Tangier has it's a red-hot black market in Spanish money. Those wise guys aren't getting any last laugh on the Trans World Record Expedition."

The trip across the Straits was over before we knew it. In 90 minutes we had traveled fifteen miles and a thousand years into a world of veiled women and turbaned men, mosques and minarets, camels and caravans. Gone were the heady orange scents of Valencia and the flamenco beat of the caves of Old Madrid, replaced by the musky smells and haunting rhythms of Africa. Gone, too, I hoped, were the problems that had plagued us so far.

From Cueta to Tangier the map shows 25 miles, but it's 65 if you have to drive it, for between the two lies the tip of the Tell, with peaks of the Ev Rif rising to 8,000 and 10,000 feet above the fields of wheat and grapes. Our heavily laden cars lumbered up the mountain, every space jammed with gear and supplies, water cans and wine bottles hanging out the sides of the jars, gas cans strapped to the front of the trailer, and our six new tires lashed to the top. The pace was slow, but the girls sang merrily, for we were back on the road and into our second continent. They sang, little realizing that we were about to have the first of a series of troubles that were to plague us day after day as we pushed across Africa.

As we climbed a particularly steep stretch, about a thousand feet above the sea, with me leading in the Land Cruiser and hauling the camper, and Al following in the Jeep, I felt a sudden lurch forward, an instant lightening of the load. I jerked around to see a shower of sparks behind me. The trailer hitch had snapped. The camper had broken loose and was careening down the mountain road. Six thousand dollars' worth of trailer and supplies was hurtling to certain destruction on the rocks below.

Al, about 40 feet behind me, had also seen the sparks and the wild

camper, and throwing the Jeep into low gear, rammed into the rear of
the trailer just before it reached the edge. The Jeep was knocked back
with the blow, almost going over the edge itself. Everything was safe,
with only a few bumper scars to give evidence of what could have
been a tragedy.

It took two hours to put on a spare hitch and replace the snapped
safety chains, so it was dark when we got to Tangier and met Woodrow and Willy. We wanted to find the camp grounds, but there were
few people about at that hour, and those who were couldn't seem to
understand what we wanted. In desperation, after a succession of
Arabs had greeted our questions with pleasant smiles but shrugged
shoulders, we dragged our small tent out of the trailer and set it up in
the street, then launched into a charade on going to sleep. We finally
made ourselves understood, and two boys volunteered to show us the
way to the camp grounds. We followed them down a wide avenue
and along the edge of the bay to a sheltered hollow of grass and sand
near the beach. But our guides had misunderstood.

Not that the spot wasn't a campsite, for it certainly was, though
the tents were so filthy it was almost impossible to make them out
in the dark. But they didn't belong to any tourists. It was a gypsy
encampment. The gypsies eyed us suspiciously at first, but after ap-
praising the value of our equipment and the vigor of our three rather
frightened females, they beckoned us to pitch out tents and join the
family. We declined the offer, and eventually found our way to the
official campsite, a secluded spot high on a lush green hill overlooking the ocean, a few hundred yards from a little-used beach.
The hill was thick with palm and pepper trees, fragrant purple bougainvillea and rich red poinsettia. There was no sound save the pounding of the distant surf and the call of unfamiliar insects, no light save
the brilliant points of starshine overhead. It was a world of our own in
the middle of a world far from our own.

Our hill was said to be the tomb of the mythological giant Antoeus
whom Hercules had slain. Other killings in the vicinity had not been so
mythological, for all around Tangier are the ruins of Phoenician,
Carthaginian, Roman and Arab colonies, as they destroyed and succeeded one another, to be followed in turn by warring Portuguese,

conquering Spaniards, colonizing English, reconquering Arabs, pirating Corsairs, bombarding Spaniards, and besieging French.

Only in the past century, when it was proclaimed an international city, did relative peace come to Tangier, for the major powers watched jealously lest any one become too powerful there. During the last war it became a center of international intrigue and espionage; after that, a gold trading center; today, capitalizing on its proximity to Europe, a pleasant den of vice where, for a price, any desire can be accommodated, whether it demands gold bars, male prostitutes, raw opium, aphrodisiacs, poisons, psychedelics, or pubescent virgins. Tangier became a home-near-home for the adventurer, the social outcast, the pervert, the mystic, the misfit, and the thrill-seeker. Whereas in North Africa the tourists sought out Cairo and Luxor, the businessmen Benghazi and Casablanca, the revolutionaries Algiers and Accra, the thrill-seekers headed for Tangier.

And there we were, though we weren't seeking thrills at the moment. Garages and welding shops were more our concern, for we had much to do before we could face Africa. We put the special tires on the Land Cruiser, replaced our SAE 30 motor oil with SAE 40 to reduce wear and heat in the deserts, greased both cars and repacked their front-wheel bearings. The storage trailer had to be assembled, our cargo shifted, film protected from the heat in Thermos chests, stoves cleaned, our Spanish money changed, food laid in. Three days. On the last of them we had to take the camper in to be welded and braced because the rough slide down the mountain had cracked the Spanish welds and put four new breaks in the undercarriage. The welders, working underneath with their torches, accidentally burned through the thin wood floor of the camper, setting afire the compartments where our clothes were stored and almost destroying the whole thing before we doused it.

By day the work tied us down, but by night we surrendered to the allure of the *casbah*, the old native section of Tangier, a fascinating labyrinth of ancient alleyways enclosed by a high wall and a fort. In our journey we would visit almost every major *medina* and *casbah* in the Arab world—at Rabat, Casablanca, Meknes, Fez, Tripoli, Algiers, Jerusalem, Damascus—but none so impressive as the *casbah* in Tangier. Here no electric bulbs impose their harsh tungsten shine, no auto fumes assault the air, no talking tubes drown the mellifluous chant of the street vendors. Here a thousand liquid tongues stir a broth of ancient Arabic, the throb of clay drums fills the night air with a solid pulse, and exotic spice and burning incense deluge the senses. Here barbers ply their trade at curbside by candlelight, tanners work the hides of goat and camel into delicate purse and rugged saddle; bearded fat candy vendors doze unconcerned while thick swarms of bees and flies gorge on their honeyed wares. Glistening kebobs sizzle on outdoor braziers, the sweet smell of Moroccan mint tea hangs heavy in the air, and the faint bluish smoke of hashish curls in mysterious cuneiform behind the turbaned pipe smokers.

The market place supplies all the entertainment and education one could ask, as buyer and seller, their haggling skills honed by generations, slowly sip and puff and do the dance of the *dirham*. A candle is a penny, a can-opener two, a ball of twine three; a dollar is a night's delight of bargaining and bickering.

Our bargaining ability was hampered by lack of both language and technique. We could do no more than ask the vendor to write on a piece of paper the price he wanted for an item that interested us, while pretending not to be really too interested, so that, whatever figure he wrote, we could look sufficiently outraged to cross it out and cut it in thirds, hoping to convince him that was as high as we were willing to go. After several blatant failures with this method, we managed to introduce a Western element into the process: competition, the heart of capitalism, the core of free enterprise, and the bane of our *casbah* shopkeepers. After establishing one vendor's lowest price, we'd reject it with boisterious dissatisfaction, loudly and directly marching to the next man who carried the same merchandise, leaving no doubts in either's mind about our motive, a trick to which the average Arab shopper, able to rely on his bargaining skill and restrained by his inbred politeness, would never have resorted. But resort to it we did, and prices fell before us. But we were still to learn that price wasn't everything, as with my purchases, for example: a clay drum and a colorful cotton bathrobe. The drum cracked in my lap the third time I played it, and as for the robe——

"What are you going to do with that dress?" Al asked.

"It's not a dress, stupid, it's a robe, the kind you wear after a bath," I retorted.

"If you wear that thing you're going to have to take two baths—the second one to wash off the dye."

I looked, and my fingers were already turning green and purple. So much for our noble endeavor to introduce the competitive spirit to the *casbah*. It was midnight, and time to quit.

The *casbah* by day and evening is a pageant of shoppers and sellers, but after the witching hour it's a netherworld of mystery. The worn stone streets rang with our lonely steps as we sought to find a way out. There were only a few faint gas lanterns to guide us. The upper floors of the houses hung over the streets and alleys, turning them into a maze of dark tunnels. Arabs squatted on corners, bent but not asleep, eyes active under their hoods, watching, waiting. Cats were everywhere; not the scrawny, frightened alleycats of home, but the imperious feline queens with shiny fur, fat on *casbah* rats. Spoiled vegetables lay dumped along the streets, and here and there the contents of a chamber pot; an old man with a water cart was hosing the mélange into the sewers. At one corner a man held another on the ground, beating him over the head with a boot; at another four young toughs lingered, just waiting.

When we reached our Land Cruiser, parked outside the walls near the Grand Socco, the hubcaps were missing. If we had had another day we could probably have bought them back; the Moroccans say that if something disappears one day you'll find it for sale in the *casbah* the next.

But we didn't have the time. We had to go to Rabat, the Moroccan capital, to apply for new Algerian visas, because the ones we had obtained in Paris had expired, thanks to our delays in Spain. Though it had once been possible to get them at the Algerian border, they were no longer being issued there because of the strained relations between the two countries; we had to drive 200 miles out of our way to get them. I envied Marco Polo; he only had to detour for rivers and robbers.

It was the 15th of May when we left Tangier, far behind our schedule, which called for us to be in Teheran, a sixth of the world away. From Cherbourg we had taken 45 days to cover a distance for which our schedule allowed eleven. If we continued at the same pace, Al calculated, our ten month journey would run to 40. We'd be on the road three and a half years!

The road to Rabat, which was a smooth and well-banked highway of French construction—the last good stretch of asphalt we'd see in Africa —ran along the Atlantic coast and gave us a breathtaking view: the sea in great green swells rolled in to meet an endless beach upon which she crashed and foamed and released the mighty power nourished by an unbroken journey of five thousand miles. There was no horizon line, for the sky and sea blended into one; there was no time, no sign or scar of civilization, no living things save us and a few camels chewing salt grass on the beach.

We couldn't reach Rabat by nightfall so we pulled off the road as evening came, into a palm-fringed clearing in the middle of a grape field. An Arab came out and introduced himself—Abdul Marrakchi, owner of 160 acres of vineyards, yet dressed like the poorest of his laborers and as work-stained as any of them—and welcomed us with plates of cooked liver and bottles of iced beer. Till the moon and his men were high, they sat around listening to Moroccan music on our radio, finished three packs of Salems and a bottle of Old Granddad, and told us stories of Morocco's battles for independence. One of them even rolled up his trouser leg to display his war wounds. By the time they left, the girls were thoroughly frightened—far from home, in the middle of a grape field in Africa, with drunken Arabs all around, strange animal sounds in the night, and tales of war and bloodshed still fresh in their ears. Thus did I agree to break a basic rule of the expedition: that the girls slept alone in the Poptent and the men in the camper. I nobly gave in to their frightened entreaties and, despite much grumbling from Al and Manu, squeezed into their tent, the girls snuggling beside me.

I had just dozed off when I felt something crawling over the foot of my sleeping bag, moving toward Barbara. I had to warn her. I shook her gently and whispered in her ear, "Barbara, Barbara, don't be alarmed, and don't panic, but there's some animal or something near the foot of your sleeping bag."

Barbara stirred, but didn't awaken. I nudged her gently again. "Barbara, Barbara, now listen. Easy. Don't be alarmed, but there's some kind of animal in the tent." She rolled closer to me.

"Quit joshing, Steve. You're a real card, you are. Go back to sleep."

When the thing jumped on her she let out a scream that carried clear back to Tangier. She tried to spring to her feet, but her sleeping bag tripped her and she fell on top of me. Liz and Mira were awake now—alarmed, hysterical, screaming, "Help! Steve! There's a bloody snake in the tent! Help! Help!"

But Steve was in no position to help anybody. All three girls were upon me. I couldn't get to my feet. I couldn't get to my flashlight. And worse, I couldn't even find my pants. Barbara and Mira were sitting on top of me, and Liz had her legs wrapped around my neck, all three of them hysterical and howling.

Finally I found the flashlight and flickered it on. There, at our feet, was the biggest, slimiest, fattest, ugliest toad I have ever seen, a foot across if he was an inch, rot-colored and wet and covered with lumps. Despite the girls' hysteria, and their legs and arms which were wrapped around me every which way, I was able to catch the toad, unzip the flap, and throw him out of the tent, exclaiming, "Okay, okay, he's gone. Now for God's sake stop screaming."

The girls settled down. Mira climbed back into her sleeping bag, and Liz returned my left arm, but Barbara was still frightened. "What if there are more of those buggers in here, Steve?" she asked.

"I'm certain that was the only one," I assured her, "but if it'll make you happy I'll shine the light around." It hardly made her happy. On top of her knapsack, surveying the scene with moist, bulging eyes, was another toad—even bigger, slimier, fatter, and uglier than his predecessor. The girls screamed, all of them, one on top of the other, and all on top of me. Mira was trying to sit on my head, Liz was shinnying up me like a telephone pole, and Barbara was crying and jumping and scratching my back. They were absolutely out of control. When I finally caught the toad, I tossed him out of the tent—and there, rolling on the ground, clutching their stomachs with laughter, yelling, "*Au revoir, crapaud,"* were Al and Manu. And I swear the damn toad nodded to them as he hopped off.

Ten minutes later all was calm and the girls settled down. "After all, it was only a toad," I'd pointed out, "and they can't hurt you. There's nothing to be afraid of."

"You're right," Liz admitted. "We're sorry we acted so silly, Steve. But those bloody frogs took us by surprise. We're okay now. Let's have a nip of wine for a nightcap and go back to bed. All right?" She reached for the wine bottle—and there was another toad, the granddaddy of them all, the biggest, slimiest, fattest, ugliest toad in Morocco. Liz screamed and dropped the bottle, spilling wine all over my sleeping bag. Then Barbara and Mira joined her, screeching at the top of their lungs and scrambling for footholds on my stomach.

I pushed them off, grabbed my pants, and moved back to the camper. Al and Manu were still laughing when I walked by.

Bad news met us in Rabat: the Algerian Embassy wanted 48 hours to process our visa applications. The girls, however, got a break; they were told that, as members of the British Commonwealth, they didn't need visas. We should have such luck. Another two days wasted.

From Rabat, after a brisk morning swim in the Atlantic, which we weren't to see again for longer than any of us dreamed, we headed east toward Algeria, visas in our pockets and a wind at our back. The land we crossed, lying between the Rif and the still snow-covered Middle Atlas Mountains, and watered by their abundant runoff, was fertile and thick with waving fields of cereal grain and dark patches of vegetables. Bright birds darted before us, and the farmers waved as we passed.

Evening found us on the outskirts of Meknes, the descending sun reflected brilliantly off the enameled tiles at the arched entrance to the *casbah.*

Meknes is Morocco's largest interior city. Beyond the *casbah* it is ultra-modern, thriving, commerical, with hotels of Miami Beach Gothic and apartments of imitation Mies Van der Rohe towering over the massive *medina* walls, updating its centuries-old reputation as a gaudy architectural showplace, a reputation first established during the reign of Sultan Mulay Ishmail who sought to turn the city into an Arab Versailles—though it's difficult to see where he found the time with 4,000 women in his harem and 876 children to his credit.

Meknes also had the last official campsite in Africa; after it, save for a thin strip along the coast, lay the barren, inhospitable North Africa of endless deserts. But when we reached the campsite, we found that the annual Meknes Fair had just begun, and the camp grounds were taken over with rides, amusements, food shops, Coca-Cola stands, farm equipment displays, livestock exhibits, and booths where the uses of fertilizer and the findings of meteorology were explained. It could have been a state fair in Kansas or Idaho, except for the big display of Russian tractors and the shop handing out Red Chinese propaganda to the dark-skinned men wearing turbans and fezzes. When we explained our problem to the director of the Fair, he apologized and listed five or ten good reasons why we couldn't camp there while the Fair was in progress—then threw them all away and invited us to stay. He cleared a spot for our tents, saw that they were protected by guards, arranged for us to come and go freely and, to top everything off, asked us to be his special guests at the opening banquet the next afternoon, the first Americans, he said, ever to be so honored.

We slept that night with our camper almost lost beside huge black goatskin tents in a maze of stake ropes as thick as an arm. We were awakened early by the fearsome bleating of a hundred sheep being slaughtered, literally on our doorstep, before being roasted on giant outdoor spits in preparation for the banquet.

The feast began shortly after midday, and we'd all skipped breakfast in anticipation. A troop of Moroccan soldiers arrived to escort us— dressed in our best, with the girls clean-scrubbed and shining—to one of the huge tents where we were seated on immense bright-colored silk pillows heaped around short tables, beside which sat scores of men— mostly in native costume, with a few government officials and busi- nessmen in Western dress—all laughing and joking and shoveling food in with their hands. The girls hesitated a moment, searching the sea of chewing faces in vain for other females.

A hundred waiters served us, and a hundred servings they brought: giant oval loaves of rye bread, still warm from the oven; huge, heaping platters of pastry stuffed with a mouth-watering mixture of chopped pigeon, scrambled eggs, brown sugar and strange spices; and lambs, whole roasted lambs, fresh and young and dripping with sweet juices; and platters of baked whole chickens covered with curry sauce.

Our Moroccan hosts ate with their fingers, tearing huge hunks of meat apart with their teeth. They shouted at the waiters for more, and grabbed meat from the platters, swallowing in gulps and tossing bones and scraps on the sawdusted ground or over their heads or out the sides of the tent with complete abandon. They ate for the sheer joy of eating, and it was a wonder to watch them. They ate as if it were their last meal on earth; they ate until their stomachs seemed about to burst—and when plates of fruit arrived they gorged themselves again.

The host at my cushion collection was the chief of the Moroccan army, a commanding young general who stuffed me like a howitzer. He yelled at every waiter to put more food on my plate, though it was always full. From one passing waiter, the general grabbed half a lamb and plopped it down on our table, showering it with salt and spice. By the time I finished my end of the lamb, I never wanted to eat again, but then they brought out the poultry, and the general smilingly threw me a whole chicken, curry sauce flying all over. He kept breaking off choice pieces of other chickens and throwing them to me across the table; as soon as I finished one piece, two more came sailing into my lap. I joined the Moroccans in tossing the bones out of the tent, but as the onslaught continued I found myself throwing whole chicken legs out the sides, even burying pieces of meat in the sand with my foot. And everybody else was still going strong. What a meal. When the food finally stopped everyone reclined on the pillows and smoked strong cigarettes and the Arabs told their favorite stories; the air beneath the goatskins was heavy with smoke and laughter and peptic rumbles of approval.

Stuffed beyond belief, we piled into the Toyota for a quick visit to Mulay Idris, a town less than an hour from Meknes, yet centuries distant, a vast *medina* undisturbed by the progress of the past thousand years. Named for the disciple of Mohammed who brought the Moslem religion to Morocco, the town retains his religious fervor to such an extent that non-Moslems are absolutely forbidden to remain within its walls after nightfall. If we tried to stay in Mulay Idris after dark, we were warned at the Fair, some fanatic *mullah* would be sure to lead an attack on us; it was bad enough, we were told, going there with unveiled women.

A girl just doesn't go unveiled in any small town or inland city of North Africa, and it is only in the big coastal cities, such as Tangier, Tunis, Casablanca, and Bizerte, which have been exposed to a hundred years of French influence, and where the women have developed European attitudes, that many have abandoned the veil completely, though most retain it in modified form. Whereas their inland sisters wear shapeless sacks of thick white cotton through which nothing shows but shadowy eye holes, the young Moslem women of the big cities wear form-fitting tunics in attractive shades of pink and blue silk, high heel shoes, and the thinnest of gossamer veils, just barely covering the nose and lips, and leaving the eyes—which are strikingly outlined with makeup—fully exposed, thus following the letter, though certainly not the spirit, of the Moslem custom. They wield their veils in the same devastatingly effective way that a Lima lady flirts behind her lace *abanico* or a Hong Kong girl coquettes with her bamboo fan. Inland, however, the women dare not flirt or look attractive to any but their husbands, and the farther east we traveled the truer we found this.

As we gaped at the veiled women scurrying out of our sight, we were conscious of the men of Mulay Idris regarding us with equal attention—though much less affection. Except for an old, one-armed man who offered to guard our car for a *dirham*, no one greeted us—a sharp contrast to the other Moroccan towns where half the population turned out to bid us welcome. As we hiked up the steep, stepped streets of the town, we had the feeling that we were being watched from behind the thick wooden doors, that in every mosque fanatical men were hatching plots to doom the infidels. The only time anyone spoke to us was when we went too close to a mosque. In Mulay Idris, as in all Morocco, it is strictly forbidden for a non-Moslem to enter a mosque, again a strange contrast to such bastions of the Arab world as Damascus and Cairo which bid the tourist welcome and are proud to display their mosques. When Willy tried to sneak into the courtyard of a mosque from which a strange chant was issuing, two guards caught him and roughed him up for his troubles. Only the little children smiled at us and posed for pictures and ate our candy—until their parents darted out of doorways to snatch them back before the heathens contaminated them. In 20 years they will probably treat their children the same way. Never have I felt so unwanted and unloved by my fellow men.

That afternoon we resolved to learn more about Islam, for its hold on its followers and its potential as a world force were more than we had imagined. Six hundred million people, a quarter of the world's population, live under its awesome power, cut off by their beliefs from the other three-quarters, taught that theirs is the only true way to worship God. A careful reading of their Koran shows they can never accept compromise or coexistence with other religions; only capitulation and conversion. We had always tried to regard religions as benign philosophical systems, each trying, in its own way, to prescribe the means of adherence to a higher law of truth and decency, to control man's baser impulses, to make for a better life on earth and beyond; but that afternoon at Mulay Idris changed all that, making us feel to the core of our bones that dark forces were at work, that a religion could become the most evil of influences.

We had been told in Meknes that one foreigner lived in Mulay Idris, an American professor who had converted to Islam and been granted a special dispensation to make his home there. Al was eager to meet him, feeling that it would be interesting material for our articles. But I couldn't bring myself to disturb him. I knew that some powerful force must have driven him to Mulay Idris, and I was sure he wouldn't want visitors from home, or intrusions like ours. But what tales he could tell, what things he must have seen—though it wasn't for us to ask him. Maybe he'll tell them himself, some day.

On the way back to our camp at Meknes we passed the ruins of Volubis, the westernmost major Roman city in Africa, an enduring witness to the six-century era when one nation ruled all of North Africa from the Atlantic to the Nile. Where 1,600 years ago 100,000 people had lived and worked in a magnificently planned and beautifully constructed city, today storks nest atop the decrowned columns and look down on a jungle of empty pedestals, a silent Forum, and Caracalla's wobbly, weathered Arch of Triumph. Where once a proud Roman highway, lined with massive Doric columns, had run from Volubis to Tangier and the farthest reaches of the Granary of Rome, today a crumbled strip of uneven rock ends in a weed-filled field, and the columns beside it are no higher than tombstones.

That night the heavens opened. Thunder rumbled across the Tell and lightning flashed onto the mountain tops. And the rains came, pounding, soaking, drenching rains, our first since Spain—our last for 10,000 miles! The next day we were to cross the Middle Atlas through the Col de Touahar near the Taza gap and enter one of the world's driest regions, an arid waste which, save for a thin strip along the Mediterranean and a few isolated oases, would stretch unbroken to the delta of the Nile. It was a region the rain gods seldom visited; so that night they came to say good-bye.

The road from Meknes led through Fez, the last city before the Taza gap, the last until the border, 150 miles away. Fez, like Mulay Idris and most of the interior cities of Morocco, is completely surrounded by a high wall built to protect it from the nomad tribes. From the outside it has little distinction, but behind the walls is a fairyland. A perpetual river meanders through the heart of the town, bringing bloom to flower gardens along its path, watering bougainvillea and citrus trees, and flowing past tiled public patios and benches where the weary or the pensive can relax. It's a city for contemplation, founded by the Moslem proselytizer Mulay Idris. Six hundred years ago, after their expulsion from Spain, the most devout Islamic scholars flocked to it. In Fez they built the famed Karaouyn University, and today another dozen *medersas* cluster around it, teaching the gospel according to Mohammed along with differential calculus and international relations. Students from all over the Arab world come to Fez, where they live in magnificent dormitories—cool, tiled complexes of living rooms, patios, chapels, cloisters, and mosques. We talked one young student into showing us the housing facilities; but the classrooms were strictly forbidden, and we could only wonder what the descendants of the Moors were planning for the descendants of those who drove them back to Africa.

It was noon before we left Fez and stopped to cook, and we were all looking forward to the meal, our first since the big feast, and a special one in another way. In our tours of the market places, we'd always been discouraged by the meat, which, since the shops had neither refrigeration nor display cases, hung on hooks in the open air where it was literally covered with flies and by midday had a grayish, pock-marked appearance that was about as appetizing as turkey vomit. A few of the more enlightened butchers would perfunctorily cover their meat with swatches of cheesecloth, but this only seemed to give the flies a better foothold. That day, however, we thought we'd beaten the system by going to the *casbah* market early in the morning, right after it opened, and choosing the freshest, reddest piece of meat we could find before any flying competitors got to it.

We dug into our lunch, then stopped and stared across the table at each other in dismay, our faces contorted. The meat was so foul-smelling we had to hold our noses to get it into our mouths—where it slipped around like a ball of rancid grease. It was so slimy it couldn't be chewed; it just squished between the teeth. It smelled and tasted almost like a camel. In fact, I realized it was a camel. I'd been compelled to live off the stuff for a wretched month when I'd crossed Afghanistan by caravan, and I swore I'd never forget the taste as long as I lived.

I went on to assure the others that camel meat was certainly edible, if hardly palatable, and that it would do them no permanent harm. They all said they believed me, but nonetheless half a dozen surprised Arabs found themselves getting a free lunch that afternoon from a slightly green group of *harib*.

We washed our hands, brushed our teeth, and bade au revoir to Morocco as we headed toward the border. Things were not going well. We were running out of wine, and ahead of us in Algeria was a mine field, a robbery, a revolution, an auto accident, and a breakdown in the desert.

Chapter 6

"The Land of a Thousand Horrors"

"What is New Zealand?"

"What do you mean, *what* is New Zealand?" Mira shot back.

"I mean what is New Zealand?" the Algerian passport officer repeated.

"It's a country. What do you think it is? It's a country just like yours —only better," she added under her breath.

"There is no such country on our list. It is perhaps part of America?"

"No, it's not part of America, never was and never will be," Barbara cut in. "It's part of the British Commonwealth. It's in the South Pacific, near Australia."

"I have never heard of it. You must go back to Rabat and apply for a visa."

"Apply for a visa?" Mira shouted.

"Go back to Rabat?" Barbara gasped.

I cut in and explained that the girls had been told by the Algerian Consulate in Rabat that they wouldn't need visas because New Zealand was part of the British Commonwealth and that British subjects could enter Algeria without visas.

"This is not a British passport," the guard answered. "These women must go back to Rabat for visas."

And so it went on for three hours. The guard wasn't going to let anybody in from a country he'd never heard of, and we'd be damned if we'd recross the breadth of Morocco.

A compromise was finally reached: the guard gave the girls a temporary entry visa, good for 72 hours, and they had to report to the Ministry of Foreign Affairs in Algiers and explain their case within that time limit or they would be put in jail.

Exhausted from the hour and the ride—which from Fez had been

66

through barren lands and mountains, and during which we'd had to labor for three hours repairing new breaks in the trailer's undercarriage—we decided to camp at the first clear spot we came to. The border area was a mess of armed soldiers, concrete tank traps, and barbed wire, but a little beyond we found a hard-caked field and pulled off into it, pitching our camper and tent about forty yards from the road. We were asleep in seconds.

"Attention! Attention!" A voice was shouting at us in French through a megaphone. It was early morning and I rubbed the sleep out of my eyes. *"Defense d'allez! Defense d'allez!"* The voice belonged to an Algerian Army officer up on the road.

Willy blanched: "He says we shouldn't move. He says we're in the middle of a mine field!"

"Mine field? I thought they'd gotten rid of those by now," Al exclaimed.

"Got rid of what?" asked Woodrow, just waking up.

"The mines. I edited a story about them at *Argosy*." Al explained that about 15,000,000 mines had been laid throughout Algeria, mostly by the rebels to blow up French troops and equipment during the war for independence, some to prevent attack from Morocco. And after the war they didn't even remember where they'd put a lot of them. They'd managed to dig up about half, but of the 7,000,000 left, a few were somewhere under, around, or in front of us.

"What does he say we should do?" I asked Willy, who was translating.

After several shouted exchanges: "He says we should stay here. He has no mine detector. He says in four or five days the mine expert is due back in this part of the country. He also says we're a bunch of stupid fools to ignore all the warnings."

Far down the road a tiny sign winked at us in the morning sun.

A four day delay would be intolerable and unsafe. The girls were afraid to try to leave, but I reminded them they'd be in jail if we didn't.

The safest and surest way to get out was probably the way we'd gotten in, but it was impossible to find our tire tracks in the hard-packed sand; so I decided to try an old trick I'd learned in the Marines. I took one of our arrows and to it tied a long piece of string, tied the string to a strong piece of cord, and attached the cord to the winch cable on our car. I shot the arrow onto the road, where the officer hauled in on the string and the cord and the winch cable until he had enough to work with.

Following our shouted instructions the officer found a big boulder, about 80 pounds. With the help of several nomads who'd stopped to see the *harib* get blown up, he rolled it to the road and hooked the end of the winch wire around it. When I started the engine to activate the winch the others took shelter beneath the camper, but I had to stay up front, my foot on the pedals, hauling in the improvised mine sweeper. The big boulder came tumbling and dragging along the ground, certain to detonate any mine in its path, and if the mine happened to be close to the car—I forced myself not to think of it, forced my mind back to thoughts of Kubla Khan and Marco Polo and the days when they didn't have mined frontiers. With a solid clink the boulder hit the bumper. The path was clear.

But was it really? The boulder had certainly swept a path big enough for a pedestrian, but was it wide enough for the car and camper? I couldn't run the risk, so I sent the others to the road, marching one at a time along the pathway. Al went last, carrying the winch wire which, on reaching the road, he hooked up to another big boulder that I planned to drag along a path parallel to the first. It was about halfway home when it hit a mine. The world erupted. My ears went deaf with the blast. The car seemed to leap straight up. Pieces of rock and dirt exploded skyward and settled over the car. But that was all. I was unharmed, the car was running, the path was cleared, and the Trans World Record Expedition was back on the road.

There was little to like about Algeria except the scenery. Prices were ridiculous: gasoline was a dollar a gallon, the highest we paid anywhere in the world; they wanted two dollars for a chicken, which in Morocco had cost forty cents; everything was three, four, or five times costlier than anywhere else in North Africa. It took hours to find a place to exchange money; no one accepted our Moroccan money, and even for dollars they offered an unfairly low rate. When Manu bought a bottle of Algerian red wine, world famous before independence, it was terrible. The farms we passed were without vigor. The Algerians had expropriated 22,000 farms when they drove out the French settlers, turning them into 2,284 "socialist production units," operated by the state in an experiment that turned out to be a disaster. Lacking the skilled managers to run them successfully, supervised by heroes of the guerrilla war who had no inclination for farm life, and worked by men who had little incentive for doing a good job, the farms had come on bad times and food prices were soaring throughout the country. Though once Algeria had earned abundant foreign exchange by selling its surplus wine, olives, citrus and wheat abroad, it was now faced with an agricultural deficit in the millions. Discontent was widespread. Every 50 miles or so a soldier behind a machine gun roadblock checked our passports and destination.

But the scenery was another matter. At Oran we hit the Mediterranean coast and drove for hours through breathtaking beauty along a cliff road overlooking the sea; every twist and turn brought with it a more magnificent view. Five hundred feet below us were virgin beaches, quiet coves, thick forests of fir trees down to the water's edge, sleepy fishing villages—the shining sands of the Costa del Sol, massive red rocks of the Riviera, wooded islands of Greece, soaring seaside cliffs of Big Sur—caves and jetties and dunes and bays, inlets and streams and waterfalls and ponds, almost every gift in Nature's cornucopia of beauty.

Al was leading in the Land Cruiser when a blue Citroen passed me doing at least 80 miles an hour on the narrow road, swaying all over the place, cutting in ahead of me just in time to avoid smashing a car coming from the other direction. At the outskirts of a little village he started to pass Al, then turned to cut perpendicularly in front of him, heading for a certain collision. Al yanked the wheel violently and smashed the brakes to bring the car and camper to a miraculous, slithering stop half an inch from the crazy Citroen. I never thought he'd make it; the Citroen seemed bent on suicide.

Al and the girls tore out of the Land Cruiser, raging at the Citroen.

The Citroen responded in French with a string of curses.

Al yelled, "Where the hell did you get your license—in a box of Crackerjacks?"

The girls let loose with some New Zealand broadsides.

And even normally complacent Manu came up with a barrage that culminated with *"Me cago en la cona de tu madre!"*

The Citroen retorted, "May a pig die on the grave of your grandmother!"

Everyone in the village was on the road, a crowd of about 40 Arabs to whom it had to be obvious from the position of the cars that the Citroen was recklessly at fault, yet all of them took his side, as if they were afraid not to—even those who had actually seen him run Al off the road. A woman came running out of the house into whose court-yard the Citroen had been turning. She was waving a broomstick, screaming in French, "Go away! Go away, foreigners. Always for-eigners. Always making trouble. Leave my husband alone!"

But Al wasn't having it. "Let me see your license," he demanded. The Citroen's mouth fell open in shock, but he didn't budge.

"I said show me your license," Al shouted, moving in on him.

"There, *that* is my license," the Citroen shot back in French, pulling a card out of his pocket.

"This isn't a driver's license, and you know it." Al barked as I caught a flash of a card that said "Ministry of Public Works" on the top. "All this probably says is you dig sewers or haul shit away. It's a very fitting card for you, I'm sure, but I want to see your driver's license. I'll see to it you never drive again."

The Citroen spat on the ground.

"OK, Frenchie, if that's the way you want it, that's the way you'll get it." Al walked behind his car and took down the license number.

That did it. The Citroen flew into a speechless rage. He ran at Al. Al pulled back to hit him. Willy kicked him in the leg. The crowd started to move in. I jumped in to break up the fight. I couldn't understand why the Citroen hadn't just made a polite apology in the first place to get rid of us; but he was in no mood to apologize now, and we couldn't take on the whole village, so I pushed Al and Willy into the Land Cruiser. As we pulled away, Al yelled at the driver, "Just wait, buddy, I got your number and I'll see that the authorities in Algiers hear about this!" The girls in the back seat merrily stuck out their tongues.

That had happened in Picard, and two hours later we were 40 miles east of there looking for a spot to camp for the night, the winding cliff

road with its rickety bridges and washed out sections having proved
too dangerous for anything but daylight driving. As we were looking, a
blue Citroen came thundering over the hill behind us, hooting the
horn, careening and swaying all over the road. But not until the car cut
in front of us did I realize it was the same motorized menace we'd
clashed with in Picard, this time with two uniformed policemen in the
rear seat.

For ten minutes the words flew hot and heavy. Al and the Citroen
took swings at each other, but their words did more damage. The
police, slightly embarrassed but obviously on the Citroen's side,
stood off a bit, holsters unbuttoned. Little by little the truth began to
emerge: the Citroen was a very important chap, Bendauche Muhamed,
the Police Commissioner for the entire district. The card he'd shown
Al from the Ministry of Public Works didn't authorize him to dig
sewers, but to arrest people, a job he'd won by being a guerrilla
leader in the war against the French.

From a quiet conversation with the policemen, I filled in the rest of
the situation: the Commissioner was an extremely bad driver whose
speeding and recklessness were notorious through the district, though
they were politely ignored in deference to his position. But we had
called attention to them. We had demanded to see his license, taken his
plate number, called him a Frenchman and a lot of things less printable,
and threatened to report him to Algiers. The only way the Commissioner could regain his village's respect was to bring us back to admit
that we were wrong.

But we had no intention of backtracking to Picard; we'd had enough
Algerian delays already, as I told the Commissioner.

"As you wish," he said, "but let us have some wine and discuss this. I
know a cafe not far from here. Come, Mr. Stephens, come with me,
and your friends can follow." I suspected a trick, but had little choice
when the policemen seconded the motion.

Not without misgivings, I got into the Citroen. The Commissioner
roared off in a cloud of dust, racing back the way we'd come, wobbling
on the wrong side of the road, careening along the twisting, potholed
asphalt, honking madly, scaring bicyclists and pedestrians, forcing oncoming cars onto the side. More than once I thought for sure we'd had

it, but the blue Citroen was known and feared by all, and neither man nor beast stood in its way; even the trees seemed to lean away when they saw us coming.

"You see, Mr. Stephens, your friend was wrong," the Commissioner boasted. "I drive very well, don't I?" My mouth was too dry to answer. In forty minutes we were back in Picard. The Land Cruiser and Jeep took another hour to make it.

The village was dark and no one was about; the Commissioner's plan was foiled, so he drove us down to the beach and told us to camp for the night, posting the two policemen to stand guard "to protect you from robbers." The police built a roaring bonfire over which the girls boiled soup and heated tins of meat; the Commissioner contributed a five-gallon jug of wine. We were all friends now, and the Commissioner was happy. He showed us a postcard of New York which a nephew had sent, and asked if we had ever been there. He told us how he had blown a train up with *plastique* during the revolution, and how he had killed fifteen French himself. He pulled out his gun and fired three shots into the night for effect. He drank until the wine ran down his cheeks. He chased Barbara around the campfire, trying in vain to drag her into the bushes, as we wondered how to limit our hospitality without giving offense. He sang bawdy French songs and roared with laughter when we played him back the tape recording. He left well after 3:00 A.M., instructing the police to bring us to his home for a banquet at noon. He got into his Citroen and blasted off in a shower of sand, knocking down a small tree as he beat a path back to the road.

At noon the policemen escorted us to the Commissioner's courtyard, adjacent to the scene of the near-tragic collision the day before. The Commissioner was at the gate to greet us, the forgiving father extending a gracious welcome to his erring children. He had arranged things well: half the villagers of Picard were gathered outside to see their hero accepting the apologies of the repentant foreigners for their reckless words and driving of the day before. The Commissioner was beaming so happily that we went along with the ruse to keep the peace.

The meal was magnificent. Although the Commissioner spent most of it joking with his brother about what had happened the day before—— ". . . and that one there, the mean-looking one, Podell, he thought I was French. Can you imagine, French! He said people who drove like me only got their licenses in Paris, and . . ."——we never wanted for attention from the brother's four veiled wives who clucked over us, keeping our plates and glasses full.

As the cheese was brought out, things took a turn for the worse, for the Commissioner made a request we had somehow to refuse. "I wish," he said, "I wish to buy that girl from you." He pointed to Barbara, blonde and chesty and glowing. I didn't blame the Commissioner a bit, but we had to get out of it—and without offending him, for a man who'd killed fifteen French during the war with guns and *plastique* wasn't going to think twice if insulted by an American.

"How much will you pay for her?" I asked, following the custom.

"How much do you wish?" he countered, and I could see we were in for some Arab haggling.

Barbara had stopped glowing. I asked the Commissioner what he thought was a fair price, and he offered fifteen hundred American dollars, in either cash or gold.

"Well, that's very generous," I answered, "but only for an average girl. It's not enough for her. Barbara here's an exception." Exceptionally pale at the moment, I noticed.

"How much do you want?"

"Well, we just couldn't part with her for less than $3,000. I mean she's no ordinary girl: lovely hair, nursing skills, nice disposition, and—"

"—and lots of meat," the Commissioner smirked, a bit of spittle driveling into his dish of *couscous*. "All right, I give you $2,500. It's too much for her, but since you're my good friend, I'll give it to you."

"I'm sorry, but we just couldn't take less than 3,000, even from a good friend like you. We turned down 2,700 for her in Marrekesh from the Sultan. We have to send half the money to her mother."

"You do not bargain, Mr. Stephens."

"Three thousand dollars is a bargain for a girl like Barbara."

"As you wish. All right. I take her."

We were astounded. My trick had backfired. I couldn't conceive of anybody paying $3,000 for a woman outside of divorce court, but there it was. Barbara looked about ready to faint, and the veiled wives were already giving her the Cinderella look when Al cut in.

"But there's one thing Mr. Stephens forgot to mention, Commissioner. You see, we had planned to sell these girls as a group. They all go together. But since you are our friend you can have the other two at a big discount, only $2,000 each, $7,000 for all three."

"No, I do not want the other two. They are too skinny. Look," he said, pinching Liz, who screamed, "No meat. All bones. I could not even get $200 for her from the nomads. I only want the other one."

"But you see—well you see—we have to sell them together. The one you want is the prize of the flock and we need her to help us sell these other two miserable ones. Nobody will buy these scrawny chickens otherwise. Come on, special for you, as our friend, only $7,000 for all three."

"No, no deal."

And with a sigh of relief we moved on to Algiers, the girls sitting in the back of the Land Cruiser singing at the top of their lungs, "Maori Battalion march to victory, Maori Battalion staunch and true, Maori Battalion march to glory . . ."

Algiers buzzed with all sorts of activity, none of it particularly conducive to a pleasant visit. Under Ben Bella, Algiers had become a center of anti-American propaganda and policies. All across Africa we'd picked up its radio programs denouncing Americans as "imperialists, exploiters, fascists, and colonialists." The city was plastered with signs and billboards extolling sacrifice, praising Socialism, lauding Nasser, saluting the Soviets, thanking Red China, and damning the United States. Ben Bella had opened Algiers to international revolutionary groups, and its streets were filled with young toughs from organizations like the Mozambique Liberation Front of the Popular Movement for the Liberation of Angola. It was a den of seedy dragons.

Behind the flags and slogans we detected unrest and discontent. High prices, low wages, half-empty stomachs, and disillusionment were everywhere. Everywhere also were guns and barbed wire; Ben Bella's palace was a fort surrounded by concrete tank traps and a high wall manned by half a hundred troops with ugly Chinese machine guns.

We searched for the pretty campsites of the tourist folders but they

were also victims of the war which had despoiled the entire Mediterranean coast around Algiers with barbed wire, watchtowers, and mine
fields; we were forced to drive twenty miles until we found a clear
beach. There we pitched our camper and rushed for the water, eager to
wash off the dirt and sweat of a week of driving. I plunged in first—and
screamed for the others to stop. The water was alive with leeches,
wriggling, slimy, ugly leeches eight inches long—thousands of filthy,
black bloodsuckers. The others ran out immediately, but I was in so far
that by the time I made it back to shore there were two leeches clinging
to my legs and another, big as a banana, sucking blood from my back.
Al pulled them off and cleansed the wounds. We sank back to the
camper, utterly dejected.

Later that night we sat around the dismal campsite getting ready for
the next long stretch to Cairo. I was studying the maps, Al was editing
photos for the sponsors, and Woodrow was computing our expenses.
Willy and Manu had gone into town to eat at a restaurant, and the
girls were packing their knapsacks, getting ready to head back home
the next day. Miles across the bay, the lights of Algiers beamed steady
in the clear air, but everywhere else around us was absolute darkness,
broken only by the glow of our hissing gas lanterns.

Suddenly Woodrow was screaming and jumping and holding his
neck. Something had bitten him hard, and blood was oozing from the
wound. But what? What kind of animal could slash a man on a North
African beach without being seen? As I was wondering about this and
helping Al bandage Woodrow's wound I heard a faint warning buzz
about ten yards away, like a rattlesnake, but lower in pitch.

I turned toward the sound and saw a blur of black leap from the
beach at my head. It caromed off the gas lantern, and vanished. It was
terrifying. On our trip we would run into everything from bull elephants
in heat to tarantulas in our trousers, but we had no idea what in the
world was after us then, and there's nothing more frightening than
the unknown.

We waited, tense and sweating. Two minutes, five, ten. Then another black buzz jumped at us. It grazed me on the chest and I swat-
ted it to the beach and pinned it with my boot. It was one of the most
disgusting creatures I've ever seen, looking more like a monster from

the laboratory of some warped scientist than any creature of Nature. It was about five inches across, dark chocolate brown in color, with big front pincers and several sets of smaller side legs. It had the general shape of a crab, the hairy appearance of a spider, and some sort of rear wings that enabled it to fly or spring about five feet in the air and twenty feet forward. And it died hard: I smashed the one at my foot ten times with an entrenching tool before it was finally stilled.

Our flashlights showed the beach was crawling with these things—— but not before one of them jumped and nipped by hand. It was apparent that they were attracted by light and converging on our campsite, so we extinguished our lanterns and sat in the dark until it was time to go to sleep and dream of mine fields and leeches and flying monsters.

The next morning brought no relief, for with it came mobs of unwashed, unruly Arab kids, all curious to see these strange foreigners who were living on the beach, and all with a touch of larceny in their hearts. With two cars and two trailers loaded with gear we had such a full time keeping an eye on things that we had to congratulate ourselves when we took inventory that evening and found we'd only lost a can opener and a stack of paper plates.

We also lost the girls that day, though not to the Arabs. They had planned to go farther with us, as far as Tunis, but the delays had put us so far behind schedule that they were already due back at their hospitals in London.

I felt very sad as I watched their steamer sail for Marseilles. Though ours was hardly a trip for women, those Kiwis had borne up beautifully. Where other girls would have constantly complained about the sun, the sand, the beds, the food, the bugs, and the flying crabs, Barbara, Mira, and Liz seldom lost their high spirits or good humor, proving a credit to their country and their calling.

In the morning we'd been eight, by evening we were only five, and I found myself wondering about those. As for Al and me, I knew that, one way or other, we would finish the trip. But Willy was disturbed about the slow progress of the expedition and some of the unexpected hardships of the journey. With Manu, it was a case of money. He had received neither funds nor word from his publisher. And with Woodrow, it was a question of health. Unable to adapt to the demands of life on the road, he was often ill and frequently homesick, and had begun to talk about leaving us in Cairo. All this with the worst of the trip to come.

Sometime during the night, as we slept, our camp had a visitor, an uninvited visitor who cut the cover on our small storage trailer and stole a suitcase loaded with winter clothing, mountain climbing equipment, and spare photographic equipment worth more than $500. We reported the theft to the police and they turned it over to the army, but the army was less interested in catching the thieves than in learning what a bunch of Americans were doing camped on a beach with ropes and crampons and telephoto lenses. We were released only after hours of interrogation.

What with the belligerent wildlife, the thieving visitors, and the antagonistic political atmosphere, none of us were eager to remain in Algiers; but we had to stay two more days because the cracks in the trailer needed welding, and the generator on the Jeep had burned out and needed rewiring. It was incredibly difficult to find anyone to handle the jobs because almost every skilled auto mechanic and machinist in the country had either been killed or had fled back to France during the war which had taken 130,000 lives and exiled a million. We went to a dozen gas stations, but that's all they were—gas, oil change, and a grease job—with not one mechanic at any of them. After hours of searching, we found a welding shop and a man in it who could rewire our generator.

"What do people do here if something really goes wrong with their cars?" I asked him. "What if they have trouble with the brakes or the steering or if the valves need to be reground? Who takes care of it?"

"If you look on the street," he said, "you will find your answer. Hundreds of cars sit idle and their owners have to go on bicycle or by foot. When something breaks it is finished. There is no one here who can do the work, and there are no parts to do the work with."

I asked him what the government was doing to prevent this.

"They are putting up signs telling us to be patient," he sighed. "They are broadcasting on the radio we should tighten our belts. They are writing in the newspaper that land reform is coming, that the first years of the socialist revolution are always difficult."

"And do your people believe the signs and the radio?" Al asked.

"In the beginning, we believed. In the beginning we were so happy to have independence we believed anything. But now we see things are not as we would like. Ben Bella is doing things we do not want. We want to be peaceful, to grow prosperous, to enjoy our neighbors. But Ben Bella has other ideas: he wants to be big man in Africa and he wants Algeria to be big power. He makes friends with Nasser, with Russia, with China. He thinks he uses them, but we think they use him. Once we were at peace with our neighbors. Morocco and Tunisia were our friends, and helped us win our independence, but Ben Bella has made them our enemies. We had no quarrel with the Jews until Nasser persuaded Ben Bella to join his Arab League. We are only partly Arabs, and we are not Communists—we don't want Nasser and we don't want the Russians and we don't want the Chinese. We are what you might call a Mediterranean people. Our strongest ties are to the Mediterranean and to the French. However we may try to deny it, we are still French in attitude and behavior. We have driven the French out, but we keep their customs. We like their way of life, their culture, their attitudes. We do not want to be driven farther from them. We should make friends again with our neighbors and with France and live in peace and prosper."

"That makes wonderful sense, but why aren't things working out that way?" Al asked.

"Ben Bella!"

"If the others are as unsatisfied as you, I imagine he'll lose the next election."

"With Ben Bella there will be no more elections. He will make himself dictator and try to stay president. No, there is only one way, a *coup d'état.* I only tell you this because you are Americans, and I am sure you have no great love for Monsieur Ben Bella. He will not be president for long. Within a short time he will be dead. We have planned well and we will overthrow him soon. But I do not think it will be safe for foreigners in Algeria when the revolution comes."

"How can you overthrow him? His palace is surrounded by hundreds of soldiers with machine guns. You wouldn't have a chance," Al said.

"I have spoken too much already, but you will see . . . We will overthrow him very soon, before the Conference meets here. The Conference is a Chinese trick to take power in Africa. We will not have it. As for his guards, have no fear, for the army leaders are with us——There, your generator is finished. I hope you have a good journey. And remember, leave Algiers as quickly as you can. I hope ours will be a happier country the next time you are here."

It was probably wishful thinking but we decided not to take any chances: we'd make tracks for Tunis in the morning.

Though we doubted the robbers would return to our camp, we realized it was possible. So as not to be caught unawares again, we stuck forked twigs in the sand in a circle around the cars and storage trailer, and ran a piece of string through them to a can full of rocks balanced on a twig in a hole under the camper beside which Al and I unrolled our sleeping bags. If anybody approached the equipment, they'd trip the string and rattle the can enough to wake us.

It was black and cramped under the camper, and I was sure the flying crabs would find us, but we managed to fall asleep. Hours later I heard something, but it wasn't the can rattling: it was someone unzipping the windows of the Land Cruiser. Al was also awake, Blackie's .38 at the ready. We slipped out from under the camper and got into position.

I flicked on the lantern. It caught three mean-looking Arabs, their arms full of our supplies. Al shouted at them to drop the stuff.

One of them did, but all three ran into the dark. We gave chase. Al warned them to stop or he'd shoot. But they kept running. He fired twice into the air, but they kept going. Then he fired at them, trying to hit their legs, though it was difficult to see in the moonless dark. On the third shot I heard a groan and thought I saw someone fall. Together we rushed to the spot. There, on the beach, next to a flying crab, was my safari hat and our binoculars and some of our clothing. The sand was torn up, but we could see three sets of tracks moving up the beach, the one in the middle dragging, and here and there a spot of what looked like blood.

Had we killed somebody? Had we just wounded him? How badly? Would he be back with a gang to get us? If he died, would his family or friends go to the police? We couldn't go to the police ourselves, for they were already suspicious and unfriendly and not likely to treat too kindly an American who'd shot an Arab—whatever the provocation. Furthermore, we had sworn at the Algerian border that we carried no firearms, knowing that if we declared our gun they'd confiscate it. The possession of that undeclared pistol alone could put us in jail, and that was the last place we wanted to be with the revolution a few days off. We decided to clear out then and there.

If the man died or made trouble, we figured the police would look for us along the coastal highway to Tunis, the best and most heavily traveled road out of the country. We also knew that hundreds of Algerian troops had been stationed along that road because of Ben Bella's argument with Tunisia; so we decided to take a chance and head south into the Sahara where we were reasonably sure nobody would be looking for us. Not that this course did not have its own dangers. When we'd inquired about the Sahara at the gas stations the day before, nobody knew if it was negotiable or what shape the roads were in, or even if there were roads; and the only map we could find showed no more than thin tracks, ominous gray veins designated on the legend as *route de viabilitie mauvaise* or *piste practicable seulement aux véhicules tous terrains;* furthermore the map indicated only one thin *piste* leading into Tunisia from the Sahara, and noted that it was subject to frequent closure by sand storms, which meant we might be forced to circle back through 800 miles of desert and mountains to link up with the World War II road through Tebessa—by which time the revolution might well have begun.

We broke camp and were on the move before dawn, and sunrise found us twisting and climbing through the Atlas Mountains, the durable barrier that protects the flourishing Mediterranean strip of North Africa from the encroachments of the great sea of sand, heading south toward the Sahara, toward what the Arabs call "the land of a thousand horrors." Al was up front in the Land Cruiser hauling the camper and I followed in the Jeep.

On a hairpin turn, just as we were cresting the mountains, I noticed the left wheel of the camper wobbling violently, and turned on my lights (our daylight distress signal) to bring Al to a stop on the narrow road. Three of the four bolts on the camper wheel had worked themselves free and were rolling around inside the hubcap; only the last bolt was holding. Another few minutes and we'd certainly have lost the wheel, probably the camper, possibly the expedition.

With all bolts back in place we continued through the mountain pass, relieved that our daily mishap had been no worse than it was. But we sighed too soon. We'd hardly gone a mile, and were just hitting a downgrade, when I saw the camper wheel wobbling again, and again stopped Al—just in time. Two bolts were out and two were on their way. A closer inspection showed why they hadn't held: the threads of the wheel were stripped and those of the bolts fused. It took an hour of delicate work to jack up the camper, which was inches from dropping off the side of the mountain, and to put on the spare tire and wheel, then another hour with a cold chisel to gouge the metal out of the thread grooves. With such problems every day on the road, it was small wonder we were so far behind schedule.

I didn't realize exactly how far behind until Al came up with a bunch of his figures.

"Steve, I've been doing a little computation——"

"So what else is new?" I sighed.

"Just listen to this. In Africa, we've been averaging only 112 miles a day for every day on the road. And that's not the worst of it. If you figure time spent for customs problems and welding repairs and servicing and getting visas and border delays and everything, our daily average breaks down to *68 miles a day!* Do you realize what that means? It will take us—based on an estimate of 40,000 land miles—*580* days to get around the world! We'd get back to New York on October 16th, 1966! That's seventeen months from now! And we're supposed to get back by this Christmas!"

"I wouldn't worry about it too much," I said, "because I'm sure things will get better. It's always a little rough shaking down at the start. Just don't mention that date to Woodrow; he'll have a fit."

"Of course not. Anyway, I'm sure you're right. We're bound to pick up the pace. I can't imagine not getting back to New York until October of next year."

Neither could I.

There were no more accidents that day, and the night was almost pleasant. We camped off the road, on the perimeter of the desert. Woodrow went to sleep early, reminding us that the robbers in Algiers had played hell with his customary nine hours. While Willy stuffed himself on my soup of creamed green beans and potatoes, Manu and Al and I sat outside under an incomparable canopy of stars. We had good food in our stomachs, music from Radio España on the shortwave, and the five-gallon bottle of potent wine the Commissioner had given us. The girls were gone, but the wilderness kept us company. It was nights like these that made all our troubles worth it.

At the start of our trip we had held the stereotyped Hollywood vision of the Sahara: a huge waste of worthless, endless sand dunes, unbearably hot by day and freezing cold at night, without rainfall or water except on a few oases, which we visualized as inviting blue ponds surrounded by beautiful gardens in the midst of an eternal desert whose life was unchanged and unchanging. These misconceptions were dispelled two days after we met her. The only aspect of our Sahara vision that proved to be valid was "huge."

The Sahara is the largest desert in the world, three million square miles, larger than the Continental United States, fourteen times the size of France. But it is not a wasteland of worthless sand dunes. The flowing dunes of the movies compose only fifteen per cent of the desert, concentrated in two or three areas. Most of the Sahara that we saw was an arid steppe, a low, hard-packed plateau of gravel, sand, rocks, and scrub grass. The rest of the Sahara is almost as varied as nature itself; it has massive mountains, high plateaus, volcanic formations, dried river beds, shadowy valleys, depressed salt basins, wind-eroded hills, and sparse plains—*hammadas, tarsos, tanezroufts, tassilis, chebkas, sebkhas, gours, regs, shotts, wadis, dayas, barkhans,* and *ergs.*

Nor is the Sahara worthless: oil, gas, coal, iron, copper, gold, tin, tungsten and manganese have all been found there recently.

Nor did we find the desert unbearably hot by day. Though the temperature went over 90 before noon and kept climbing, the heat was by no means intolerable because the air was so dry and in such constant motion that perspiration evaporated instantly, keeping the body cool and dry. We did require salt pills and a constant intake of water to keep our bodies' air-conditioning apparatus working, and we had to keep heavy foods to a minimum, but as long as we stuck to this regimen the Sahara was in no way unpleasant. I found its climate in many ways more enjoyable than that of Coney Island in July or Palm Springs in September.

Nor did we find it freezing cold by night. To be sure, the great desert cools quickly once the sun goes down; with a cloudless sky overhead, the sand rapidly loses its heat by radiation, and there are no large bodies of water near enough to mitigate the temperature shift. But we never found it unpleasant. I doubt if it ever dropped below 60.

We also learned that the Sahara does receive rain, though it didn't when we were there, and has plenty of water, if you know where to look. During the winter some parts of the Sahara get four inches of rain which, while hardly enough to sustain agriculture, is just enough to encourage dormant seeds to germinate, dotting the desert with patches of green and bursts of bloom. As for water, the Sahara has neither conventional lakes nor rivers; they couldn't possibly survive, for the hot, dry air can evaporate a thirteen foot depth of surface water in a year. But below the surface, there is another world: fed by centuries of runoff from the Atlas Mountains and underground streams trapped in layers of cretaceous mantle rock, the world beneath the sand is aflood with waters waiting to be tapped. Some of them rose to the surface centuries ago in the form of springs or pools to make the oases, but most of the water lay unknown and unused until the past 20 years when geologists discovered its secret and found that it could be called forth. In some places the water table is close to the surface, and all along the road south we found wells less than 40 or 50 feet deep. Though we were never sure, they seemed to be open to any traveler, a pulley and bucket ready and waiting, never any warning signs, never any fences around them.

Since we drank insatiably, every other hour draining our five individual quart-size Thermos bottles and the two two-gallon jugs we shared among us, we found ourselves forced to stop every thirty miles or so to fill up again; yet we never lacked for water wells in that part of the Sahara. There are few such wells farther south, in the heart of the Sahara, but even there the water is abundant, though much deeper below the surface. Recent surveys show that all the wells, springs, and irrigation ditches in the entire Sahara are using its water at only one fourth the rate it flows in; millions of acre feet remain to be tapped, and the Sahara may some day bloom and thrive. It was all rather shattering to our vision of the world's greatest desert.

Even more shattering were the oases, which we had envisioned as cool pools surrounded by beautiful gardens. From the distance they seemed to live up to their reputation; from miles away in the clear desert air we could see the brilliant green tops of the palm trees. But as we drew closer, the vision faded. There was little green to be seen at eye-level, just brown tree trunks, and brownish-red mud, and rocks, and ugly houses, and barbed wire, and struggling gardens. The water is highly prized and closely guarded, and usually runs from heavily fenced-in springs, along dirty canals that border the streets, into portions of private land dammed with rocks and unsightly boards and protected by rusting barbed wire. Everything has a brown coat of dust or sand from the encroaching desert and the ceaseless wind. The houses are made of weathered mud or yellow clay; only a few of the fancier ones are touched up with whitewash.

The bleakness is little relieved by the gardens, for they are often a tangle of weeds or rodent-gnawed vegetables. And they are unprofitably small, having been passed on for generations, divided among brothers, split and split again, until they are often no more than three feet by five, with the biggest seldom more than 60 square feet.

Many of the younger people refuse to accept this way of life as the will of Allah. In contact with European civilization, hearing about the wonders of science and industry and the 20th century, able to catch a truck ride and quit the desert in a few days, hundreds of young men are heading for the cities of the coast, deserting the oases, seeking a better life, leaving the old people to tend the dying gardens.

Nor are these the only changes taking place on a desert we once thought of as changeless. The other upholders of the old way of life, the nomads, are also undergoing a major transformation and may soon be men of the past.

The nomads came to the Sahara when the camel was introduced there from Egypt shortly before the decline of Roman influence in Africa. Until then, the desert dwellers had been tied to the oases, unable to move about, for they had only oxen and small elephants, neither of which were of much use in the desert; but the camel gave the nomads mobility, enabling them to travel for days without water or food since the camel could live on the tough desert grasses and the nomads could live on the camel's milk. They prospered. They organized caravans to carry goods across the desert; they raided competing caravans and sold protection to others. When the grazing ran short they were powerful enough to attack the oasis dwellers and graze their camels on their gardens.

The 20th century brought the truck, killing the caravan trade. And there were other economic factors at work—the depletion of the desert gold mines, the introduction of cheap salt from Europe, and the decline of the ostrich feather business—all of which diminished the size and importance of the caravans. The French threw in two serious blows when they abolished the lucrative slave trade and the feudal dues paid the nomads by the oasis dwellers. The nomads then tried stock breeding as a source of income, but the decline of the caravan trade decreased the market for camels, and droughts devastated the sheep herds.

Today the powerful nomad tribes are breaking up, their members setting out on their own; the authority of the chiefs has been weakened, and families are moving about at will. In our drive across all of North Africa we saw only one large tribe of nomads. Everywhere else there were just families (four or five people, 30 camels, a few sheep), looking for pasturage, heading into the setting sun. Many nomads have given up their old way of life completely, settling on oases, buying a few date palms and some cereal seeds, and making a try at agriculture, forced by the 20th century to become rooted peasants rather than free wanderers—forced to join in the great revolution now sweeping the Sahara, which is just beginning, after untold millennia, to be bored by oil rigs, crossed by roads, crisscrossed by geologists, bisected by pipelines, straddled by air strips, carved by mines, and tapped by water wells. The revolution is just under way, but the future is clear. The demands of modern life will bring drastic changes to the Sahara in the years ahead, and we're glad we saw it while it was still awesome and proud and not yet quite conquered.

After three days we were far enough south of the Tebessa Mountains to try to make a run for Tunisia, hoping we could get through. The lack of reliable road maps was worrisome, for once we left France there were no more gasoline station handouts, and when we tried to depend on what the national tourist ministries furnished, we were frequently misled. Their maps were generally glossy and colorful, but I'm convinced the tourist ministries filled in the thick reds and blues more for the sake of artistic effect than cartographic accuracy. There were often thick red bands indicating superhighways where camel trails could barely be discerned. It was usually impossible to determine anything about road conditions from the rural Arabs, few of whom had ever been more than 50 miles from their mud doorsteps. They were, however, of a different breed from the Spanish peasants who always boasted of their superhighways. In fact, they were two breeds: one, fatalistic and untraveled, invariably telling us that the road ended just beyond his oasis and that we couldn't move farther without a camel; the other, anxious to please and reluctant to give offense, invariably telling us to continue in the direction we were heading lest it be thought he was calling attention to our error. There was also a third breed, and at times they seemed to predominate: those who didn't understand a word of what we were asking.

We turned north and east at El Qued, last of Algeria's big oasis cities, set in the midst of some of the loveliest dunes in all the Sahara, many of them as high as small mountains, their lines different from every angle, always graceful, never tiring. They were as picturesque as the Hollywood version, and we found ourselves waiting in anticipation for a rider in a white robe and flowing turban to come charging over a dune waving a sword, his horse leaving a flowing trail in the golden sand. But no rider came, only flies.

As a final homage to the great Sahara, now in its last days of untamed glory, we had stopped the cars and Manu and Al and I had raced to the tops of these golden hills, tumbling and sliding, laughing and playing, making tracks where perhaps no human had ever trod before, thrilled by the vast unspoiled emptiness of the great dunes, at one with Nature. The minute we rested the flies set upon us, vicious biting flies, twice as big as our biggest horsefly, with teeth as sharp as a dragon's. Their presence in the middle of the barren dunes, miles from any food or breeding spots, was a puzzle to us, as surprising as the flying crabs in Algiers. Where did they come from? What did they eat? How did they live in the middle of nowhere? From the relentlessness of their attacks, I gathered that our expedition must have been the first food they'd seen in months. We rushed back to our car where Woodrow greeted us: "You've been gone more than half an hour! What were you running up and down the sand dunes for? It's too hot. What fun is that?" Fortunately, the flies departed when the sun set, even if Woodrow didn't. God only knows where they go. They're back with the sun at five in the morning, an infallible, unbreakable, unstoppable alarm clock.

But they aren't there after dusk, thus permitting the Sahara traveler to relax and enjoy its sunset, one of nature's most dramatic spectacles. Since there are neither clouds above the desert nor moisture in the air to diffuse or refract, the sun descends in a brilliant hard-edged crimson circle. In but a few minutes the dunes lose their dazzling glare and turn to soft colors, their lines now muted, even more graceful, as long shadows of purple, like pools of deep water, replace the bright harshness of the day. The night comes quickly, and its stars are startling in their number and stunning in their brilliance. There is no sound for a hundred miles save the murmur of the cooling sands, no human, save yourself; and you find yourself wishing that the Sahara, however it changes, may never lose this magic.

The road from El Qued toward Tunisia was not as bad as we'd feared, nor as good as we'd hoped. It was asphalted in parts, but badly potholed, and clogged with camels who refused to get out of our way. Worst of all, it was covered with sand for long stretches at a time, making the going slow, slippery and confusing. Loose blown

sand on the roads is the worst enemy of the Sahara traveler, and the
farther in, the worse it gets. On his 1956 trip Peter Townsend reported
meeting a driver who had taken *two full days to cover 100 yards*
through heavy sand. Townsend himself had to stop repeatedly to make
life and death decisions as to which was the real road and which a false
track. Rocks can puncture tires, potholes crack springs, and mud mire
you down, but nothing is as vicious as the Sahara sand which at one
and the same time obliterates your route, batters your equipment, and
assaults you personally.

It was nearing nightfall when we reached the border station, hoping
that news of neither our shooting incident nor the impending revolution had reached this isolated outpost. In that respect, we were
in luck, for the border post was completely cut off, with no phone or
telegraph for a hundred miles. Yet the guards refused to let us pass.
By Algerian law (as well as by the laws of almost all dictatorships) any
foreigner trying to leave the country must have an exit permit, a stamp
of good conduct put in his passport to show he's done nothing wrong
and that the government has no objections to his departure. The border
guards insisted we get them, even though it meant we had to return
to El Qued, five hours back in the Sahara. We pleaded and cajoled, but
it was no use; we'd have to go back in the morning for the permits.

The guards offered us the hospitality of the post for the night. We
accepted, but we learned something at the barracks that changed our
minds: a detachment of troops was expected from Algiers the next
day to bolster the border post. Algeria's Ben Bella, furious over a
speech Tunisia's president had made criticizing him, was again pushing his war-weary people into an argument for which they had little
desire.

Our concern was only partly with the warfare that might erupt; we
were more worried that the troops might bring news of the revolution
or of our shooting in Algiers. In either case, we knew we had to be
gone before they got there. In a panic, and late at night, we raced back
toward El Qued for our exit permits, dodging sand drifts here and
huge potholes there. By night there was even less of a road to be seen
beneath the sand, but we pressed on. The wind-whipped sand was
blowing thick off the desert, making it impossible to see; our lights

merely reflected back and blinded us. Herds of camels clogged the road, refusing to move, and when we honked or yelled they turned their heads and bared their teeth at us. Once past the camels we picked up the pace, speeding 60 miles an hour on the dangerous road. We blasted through a couple of small sand drifts, almost skidding off the road, before we plowed full speed into a deep one which flipped us over on our side. We were shaken up, but unhurt; however, we couldn't right the car. We had to wait an hour until a nomad herder came by with some camels who reluctantly helped us pull the car back.

We arrived after midnight at El Qued, where the drowsing duty officer was anything but glad to see us, suggesting we come back in the morning when the telegraph to headquarters was open and he could get authorization for our exit permits. A small bribe convinced him that midnight was a much better time to do business. Before the sun was up we were back at the border.

The border didn't open until eight, but since it was too late to sleep, we explored the post and, to our delight, found a wide pipe gushing pure, cold water into a shallow pool where the cavalry's camels drank. We hadn't had a shower since the *casbah* in Algiers. The Sahara is so dry and you sweat so little you can go for long periods without bathing; but there are limits, especially for those accustomed to daily baths. With a roar and a rush we ran toward the pool, yelling at the top of our lungs. The frightened camels dashed out, all except for an ugly albino veteran whom I had to slap hard in the rump. For half an hour we bathed in the pool and stood under the gushing pipe, letting the water soak into every dehydrated pore of our bodies. Even Woodrow dropped in and got wet, though he kept his clothes on. It was heaven, until the camels regrouped and, led by the albino avenger, came back boldly to reassert their rights. It was our turn to retreat. Besides, the border was about to open.

When we began our trip, Al and I had been particularly looking forward to our drive through Tunisia. We had planned to take the beautiful Mediterranean coastal route into Tunis, on past the ruins of once-mighty Carthage, then for hundreds of more miles south along the Gulfs of Hammamet and Gabes. After our Algerian difficulties, we had also looked forward to Tunisia because of its friendly attitude toward Americans. Aside from Morocco, Tunisia is the only country in Africa for which an American requires no special visa or permission to enter, the only country in our 8,000 miles east to Thailand where Americans are welcomed as friends rather than suspected as enemies or fleeced as wealthy tourists.

Even more important, we were anxious to visit Tunisia to see what Bourguiba had wrought. This complex, compelling political maverick is one of the world's most enlightened statesmen, the most progressive leader in any Arab nation. He stands apart in that part of the world from dictators bent on revolution and hereditary rulers bent on reaction and personal profit. If he succeeds, many in the West see a bright future for all the Moslem world; if he fails, they see only darkness.

He had passed the Code of Personal Status which challenged the most cherished Moslem traditions, made marriage a voluntary contract between a man and woman each acting as a free agent, set a minimum age for marriage, required the bride's consent, outlawed the custom of selling young girls, and abolished polygamy. The husband no longer had the right to divorce his wife arbitrarily. More than that, the wife was given the right to institute divorce proceedings against her husband. Bourguiba gave Moslem women the right to vote, and he told them to take off their veils. "It is unthinkable that half the population be cut off from life and hidden like a disgraceful thing behind an odious rag." He opposed the Moslem custom of fasting during the month of Ramadan, pointing out that a country struggling into the present after a thousand years of backwardness was in no position to sacrifice a month of labor each year. He challenged the blind faith demanded of the people by the Moslem priests.

A less secure leader in the Moslem country could have been overthrown for any one of these drastic innovations, but Bourguiba was in a unique position: he was the original leader of his people's fight for independence, the George Washington of Tunisia, the father of his country, and this gave him the rare opportunity to shape the destiny of his people, and to point the way for 600,000,000 other Moslems.

His revered position in this country explained why he had been able to launch these ambitious reforms, and why he had not needed to resort to anti-Western outbursts. As he once said, and as we found to be true from Algeria to Egypt to Pakistan to Indonesia: "In many underdeveloped countries, the leaders veil their internal political problems. They are constantly searching for distractions to channel popular passions. . . . Those who excite the crowd, as an instrument of power, must always be denouncing enemies. The most fashionable enemy is colonialism or neo-colonialism. . . . If there is no progress, it is because colonialism is still there . . . so that one can justify all failures. With this psychosis, the people remain in a permanent state of mobilization. They think they're fighting enemies. The leaders repeat that they don't have time to worry about the price of bread. . . . Colonialism is holding them by the throat. Sad alibi! Convenient scapegoat!"

We were eager to see what this political marvel had been able to reap in fields where his counterparts had not even dared sow, but we were destined to be disappointed. Because of the Saharan detour necessitated by our trouble in Algiers, we entered Tunisia in a region barely inhabited. Even the road ended at the Algerian border, leaving us nothing but a rutted dirt track that twisted its way through a no man's land toward the customs post at Nefta, 25 miles away. By ten o'clock the air was scorching and we were parched, for there were no water wells on this dirt track, nor cars, nor camels, nor anything but the toughest of withered salt grasses clinging to life.

The morning sun, into which we were forced to drive, began performing tricks, amusing us every minute with new mirages—trees, ponds, pools, oases—until it decided to play a deadly one. I was driving the Jeep, and Woodrow sat beside me, staring out at the shimmering sand. He thought he saw something fall out of the Land Cruiser up ahead, and in a trance he rose from the seat, saying, "I'll get it," as he stepped out the door of the moving Jeep. He hit hard, smashing into the road at 25 miles an hour, scraping and tumbling along head over heels as I jammed on the brakes. When I reached him he was lying in the middle of the road, his arms and face covered with blood, his knees and legs cut and bleeding. He sat up and began beating himself in anger, pounding his shoulders and thighs with his pulpy hands. "You idiot!" he was screaming at himself. "You stupid idiot. You ass. You ass. Look what you've done! How could you do that? How did you do such a thing? What an ass. What an ass." He started crying and began hitting himself hard in the face.

We put him in the Jeep and rushed to the customs post. The medic there cleansed and bound his wounds. When he stepped out of the building, his hands and legs swathed in bandages, he looked like a war-torn Legionnaire. His driving was finished for the next two weeks; though if we'd been going any faster, I realized soberly, a lot more than that might have been finished. As it was, it meant Al and I would have to do 2,000 miles of rough desert driving ourselves.

Willy had proven so reckless behind the wheel I'd had to forbid his driving. On my previous trip, through Russia, I'd let him drive once—and only once. He had rocketed us along the wretched Soviet highways at breakneck speeds, time and again taking his eyes off the road and his hands off the wheel to photograph peasants and livestock and buildings and whatever else caught his fancy—at seventy miles an hour. When I invited him to join our expedition I hoped that he had settled down, but he was still a wild driver, weaving all over the pavement, dipping a wheel on the shoulder, taking dangerous blind turns on the wrong side of the road "the way a race car driver showed me." The last time I'd let him drive was on the winding cliff road along the Algerian coast. I was dead tired and had asked him to relieve me so I could take a quick nap. In ten minutes I was shaken awake by the violent swaying of the car. Willy had taken his shoes off and was steering with his bare feet.

Manu was another problem. When we'd invited him in Spain to join the expedition he'd assured us he could drive. "We Spanish can do anything," I remembered him saying. "Especially Spanish from the Basque country. Anything." I didn't learn the truth until Tangier when I asked him to take the Land Cruiser into town for some supplies. He was delighted, gave me a big salute, and leaped into the car. After five minutes of fiddling around all he'd managed to do was turn on the windshield wipers and unwind the winch. "We have no Jeep in Basque country," he explained. "Show me, and I drive in one day."

Well, Al did show him, for five days, and on the road from Rabat, Manu had told me he'd mastered the art. I'd let him take the wheel. He'd turned the key with the consummate skill that only a noble Basque could display, and we'd roared off in a merry grinding of gears, Manu the happiest man in the world. I was not unhappy, for it would be good to have someone to relieve Al and Woodrow and me of some driving. Manu drove without an accident for five minutes, but when three camels blocked the road ahead of him he started turning the wheel to go off into the desert. "No, Manu," I'd shouted, "you can't do that. The brake, Manu! Put on the brake!"

"Brake? Brake? Al hasn't shown me the brake."

Al did show him, five more times, but his driving never got better. He was just too carefree, and no lecture could convince him of the dangers of driving or the respect due machinery. He took it as light and gay as everything else, and we found it a lot less of a strain to drive ourselves than to supervise our man from the Basque country.

We followed the dirt track toward the east, and as the sun came hotter into the sky we began to feel the effects of dehydration. Our eyes burned and our lips cracked. There were no water wells in this part of the desert. There was not a tree anywhere, not even a boulder to give shade. Then, suddenly, as we peaked a slight rise, we saw a glorious sight: a lake stretched in front of us as far as the eye could see, a huge lake in the desert. We all saw it and cheered. Al and I gunned the engines, turned off the road, raced the cars toward the water's edge. We soon left the soft sand of the desert and reached the hard-crusted surface that marked the periphery of the lake. But the water itself, that great, wonderful, beckoning water, was still distant, still farther than we thought. The faster we drove, the faster the water receded in the distance, until we gradually came to realize we'd been tricked. It was a mirage after all, a classic deception of those shimmering sands, but a deception of such magnitude that we were all stunned.

We got out of the car and examined the ground. It was packed sand and salt deposits interlaced with a network of the tiniest fissures. It must have been a dried lake bed. The map confirmed it: it was Chott Djerid, the biggest dried lake in the Sahara, half as wide as Tunisia itself, half as long as Lake Erie, but absolutely waterless and barren. It held not a stone or bush or mound of any sort; the horizon was as hard as the edge of the sea, the sand around us as flat as Bonneville. We forgot our thirst just thinking of this marvel, and laughing over how we, supposedly old desert hands by then, had been deceived by an empty mirage; but the real desert hands know you can never outwit a mirage, that it'll get you every time.

Relying on our map and compass, we decided to continue across the lake for a while, for it was a relief not having to dodge rocks and potholes, and a thrill to be driving where no car had ever gone before, leaving tracks on the virgin sand.

But we still had problems, as we found when we arrived at Tozeur, the only town in that part of Tunisia. We had exhausted our food supply; we had consumed most of the 110 gallons of gas we had carried from Algiers; and we had no Tunisian money to buy anything— the banks were closed. In fact, everything was closed. Listless banners on the empty streets proclaimed the annual *Fête des Sports*, a four day Tunisian holiday during which everybody evidently went somewhere else. The same was true when we reached Gafsa, halfway across the country: there wasn't a soul to be seen anywhere. We'd been looking forward to meeting the Tunisians, checking out the unveiled women, and finding out what the men thought about democracy and progress and Bourguiba; but we couldn't even find anyone to sell us gas or food or tell us what they thought of the road to Libya. With four stomachs and two gas tanks about on empty, we decided to push on for Gabes, the big city where the desert road reached the coast.

A few miles out of Gafsa the hitch on our small storage trailer slipped, and the unharnessed trailer broke loose from the Jeep, careening and tumbling down the highway, spilling our supplies everywhere and coming to rest upside down. A dozen bottles of bugspray were broken, a spare Thermos cracked, a clock smashed, clothing torn, and a big split put in the wooden side of the trailer; even worse, though we didn't realize it until the next day, the trailer's axle had been knocked out of line. It was dark by the time we finished repairing and repacking, so we camped where we were, hungry and unhappy.

Woodrow was particularly upset, about both his accident and ours.

"We won't make it," he walked around muttering. "We'll never make it. We can't do it. Something happens every day. We'll never finish the trip."

Manu, in contrast, was shaping up, even if he hadn't learned how to drive. Whereas at the start of the trip he'd been the Spanish gentleman who had never worked a day with his hands in his life, nor ever even had a dirty day, by Tunisia he was shaving only once a week, working up a good desert tan, and helping on his own to maintain the equipment, beginning to realize that our survival depended on each doing his share.

Al was at the other extreme from Woodrow. Whenever the trailer would break, or a hitch snap, Al would dash out, calling for Willy to take pictures, assuring us, "It could have been a lot worse. Don't worry about it. It'll make a good picture. Now let's see how we can fix this." His attitude was almost too lighthearted; but it cheered us up, and it was refreshing to know that the worse things got the better material Al felt it made for our magazine articles. Even when he became very ill later in the trip, he tried to make light of it, saying, "It will make a good story." Fortunately for him, he didn't air his feelings when I got sick, although I could hardly get a hangnail without his mailing a report of it to half the newspapers in the United States.

The next morning, however, even Al wasn't particularly jovial as we headed toward Gabes, without food or gas or Tunisian money to buy either. The Jeep ran dry five miles out of Gabes and the Land Cruiser only made it there on fumes and momentum. The banks were closed; so no money. Only three shops in the whole town were open, and their keepers looked at our traveler's checks as if they were expired laundry tickets. They also pointed out that Tunisia requires, as do many countries with currency problems, that foreign money be exchanged only in the banks and certified on an official paper, a paper we didn't even have since we'd come into the country so far off the usual tourist route. The banks would open after the holiday, in three days, but force of habit made us reluctant to go that long before eating.

Contrary to the precepts of the International Monetary Fund, it was our experience that the most universally acceptable medium of exchange was the American cigarette. Having drawn a blank with the traveler's checks, we decided to barter with the butts, four cartons of which Al and I had laid in for just such emergencies.

I took a carton of Pall Malls to the three open shops and Al followed with his Salems. Despite my pitch, the first two shops didn't want them, had never heard of them, and wouldn't believe they were American cigarettes, even after they conned me into opening a pack and giving them free samples. Their customers wanted Camels, Chesterfields, and Luckies, the brands the GI's had introduced twenty years before; so when the third store offered me the Tunisian equivalent of three dollars, I took it. Al fared much better with the Salems whose mentholated novelty had made them famous in Oriental countries, where they served as instant status symbols. He got $6.20 for the carton after spirited bidding.

When we reached the Tunisian border, we had trouble: the guards wouldn't believe we had crossed the entire width of their country without Tunisian money. We had no documents crediting us with official exchanges, and our sale of the cigarettes was illegal under Tunisian customs regulations and couldn't be mentioned. Only after an hour of interrogation did we convince them we carried enough food and gas to get us anywhere, a baldfaced lie since our stomachs and gas tank were both back on empty after their insufficient refill in Gabes. By then the border was closed for the night.

The guards raised the barrier the next morning and we headed toward Libya. We had come to Tunisia to see the ancient Carthage and the modern Tunis; the forest-covered hills and the beautiful coast; the unveiled women and the march of Moslem democracy. We had instead seen a desert, a dried lake, a first aid station, the inside of three shops, the customs office, and a mirage.

We hoped for better luck in Libya, another land with an amazing story to tell. Seldom has there been a country which joined the family of nations with heavier burdens on her back. Fourteen years before, her assets were nil, her liabilities immense. Her per capita income was thirty dollars. Her proven natural resources were negligible. Her major industries were the selling of salt from the ocean and the collection of scrap metal from the war wreckage that littered her devastated country-side. Most of her towns were in ruins. Five million land mines lay buried beneath her sand along with thousands of unexploded shells and grenades. Disease was widespread: three out of every ten babies died at birth, and those who survived were subject to cholera, smallpox, plague, and the dreaded trachoma. Most of the natives subsisted on 1,600 calories a day. In a territory of 680,000 square miles, nearly the size of the United States east of the Mississippi, there were less than 1,250,000 people, sixteen of them with university degrees. Cut off from European influence during a thousand years of Arab rule, and taught little by her 20th century Italian conquerors, she was one of the most backward countries on earth. She wasn't even a country in the true sense of the word. Her people had no common identity, no feeling of nationalism, regarding themselves as Tripolitanians, or Cyrenaicians, or Fezzanians, or just plain nomads. There were nothing but camel routes linking the settlements, and only one paved road in the whole vast region. Libya as a nation was more a notion than a reality.

Yet it was this poor, backward, diseased, disunited, and war-torn land that was to emerge as one of the most successful experiments of the United Nations. It was on this unhospitable soil that the pioneering UN created the first newly independent country in all of Africa after the war, and it is to the credit of whatever gods rule the destinies of men and the flow of oil beneath the desert sands that the experiment worked as well as it did.

It worked so well that I found myself looking into the gold inlays of a Libyan customs officer who'd come back from his inspection of our cars smirking as if he'd trapped an arch criminal. In the flickering glow of the kerosene lantern he looked absolutely sinister as he reread our entry declaration, his finger pointing to the part where we'd sworn we had no guns with us.

"Have you guns?" he asked, with what must have been his favorite English phrase.

"No," I replied, for there was nothing else I could say. It was too late to confess that I had a pistol hidden under the seat. It had proven so useful in driving off the Algerian robbers that I was determined to take it with us, however many countries it meant smuggling it into and whatever the risks involved.

"No guns? No guns! *Vieni!*" He led us into the courtyard where we'd parked and where the other three officers, two holding rifles, were standing guard over our Land Cruiser. If he had found the pistol we'd be in serious trouble.

"No guns?" he asked, pointing to the Land Cruiser, giving us more than enough rope to hang ourselves.

"No, no guns."

The officer flung open the door of the Land Cruiser and pointed inside. I wiped the sweat from my eyes and went closer. He was pointing up, up to the three long leather cases we carried strapped to the underside of the roof and which he thought held rifles.

I unzipped the cases and pulled out our hunting bows. The officer was shattered; his gun runner was a mirage. Then he started smiling, and soon he and his men were laughing and roaring: "Pow! Pow! You cowboy and Indian, like American movie. Haaah, haaah. Bang! Bang! Sssshhhttt. Sssshhhttt."

To make up for the delays, we drove until very late that night. When we'd been planning the trip, we'd figured on making camp every night before sunset, but the farther behind schedule we got, the harder we pushed and the later we drove. In Europe we rarely made camp before nine at night; in French North Africa seldom before midnight; now we were sometimes pushing on until two in the morning, trying to make up for lost miles, trying to catch up to an impossible schedule that called for us to be clearing India.

But camping in the dead of night had its hazards, as we learned time and again. That first night in Libya we pulled beneath some trees to sleep, too exhausted to reconnoiter the area. In the morning we woke to find we'd camped in an olive grove; and the farmer, his children, and half the dogs in Tripolitania were there to see what we were up to. We apologized for trespassing and packed up quickly, but we couldn't get out; we were stuck fast. The sand between the trees was as dry as talc, and our rough treads cut in like a trench digging machine; in a minute we were in up to our axle. For three hot, sweaty hours we worked to free the equipment, deflating the tires, piling sticks and stones and blankets underneath, winching car against camper. In the direct heat of the sun and the humidity of the coastal region it was exhausting work, and we were dead tired and depressed when we finished.

The month in Africa had taken its toll on us; the detours and delays, the run-ins with robbers and mine fields, the passport troubles and customs problems, the breakdowns and breakups, and the red tape and suspicion we met everywhere had exhausted us.

A spirit raiser was scheduled to be Sabratha, the unearthed Roman city on the shores of the sparkling Mediterranean, and it was there we headed after our extrication from the olive grove. Hardly had we gone five miles when our jinx struck again: the hitch snapped and the small trailer broke loose, bouncing and banging down the road until it lost a wheel and ground to a stop, its spindle broken, its axle bent far out of line. We had to empty the trailer and carry it by hand three miserable miles to a mechanic. Repairs would take all day.

We spent the day at the ruins of Sabratha. There all was still as the desert night, lifeless as the desert day, and sea wind and weather were threatening to reduce to limestone dust what had once been part of the glory of Rome.

We're travelers, not philosophers, and we made this trip to see the world's past and present, not to speculate about its future; but one must give rise to the other, and the thoughts forced themselves upon us. No one can visit the Roman ruins in Volubus or Sabratha or Leptis and not speculate about the destiny of nations; you can't isolate them architecturally or artistically; you can't come away thinking only of the spatial relation of the Forum to the baths or the proportions of the columns; you are compelled to think: this was once a living city in a mighty empire, a thriving city in a civilization that ruled most of the then known world for 800 years, a civilization that brought engineers and aqueducts and teachers and libraries to the most distant corners of the darkness—an empire measurably more powerful in its time than our own country in its, an empire whose enemies were just heathens on horseback and nomads on camels—yet an empire of which only these tombstones remain. And you can't help but wonder what fate lies in store for your United States, a mere infant in only its second century of existence and its third decade of world leadership, but already besieged on all sides by powerful enemies; spending its youth and vigor on far-flung battle fields; and you wonder what lessons can be learned from these old Roman ruins on this forsaken desert—and you remember you're a traveler, not a philosopher, so you push on.

It was too late to push farther that night; so we laid our sleeping bags among the ruins on the shores of the sea and slept to the gentle lapping of the waves. Toward midnight a new sound drowned out the waves and wakened us: Manu was groaning. He began tossing and turning, clutching his stomach in pain. He was running a high fever. We gave him aspirin and Enterovioform, but they did little good; the fever and pain grew worse. He had a bad case of dysentery. There was little more we could do than give him water to prevent dehydration as we rushed him to a doctor in Tripoli.

The doctor insisted Manu needed at least three days in bed. Since he was thus confined, the rest of us set out to explore the city. We found it a delight, the Riviera blended with the *casbahs* of Africa. It had broad boulevards, spotless shops and sidewalks, a shady canopy of palm trees, a bazaar where the best gold and silverwork in Africa could be bought, and an ancient Moorish castle which looked out upon the harbor and which 160 years before had seen a young U.S. Navy lieutenant named Stephen Decatur slip under the noses of the Barbary pirates to burn and blow up one of their ships and put an end to their depredations on American merchantmen in what England's Admiral Lord Nelson called "the most daring act of the age."

The pride of Tripoli is the spacious, palm-fringed boulevard that runs along her beach-studded harbor. It is one of the most impressive streets in the world, built by the Italians as a grandiose showplace and lined with magnificent hotels, apartment buildings, arcades, public squares, and hospitals. When Libya was their colony the Italians called it the Lungomare; when she became independent the Libyans renamed it Sharia Adrian Pelt in honor of the United Nations statesman who prepared them for self-government.

Sharia Adrian Pelt also housed the headquarters of Soussi Brothers, the only Toyota distributor in North Africa. We'd alerted them from

New York about our trip, telling them to expect us in mid-April. It was now June. When we walked into the Soussi office they looked as if they were seeing ghosts; they had thought we'd turned back or perished on the desert.

We were introduced to Mohammed Soussi, the young English-educated heir to the Soussi enterprises which are introducing to Libya the products of the modern world. Everything from autos to office equipment, from washers to water pumps is imported, distributed, manufactured, serviced, rented, sold, leased, contracted for, or represented by Soussi Brothers. With somewhat of a shock we found that Madison Avenue had also moved to Libya, a country that 50 years ago hadn't even heard of New York. In seconds Mohammed was on the phone, calling his press agent, Publilibya, ringing up newspapers, inviting ministers, reserving rooms; in minutes he had arranged a press conference, a banquet in our honor, and a demonstration of our Land Cruiser for the most important people in the city.

The Soussis insisted we be their guests until Manu was well enough to travel. They wouldn't hear of our living in the camper; so they moved us to a hotel where we slept between sheets for the first time since the *Queen Elizabeth,* had our first haircuts since Jerez, and our first hot showers since Algiers. Our prospects seemed suddenly brighter.

The next day, headlines proclaimed our arrival in Arabic, Italian, and English, and the newspapers devoted so much space to our trip that one would have thought that Columbus, Magellan, and Kim Novak all rode in our Land Cruiser. The papers announced we would demonstrate our car under rough conditions at the Underwater Sports Club for a select assemblage of dignitaries including Libya's Minister of Transportation, his three top assistants, the general in charge of the Quartermaster Corps of the Libyan Army, and his aides, and the purchasing agents of every major oil company operating in the Kingdom.

Later that morning, before these distinguished guests gathered for the banquet, the Soussis and Al, who was to do the driving, went through a clandestine rehearsal, running the Land Cruiser through soft sand, over jagged rocks, across barbed wire, into the ocean up over its hubcaps, up a slippery hill, and through ditches and depressions, until they knew just exactly how to take the car to the brink and how to make it appear to attempt the impossible yet barrel through with flying colors.

There were so many titles and decorations at the banquet that it seemed more like a meeting of the Libyan cabinet than an automobile promotion, save for the Soussi crew spotted among the guests, exchanging polite conversation and now and then slipping in a plug for the Land Cruiser, which was the perfect vehicle, they explained (depending on whom they were talking to), for surveyers, soldiers, postmen, engineers, or geologists.

When the big demonstration came, Al was so stuffed he could barely squeeze behind the wheel. He safety-belted himself in with mock severity, raced the engine, and roared off along the course he and the Soussis had secretly laid out that morning. The crowd had its heart in its mouth (indeed, there was little room for it anywhere else after that meal) as Al plunged into the Mediterranean and seemed about to float away. The water was over the tops of the tires and the tailpipe sounded like an outboard engine about to give up the ghost; but he pulled it through, and roared to the crest of a rocky escarpment bounding the sea, charging up a stone hill so steep and slippery you'd have sworn he was going to fall over backwards and crash into the ocean. This was followed by a flat-out run across the open ground, churning through sand, bouncing over rocks, leaping across ditches. It was a hell of a way to treat a car that was supposed to take us the rest of the way around the world. For a grande finale, Al charged a gaping trench that had not been on his practice run. It was six feet deep and sheer as a cliff but Al charged it anyway. The crowd gasped, I gulped, and the Soussis held their breath as the front of the Land Cruiser went crashing straight down to the bottom of the trench—and stayed there.

It was the worst hangup I've ever seen. The front wheels barely rested on the bottom of the trench and the back wheels were suspended from the upper edge, leaving the car almost straight up and down. There was no room to maneuver and no direction to maneuver in. Al sweated and swore and shifted gears and ground into reverse, but nothing worked; a tank couldn't have gotten out. By now all the dignitaries had gathered on the rim of the trench; it reminded me of a funeral.

After half an hour Al had to submit to the final indignity: I rumbled over in my old Jeep, threw a winch around the Land Cruiser's rear end, and hauled it out of the hole.

The Soussis must have worked late that night: next morning the newspapers only reported that "The car's ability to negotiate sand, rock, and shallow water was clearly shown."

Mohammed Soussi gave us a farewell dinner, and after the other guests had gone we sat on a terrace overlooking the city and talked. Somehow the conversation turned to religion, and Mohammed gave me an insight into his. I had previously believed Islam was a religion of the masses, a dogmatic bunch of superstitious mumbo-jumbo in which only the uneducated could believe; but here was a very intelligent young man, who'd been schooled in England and who skillfully ran a modern business enterprise, telling me that:

"Islam gives meaning to my whole life. I could not live without it. It tells me everything I need to know and every way how to act. It is the greatest religion, the only true religion. I have studied your Catholicism, but it is a fairy tale with miracles and sons of God and Trinities. And your Protestantism has no meaning; you have Baptists and Methodists and Lutherans and fifty different denominations, each claiming to know best how to praise and obey God, and each doing things different. But with Islam there is only one God and he is all powerful. We grant that Moses and Jesus may have been prophets—but Mohammed was the final one. Mohammed is the true prophet of God, and his writings are the only way that the divine will can be learned. The Koran is the final revelation. We need look no farther and we need accept no other. The Koran tells us all we need to know about how to conduct our lives and how to submit to the will of God."

"But surely, Mohammed, you cannot believe——"

"It is difficult to explain to you, for it is complicated, and you are of another world with different standards. I saw that world in London, but I am not a part of it. I am Muslim. All I can explain to you is what my belief does for me. I never worry, I never drink alcohol. I do not covet young girls, and I will make my marriage with the help of my father. I never think of suicide and I never think of taking drugs. I work hard—but I enjoy it. I don't worry; I am not, like so many in the

West, troubled by doubts and fears and neuroses. I know that Allah watches over everything we do, and that if we do everything as he has caused to be written in the Koran we shall have our reward. I am serene and at peace with myself and the world. I am delighted with the sunrise, because it is the work of God, and with the sunset, because that is also his doing. And when I say my prayers and praise him, I am sure that he hears them, and that I need fear nothing. I do not mean to boast, and I know it is difficult for you to understand me, but our God gives me peace. Does yours?"

The next morning we were ready to leave Tripoli. Manu had recovered somewhat from his illness and Al from the knowledge that he didn't have a future as an automobile test pilot. The Soussis had shined and serviced our cars, and they'd found an Italian machinist named Guglielmo Scianno who, with loving care, had made a completely new axle and spindle for our little trailer, made them so well that we wouldn't have a bit of trouble with them again. If you're ever in Tripoli and need a new axle, look up Guglielmo Scianno.

As we were leaving town, Woodrow realized he still didn't have his visa for Egypt; and no one knew if he could get one elsewhere in Libya, for its capital city keeps shifting with the seasons and the disposition of the King. The rest of us had gotten our Egyptian visas in New York or Algiers, but Woodrow had never been up to it.

Rather than hold up both cars while Woodrow went for his visa, I told Al to take off with Manu and Willy and I'd catch up with them. I could move faster with the little trailer than they could with the camper, and assumed I'd catch them by night. It took five hours for Woodrow to get his visa; so it was early afternoon before we left Tripoli for Benghazi, 660 desolate desert miles away.

In spite of the delay, I had to stop for a quick view of Leptis Magna, though I would have preferred to spend a week. Far bigger and more beautiful than Sabratha, Leptis had been one of the showplaces of the Empire, a handsome city of colonnaded avenues, amphitheaters, meeting halls, fountains, baths, basilicas, forums, libraries, arches, and some 40 major buildings. Unlike Sabratha, which had been built from local limestone, Leptis was fashioned from beautiful multi-colored marble

brought from Greece and Italy and Asia Minor and the far corners of
the Empire, and its noble stone still stood as it had before the birth
of Christ.

After Leptis there was nothing save the tiniest of villages and the
dullest of deserts. The road we followed was the Strada Imperial, built
in the 1930's by the Italian militarists. It still bore the scars of war where
it had been chewed up by tanks and blasted by dive bombers. Land
mines and artillery shells had also taken their toll on it. The craters
were strategically spaced and impossible to avoid; if we swerved to
miss a hole with our right wheel, our left got clobbered, and vice versa,
really clobbered. The roadside was strewn with the carcasses of huge
tires that had literally been torn to shreds by the potholes and the
desert heat. Many of the devastated tires were three feet in diameter,
and laced with metal mesh, so heavy the two of us couldn't lift them;
but the road had shattered them. The only thing in the road's favor
was that it was straight, arrowing across the desert, often going 30 or
40 miles without a turn or bend, as monotonous as the desert itself.

By dusk we were tired and would have liked to set up camp, but we
had to close the miles between us and the others. To save time we ate
our evening meal—two cans of sardines and some salted crackers we'd
bought in Tripoli—standing in front of the headlights, our backs against
the wind and dust. We washed the meal down with water from the
thermos, but even it was thick with sand. We drove on in the darkness.

It was ten o'clock when I felt pains. They were deep in the stomach
and came with a severe blow that gave no warning. I then began to
vomit. I stopped the Jeep and tried to take water, but it only made the
vomiting worse. I tried driving again, but after half an hour I had to
stop. The pains had become so severe that I was bent over in agony. I
couldn't go farther.

I tried to help Woodrow set up the Poptent against the howling
desert wind, but I couldn't. I was hit with acute diarrhea. Next I
started vomiting great amounts of blood. Then came fever and chills.
I knew then that I had food poisoning.

Woodrow was so frightened he was stuttering, and I knew I'd get no
help from him. When he went into the tent, I took a blanket and
crawled off into the desert.

I grew delirious. I remember tearing off my clothes. I fell to the ground, wracked with convulsions. Covered with vomit and blood I rolled naked and shivering in the sand. Grotesque figures and images appeared before me. The world was fluid and I was swimming. No, I was being carried away through a deep chasm of blackness. Then there were moments of peace and joy. It would be so easy to give in, to struggle no longer. But I held on. I called to Woodrow for help, but he didn't come. I started crawling back toward the road. Al would find me. He would know what to do and give me something from his bunch of pills. I kept calling out to Al, "Here, I'm over here," and I didn't remember that he was hundreds of miles away.

When I opened my eyes and saw the first light of dawn it was all life and hope. Woodrow found me several hundred yards from the tent. He was pale and shaken. He swore he hadn't heard me calling in the night.

I was so dehydrated that I was aching with pains of thirst, but when I took water, even a sip, the vomiting began and more blood came. Woodrow would have to drive, even though his hands weren't completely healed from his fall. He would have to drive until we reached a doctor at Marsa Brega, 300 miles away. I tied myself into the Jeep and we set off.

The sun was as hot as ever, but now it felt pleasant to me, and whenever we stopped I untied myself and lay in the sand. And it felt good. Struggling back into the Jeep was the most difficult. Each mile we drove was like a day of torture. Hours later, my stomach would still not hold food or water. And so we crawled on—for 300 miles— without seeing a living soul.

By six that evening we reached Marsa Brega, the big Standard Oil complex on the Gulf of Sirte. I was never so glad to see an Esso sign in my life. We found the hospital, and nothing mattered anymore. When I awoke the next day, the doctor told me that I had had type-E botulism, which I had suspected, and that I had come within a breath of dying, which I had known.

Marsa Brega is an artificial port city, built almost entirely by Esso, on the terminus of its 200-mile pipeline from the desert oil fields; and it was a heavenly place to recuperate. Everything had been done to make the employee inhabitants comfortable. Its dining tables held fresh fruits and vegetables and thick slabs of steak. It must be the only air-conditioned city in North Africa. And it had ice water! Since we'd hit Africa, the water had been warm, muddy, dirty, minerally, animally, and full of bacteria. We'd filter it through a cloth, throw in a few halazone pills, and force ourselves to drink it—abominable! But Marsa Brega had delicious ice water from electric water coolers, and I practically lived next to one of them for a day. Thanks to a letter of introduction we'd gotten from a friend of the Soussis in Tripoli, the Esso people gave us the run of the place, and I gained back some strength from American food, ham and eggs, buttered toast, and hot coffee—a few of the luxuries we'd foregone in our month of camel meat and *couscous*.

One of the purposes of our trip was to eat and sleep and live as close to the natives in each country as possible, and to avoid, at all costs, the air-conditioned hotels and tourist restaurants where everything was certified safe and sterile and innocuous. Our tent on wheels was as close as we could reasonably come to duplicating native living conditions in three dozen countries. It would not isolate us from the elements of nature which exert such a controlling influence over the people outside the western world; it would give us no more protection from the desert sun than any nomad tent in Libya, nor more relief from the dust storms than any native hut in Afghanistan; it would be as susceptible to monsoon dampness as any Indian village shack, as penetrable to the creatures of the forest as any jungle hut in Thailand or Panama; and we felt that our exposure to the forces and fears that shaped the lives of the people would better enable us to understand them. We would eat what the natives ate and drink what they drank; we would shop at the native markets, sup at the native stalls, drink from the native wells, and take most of the chances they took. We'd toss some halazone in the water, peel all raw fruits and vegetables, and supplement our meals with vitamins and protein powder, but these were our only concessions to civilization.

When I was well enough to travel I found the desert inferno
waiting for us right outside the gates of Marsa Brega. The air was so
dry we could actually feel our bodies dehydrating. Then the *ghibli*
began, the dread desert wind that is the scourge of Libya. The old-
timers had warned us about the *ghibli,* but it goes beyond description
and further than imagination. It was a blast of pure heat unlike anything I have ever met before. I could not conceive of a wind being
anything but cooling, but this was the discharge of a blast furnace. The
temperature inside the car soon rose to over 120°! Whether we drove
fast or slow, there was no getting away from the desert blowtorch. It
stopped our breath, dried our perspiration before it formed, blistered
our eyes, cracked the insides of our noses, and parched our throats. We
were being baked alive; but there was absolutely no escape from the
searing wind until it died of its own accord two hours later. I would
gladly take my chances in a tornado, swim in a hurricane, or spend a
month in a monsoon before I'd want to meet another *ghibli* face to
face.

The *ghibli* is so much the scourge of Libya that it can take almost
sole credit for the desert that covers 98 per cent of the country.
Irrigation and fertilizers can help make the desert bloom, but they
can't beat the *ghibli.* Flourishing fields have been decimated in a day,
farmers wiped out in hours. Only the hardiest of olive trees and date
palms manage to survive. Because of the *ghibli* Libya cannot be considered an underdeveloped nation. "She's as developed as she's ever
going to be," one old-timer told us, "as long as she has the *ghibli.* Once
that wind hits there's nothing left to develop."

Bad news met us in Benghazi. I found Al at the Soussi Brothers
garage, supervising a crew of mechanics. The potholed desert road had
shattered the camper's undercarriage, and to repair it the mechanics
had to reinforce it with heavy angle irons. And a tricky short somewhere in the camper lights was blowing the fuses in the Land Cruiser
and defying every effort to pin it down. We'd be stuck at least three
days until repairs were finished.

Benghazi is not the best place in the world to be stuck for three
days—or even three hours. The second largest city (pop. 60,000) in

Libya, Benghazi owes that distinction less to its attractiveness as a place to live than to the simple fact that there is only one other city. Among Benghazi's other claims to fame: it is one of the world's most bombed-out cities, having been the object of one thousand air raids by Allied and Axis pilots during the war, and one of the world's most expensive, being presently the site of most of the business activity connected with Libya's great oil boom. A reconnaissance of Benghazi's tourist attractions (which consumed eleven minutes) and a light lunch in one of its cheaper restaurants (which consumed as much as we'd spent for a week's food in Morocco) convinced us that we'd seen all we wanted to of Benghazi.

We decided to take a flight into the desert while we waited. A men's magazine had commissioned us to watch for good adventure stories, and we'd just come across one of the best of them, the story of the desert pilots. When oil was first found in Libya and the boom began, there wasn't an airline in the country; but the oil companies needed them. The drilling rigs were two, four, or six hundred roadless miles from the coast, and the cross-country trip by car was exhausting and dangerous. Planes were needed to take workers to the drilling rigs and to bring them fresh fruit and meat, and mail, and urgently needed parts; so little companies were formed to meet the demand—and the desert pilots took up the challenge.

We hung around Benghazi Airport for a day interviewing the men who flew the desert runs. They were all rovers and adventurers; no other kind would take the job. There were jet fighter pilots from the Korean War, jungle pilots from South America, a guy who'd been King Saud's pilot in Arabia for five years, and another who'd flown for the UN in the Congo and then flown against the UN when he got a better offer from the rebels. They told us matter-of-factly of the dangers of their run: lack of landing fields, dust storms and *ghiblis,* the way the desert obliterated all landmarks, the fact that in an area as big as the United States east of the Mississippi there were only two strong navigational beams. Most of the planes that day had delivered explosives and equipment to fire fighter Red Adair who was trying to cap six blazing wells; but there was a flight into the desert the next morning, and we were invited along. We didn't need a ticket—just our signature on a form releasing the desert air service from any responsibility in case we didn't make it back.

From the air Libya is astounding. Benghazi is no longer a city; it is an oasis of brick and cement on the edge of an endless desert. It looked as if a good sandstorm could cover it over—or maybe that was just wishful thinking. Marsa Brega from 8,000 feet is a pathetic speck surviving only at the mercy of the desert.

At Marsa Brega we turned south, leaving the Mediterranean behind, heading straight into nothingness. Our cargo: meat, fresh vegetables, and ten Arab laborers who sat on the floor and got airsick the minute we took off. Our destination: Sugar Seven, a fly spot on the map, a prospecting rig 300 miles from anything. Our pilot, Captain Steve Toich: "Look below and you'll see our problem. Every mile looks the same as every other mile. There's a cliff or a bunch of hills, but mostly it's like this—miles of flat sand. It's a bitch to tell where you're at. The radio beacons are so weak you're sometimes out of touch in half an hour. You try to memorize a few landmarks; then a *ghibli* comes along and wipes them out, and if you're up here when a *ghibli* hits!——Then you've had it. You'll never know where you're at—can't even tell if you're upside down. We try to fly a tight pattern until it blows over, but sometimes those mothers last for two days. See—down there—that plane, almost covered by sand—went down in a *ghibli* last winter and they still haven't figured how to get it out.

"Sometimes we fly by the smoke, but that only works when we're near the wells. Libya doesn't use its natural gas—no pipelines and no local customers—so the oil companies burn it off. Makes a big blaze, 50 feet high, and lots of smoke. There—there's one now—that's Zeltan One, the grand old daddy of them all, the baby that put us in business.

"Another problem? The air fields. The only way I can tell them from the rest of the desert is 'cause they got camel droppings all around. These guys on the rigs don't have time to put in a pro strip; so they just find the nearest piece of flat ground, run a bulldozer over it, line it with oil drums, stick a windsock at one end—and call it an airfield. Most of the times they've laid it across the wind or in the middle of a kangaroo rat colony."

Sugar Seven was a drilling rig, a water pump, a storage shed, and half a dozen quonset huts in the middle of an immensity of desert. But everything was air-conditioned, and there were recreation rooms, and radios, and movie shows, and a dining room handing out freshly baked Danish and pitchers of iced lemonade and bowls of ice cream. All the men had to do was work like hell and—if they didn't get lost in the desert—collect a big bundle at the Benghazi bank when the job was done. The wages ran high: the rig at Sugar Seven was on a subcontract to drill a hole for $2,000,000.

Back in Benghazi the welders were just finishing the new undercarriage. It was as solid and substantial as we could ask, and the head welder assured us it would get us around the world. But in the process of building he'd accidentally done something which was to wreck us a few days later and hang over our heads for the rest of the trip.

Minutes out of Benghazi we were back in the desert, a wasteland still littered with the wreckage of war. In the rainless climate, where nothing rusts or rots completely, we could still see the crushed C-ration cans and garbage piles where armies had camped in preparation for battle 23 years before, and where now there were solitary Bedouin tents. Where battles had been fought there were now only turbaned scavengers picking through the shell casings—and occasionally blowing themselves to bits on an unexploded mine, an estimated five million of which make nomad life in Libya an especially risky business.

More than half the people of Libya are still nomads, and we began to see more of them as we left the desert floor and slowly climbed toward the hills of the Jabal Al Akhdar. Here and there were bits of stubble and tufts of grass, and the scrawny goats and sheep and camels moved about them and chewed them into something edible. The sun beat down without mercy and there was absolutely no shade, not a bush or a tree anywhere. I felt sorry for the animals who had never known the shade of a tree, or seen a green meadow, or stood in a cool brook.

When we stopped for lunch I checked over the Land Cruiser and found the headlight fuse had blown. I put in a new one and it blew as soon as we moved. Al and I searched around with the wiring diagrams, but we couldn't find the trouble. We'd either have to go back to Benghazi or drive without lights all the way to Cairo. We went back to Benghazi, and it was another day wasted, on top of the three spent for welding, on top of the two spent for my illness, on top of the three spent for Manu's illness, on top of this on top of that. Were we never going to have a day without trouble or delays?

We almost made it the next day. By nightfall we were in Derna, a small town 200 miles from Benghazi and halfway to the Egyptian border, and we hadn't had a bit of trouble. When we turned on our lights, the fuse on the Land Cruiser blew in a flash, and the red generator warning signal in the Jeep went on. Now it was double trouble, but I'd be damned if we were going back to Benghazi; we'd find a mechanic in Derna.

Derna is known for two things: it grows delicious little bananas, highly prized for their alleged aphrodisiac properties, and it was the site, in 1805, of a famous raid by American forces. When the young United States had refused to submit to the demands of the Barbary pirates, the Pasha of Tripoli had declared war on American shipping. Outraged by this, the American Consul at Tunis, one William Eaton, went to Egypt, where he organized, out of his own purse and without official sanction, an army of 400 men, including 38 Greek mercenaries, assorted Italians, Englishmen and Arabs, 190 camels, and eight American Marines. For six weeks they made an incredible overland march through the Egyptian desert to Derna. There they captured and held the fortress. Made bold by their victory, they were planning to march on Tripoli itself when the Pasha and the American government made peace. They never got farther than Derna, but their daring sortie is forever enshrined in American annals—with a thousand miles of geographical inaccuracy—as part of the Marine Corps hymn: "From the halls of Montezuma to the shores of Tripoli . . ."

Anyway, that's what Derna is known for: bananas and the raid. It is not known for having any auto mechanics, nor did we find any. But if the Trans World Record Expedition was ever to move itself from the shores of Tripoli to the halls of Montezuma, we had to do something. Al and I spent half the night with the wiring diagrams until we found the trouble, a smashed connection on the Land Cruiser's trailer socket and a loose wire on the Jeep's voltage regulator. We went to sleep late, wondering what disaster the next day would bring.

It brought a beauty, the prize of them all, which hit us 170 miles from Derna on what is probably as deserted a stretch of road as exists anywhere in the world. I was driving the Land Cruiser when I heard a loud thump behind me. I turned around and saw the left wheel of our camper bounding high in the air and bouncing off into the desert, followed immediately by a spray of sparks and the shrill cry of tortured steel as the naked axle dug into the road. The camper scraped on its belly for the length of a football field before I could stop. It was a mess: the floor was splintered, the sides buckled, the struts bent, and the new undercarriage cracked through in three places. Woodrow was almost in tears, and even Al wasn't smiling as he and Willy snapped another set of "disaster photos."

The accident was a mystery until I took a look under the trailer: the welder in Benghazi, in the process of fitting the new frame, had had to remove a small bend in the axle that had been put there by the manufacturer to give the wheels the proper camber. After he had straightened the axle in a gigantic heat press the wheels were thrown out of camber, and the entire weight of the camper and its contents shifted to the spindles, one of which had snapped.

It could only be repaired in a welding shop, and the nearest one was in Tobruk, many hours back the way we'd come. Since it was impossible to pull the camper on one wheel, we'd have to take off the entire axle, put it in one of the cars, and take it back to Tobruk to have a new spindle welded onto it. It was an immense job. Even getting the camper off the road and onto the level desert floor was an immense job, and we sweated over it for an hour. Next we had to jack up the trailer on all four sides to get it high enough off the ground and steady enough so we could remove the axle. It took two hours in the broiling desert to find and carry back enough big rocks to do the job, and we were sun baked and dirt covered by the time the camper was propped up. I then spent a tense thirty minutes under the trailer, unbolting the axle, knowing the slightest shift of one rock would bring two tons of trailer crashing down on me; but there was no other way. The sun was down by the time we had the axle off. It was too late to take it back to Tobruk, and since the next day was Friday, the Moslem Sabbath, when all shops are closed, we were stuck in the desert for two days.

By nightfall all our food and water were gone, except the box of matzos which Al insisted we had to save for the Pyramids. We'd been traveling light on rations because of the exorbitant prices in Benghazi, planning to stock up in Egypt where food was reportedly cheaper, and we'd drunk our water cans dry in a couple of hours from our exertions. Only one car passed all day, and they had no water to spare.

We were preparing to settle down for a parched and hungry night when a green Land Rover pulled up beside us, and out jumped a young Libyan Army lieutenant who offered us his canteen. No genie jumping out of a lamp could have materialized at a better time.

The lieutenant was an instructor at a desert camp near the Egyptian border, about 50 miles distant, where he taught guerrilla warfare, counterinsurgency techniques, demolition, traps, and sabotage to a band of commando trainees. He'd been home on leave to Benghazi to visit his wife, he explained, and was returning to his camp when he saw us.

I asked if he had any food, and he thought for a moment, then pointed south, into the desert. "We will get food from the nomads. They are passing through here on their way to summer pasture in the hills. I visited their camp a few days ago."

"But aren't the nomads dangerous? Don't they beat up strangers, and rob them?" Woodrow asked.

"Only the nomads with the five-sided tents; even I stay away from them. But these are different, and they will not bother you if I am with you."

"You mean they're afraid of the army?" Al asked.

"Not at all. We have no control over them. When we got our independence we promised the nomads they could come and go as they pleased. We let them keep all their guns. They have no passports; they cross the borders as they wish. Our country is trying to persuade them to settle down and become farmers, but it will take years. It is difficult to build a nation when half its people are never in the same place from one month to the next. But they are too proud to be told what to do. It was their great-great-ancestors who destroyed the towns along the coast when the Romans left, and it was their sheep and camels a thousand years ago who pastured on the farms and ate all the grasses and pulled down all the forests. Our legends tell us that once a man could walk all the way from Tripoli to Tangier in the shade of trees and gardens, but these nomads destroyed them all. They want to stay with their old ways. Every year more of them die. When there is no rain and no grass, you see everywhere the bones of their baby sheep and goats. The herds get smaller every year. Many of the families have only enough left to keep alive."

"Then how will they be able to help us?"

"The Bedouins here do well. They are near Cyrene and the hills, where there is always rain and grass. Their goats and sheep survive."

"Then why don't all the Bedouins come here?"

"It is forbidden. It would be war. The Bedouin tribes graze where they have grazed for a thousand years. In this desert, each tribe has a boundary. If they find another tribe on their grazing land, they kill them."

"That doesn't sound like a very charitable attitude," Al remarked.

"The Bedouins are not known for their charity."

"Then what makes you think they'll give us food?" I asked.

"You will give them a present, of course. Some clothing is always good, or jewelry. Also bring your rifles; we must show the nomads you are armed so they won't come back and rob you when you sleep."

"The only extra clothing we have is shoes, and we don't have rifles, just bows and arrows," I answered.

"That will do. The nomads wear shoes. And they will respect you as warriors if you bring bows and arrows, for their fathers used them before the British gave them guns in the war."

We drove about four miles straight south into the desert before the lieutenant stopped us: "We will walk the rest of the way," he said, "so that we don't disturb their animals."

It looked like the middle of nowhere, but soon I could see black tents against the blackness of the desert night. What seemed like open space between the tents was crisscrossed with guy ropes, and by the time we'd stumbled our way through them, the whole camp was aware of our presence. Sheep and goats pulled away, chickens and children scurried in front of us, tethered camels snorted beside the huge hide tents. The scent of tea and baking bread was fragrant on the night air.

The lieutenant led the way to the *sharif's* tent, at whose threshold we laid our bows to show we came in peace, and bowed to the smiling old Arab who bade us enter. We removed our shoes and left them outside, save for the pair we brought to barter. The lieutenant, after a round of Arabic courtesies and formalities, explained the purpose of our visit, pointing to our gift. The Arab in turn pointed to our bows on the threshold, whereupon they went into a long discussion before seeming to reach an agreement.

In the meantime I'd been inspecting the surprisingly comfortable tent. It was about 40 feet in diameter and fifteen feet high, with a floor of bare earth covered with straw mats and thick rugs. The top, which showed wide holes at the seams where air and light came through, certainly wasn't rainproof, but in a country where it sometimes doesn't rain for a year I guess that wasn't a consideration. As we entered someone drew a curtain across one part of the tent: this was the women's quarters and the kitchen. When strangers are about they are hidden so as not to see or be seen.

The most amazing thing about the tent was its contents. Stacked against half the length of the wall to a height of three feet were dozens of folded rugs, each exquisitely embroidered, each worth a fortune. The chief proudly displayed them to us. I saw something protruding from one of the rugs that looked like a rifle butt. The chief caught my gaze and pulled out an ancient Italian rifle wrapped in rags. I looked up to the center post, which was crisscrossed with cords and burlap, and there hung other rifles. There was even a rifle tucked under the chief's cushion. Four or five chests stood beside the stacked rugs, each a sturdy trunk studded with decorative nail heads; I could only guess what was in them.

The old man opened a smaller chest to pull out a box; inside I caught a glimpse of sparkle and shine and heard the clinking of coins. From the box he withdrew four small glasses with gold rims. One of his wives came from behind the curtain bringing an old British Army canteen filled with steaming water; she was shy and hid her head from us a bit, but she was too curious to hide completely. She was about sixteen, dressed in a scarlet skirt and white blouse with gold bracelets on her wrists and ankles. She was full-breasted and seemed full of life, and I found her quite appealing save for some bluish tattoo marks on her chin and between her eyes. It was hard to hide our admiration from her husband—and our envy of him. I found something overwhelmingly compelling about this old man and his nomad life. It was a life with no bonds and no borders, no bosses and no timeclocks, no PTA meetings and no Chamber of Commerce. It was moving with the sun, blowing with the wind, making love in a great airy tent on an empty desert beneath a canopy of stars.

The old man began an elaborate tea ritual. It reminded me of the Japanese tea ceremony, and what he lacked in the grace of a geisha, he made up for the obvious love he put into his labors. Another of his wives came in with a flat piece of tin that held burning coals. The old man poured the canteen of water into an iron pot placed on the coals. He added a handful of tea. Then a pinch more. Then came the sugar. One heaping spoon, two, three, four—endless spoons of sugar into a pot that held little more than a pint of tea. He mixed the brew, then poured tea into each glass, then back into the pot, then back into the glasses and back again into the pot, caressing the glasses, stirring the pot, for fifteen minutes. Each time he poured he held the pot higher; soon it was two feet above the tiny glass, but he poured without spilling a drop. When at last he considered it suitable for serving, it was as sweet as honey, thick as blood, and hot as fire. The nomad drank his without cooling it, and the lieutenant told us to do the same. It blistered the lips, melted the teeth, and warmed the soul. The chief pressed another cup on us; then another. There was no refusing.

When the tea was finished the chief clapped his hands. The two wives came from behind the curtain laden with food which they placed at our feet: a big porcelain pitcher of thick goat's milk, a pile of flat brown bread, and a metal bowl holding several dozen small eggs.

"That's a good haul for a pair of shoes," Al said when we were clear of the camp. "You're some bargainer, lieutenant; I wish we had you with us for the whole trip."

After a minute of silence the lieutenant confessed, "I'm afraid I had to promise him more than the shoes."

"What?"

The officer explained that the nomads wanted us to help them hunt a gazelle. They didn't want to kill their sheep or goats at that time of the year, he elaborated, but they wanted meat. They couldn't hunt the gazelles on foot, because they'd grown wary and wouldn't let men get that close, nor could they hunt from their camels, because the gazelles were too fast. So the nomad chief told the officer they wanted to hunt from our car.

I told the officer I thought it was ridiculous.

He said the nomads didn't think so.

I told the officer I wouldn't do it.

He said I would. "You can't refuse, or the nomads will be angry. I have already told them you were a great hunter in America. The chief expects you back as soon as you give the food to your men. But don't worry, I'll go with you. I would let them use my Land Rover, but the top doesn't come off, and the chief wants to be able to shoot from the car. Besides, the Army already warned me—here, have some milk."

Not without misgivings, but without much alternative, Al and I took the canvas top off the Land Cruiser and emptied out the supplies, leaving the others behind to guard them and the crippled trailer. When we drove into the encampment the nomads were hopping happily up and down as if I were some sort of brown-bearded Santa Claus about to give them a ride in his sleigh.

In a twinkling, eleven of them had jammed into the back of the car, all chuckling and talking and joking and spitting on the upholstery. They smelled as if they'd had scampi and garlic bread for dinner, and their last bath a year ago. They were all jammed together in the back, all trying to stand up at the same time, all ready for action, their guns bristling in every direction, so that the Land Cruiser resembled nothing so much as a red porcupine. They had a specimen of almost every piece of armament in the books——270's and 30.06's and 30—30's and even a twelve-gauge shotgun. I expected one of them to go running back for their trench mortar. The chief had the best rifle in the bunch, a shiny new Magnum Express that could easily dispatch an elephant. One little old nomad who reminded me of Sneezy the Dwarf came running up with a blunderbuss that looked as if it must have been left over from the war—the War of 1812. There didn't seem to be any room for him, so he scooted over me and wedged himself right behind the driver's seat, his powderhorn swinging against the back of my neck as we headed off into the desert.

I drove, Al scouted from the window seat, and the officer sat between us up front, pointing out the way through a haze of cigar smoke.

When I complained that I didn't really think it was ethical to shoot an animal from a moving car, all I got for my trouble was a lecture from the lieutenant about the survival of the fittest and the laws of the desert and that the animals belonged to the nomads and that Americans couldn't understand because they were always fat and well-fed.

Al cut in to point out that our nomad friends had far from empty bellies and probably enough treasure stashed away to buy a controlling interest in IBM, when the officer turned out the headlights. The light could be seen fifteen or twenty miles in the clear desert air, he explained, and would spook any game around.

He might as well have blindfolded me, the thin slice of fading moon gave so little light. I was soon driving more by touch than by sight, and I seemed to be touching every ditch, rock, mound, bump, and hole west of El Alamein. I was down to fifteen miles an hour, but the results were still devastating. I was cinched in tight with my safety belt, but still seemed to be steering with my stomach and shifting with my knees most of the time, with the little nomad swaying back and forth over my head like a yoyo, spilling gunpowder down my neck. The car sounded as if it would break apart, and I began to wonder if this was a technique our khakied friend taught at his demolition school.

After a shaken-up eternity, someone spotted a gazelle, far to the southwest, silhouetted against the night sky. I reluctantly increased speed, heading toward it, my lights still out, wishing I'd installed radar in the car instead of a Ramsey winch, when the nomads opened fire. At first I thought a small volcano had erupted under us. Then the little nomad behind me discharged his blunderbuss, sending smoke and fumes and grapeshot all over the place. I knew it was Vesuvius. The nomads urged me forward, but with the bouncing of the car in the dark I don't know how they hoped to hit anything edible. Half the shots were winging off in the direction of Uranus and two or three peppered the dirt in front of us. I couldn't see a thing through the smoke and smell, and the only thing I was certain of was that the gazelle was a lot safer than I.

Later, as we drove back toward our camp, Al said to the lieutenant, "I hope the nomad chief wasn't too disappointed about not getting a gazelle."

"I don't think so," the officer smiled. "He's always wanted a ride in an automobile. And—oh yes—he wonders if you might have another pair of shoes. A little smaller."

All the next day we toiled in the scorching desert sun, nailing and boarding the camper floor back together, pounding the buckled sides into place, straightening the struts underneath. The following morning I took the axle and one of our spare spindles to the welding shop in Tobruk. It was late afternoon before the work was finished and we were ready to roll. We'd lost two full days, and the undercarriage still had three bad cracks that we'd have to weld in Cairo, but at least we were back on the road. Our Sahara adventure was finished. We'd overturned the small trailer twice, smashed the camper, broken an axle, snapped a spindle; we'd been attacked by leeches and flying crabs, looted by robbers; we'd fallen out of moving cars, been caught in sand traps, baked by the *ghibli,* and stranded in the desert. But we were pushing on.

Just as we were leaving, the little nomad came trotting to our camp on his camel. The chief had sent him. Did we happen to have any shoe polish? Brown?

Chapter 7
One Day

As we neared Saloom, the Egyptian border town, the sun was directly behind us and setting, a crimson wafer quickly consumed by the huge appetite of the Sahara. Our timing was perfect, we hoped, for experience had shown that dusk was the best time to reach a border post. If we arrived any later, the border was often closed for the night; if we arrived much earlier, the guards had time to waste, and they'd often waste ours in the process; but if we arrived at dusk, when the guards were anxious to finish duty, they usually wouldn't bother with a thorough search of our equipment. And a thorough search was the last thing we wanted that day since our prohibited items included an unregistered pistol, several hundred undeclared dollars, and a half case of bourbon. I was also concerned because Egypt requires travelers—even those with visas—to prove that they are not Jewish, and Al could not.

We peaked the rise of the bald, round mountain we'd been climbing, and Egypt spread before us, four still distinct strips in the dimming twilight. To the far left, and stretching over the horizon, the darkened Mediterranean broke black and white on the beach; to the right of it, the coastal strip, perhaps a mile wide, containing the beach, the border town of Saloom, and the thin trail of asphalt stretching toward Alexandria; then the escarpment of rugged, barren hills, straight-rising and straight in line, a geological arrow aiming east southeast; last was inland Egypt, mile after mile after endless mile of dry and lifeless sand, not the glistening golden grains of the Sahara *ergs*, but a coarser, dirtier, rockier sand devoid of life and hope.

We coasted down the winding road to the base of the mountain

121

where a guard waved us off the road and toward the passport office. The big room was dark and filled with thick cigar smoke. It was furnished with splintering wooden desks, cracked leather armchairs, two pictures of Nasser, two pictures of the Aswan Dam construction, and four army officers. In the United States and most European nations, passport control is handled by a special department; but in Egypt, as in most Arab countries, the Army controls the frontiers. The officers were in their undershirts, their fat arms and faces sweating in the airless room. They were suspicious, arrogant, and in no hurry to get home.

We entered the passport office a little before six; it was well after nine when we cleared. The official business transacted in that time could have been finished in fifteen minutes; the rest of the time was a waste—and an indignity. For the first hour, the officers, once they'd learned that three of us were Americans, ignored us while they busied themselves lighting their kerosene lanterns and extolling the virtues of their Cuban cigars. For the following hour we were scrutinized like bugs under a microscope. Why had we come to Egypt? Where had we been? Where would we be staying each night? How much money did we have with us? Were we planning to take pictures of the Palestine refugees? What kind of work did we do? Where were our parents born? Were we connected with the American government in any way? Why did we have a trailer with us? Had we ever visited Egypt before? Had we ever been thrown out of Egypt or arrested? Had we ever been to Israel? Were we planning to go to Israel?

I was annoyed; but the officers were just waiting for one of us to lose his temper. When we had gotten our visas weeks before we had filled out forms and answered all the relevant questions; our passports and visas were in perfect order, but the officers were determined to continue their game.

"You, what work do you do?" they asked Al.

"I'm an art director—you know—for advertisements." He was using the cover story we'd contrived for those countries that don't like foreign journalists prowling around, but which would still serve to explain the presence of all our film and cameras.

"What do you do, Mr. Stephens?"

"I teach school in Washington."

"And you, Mr. Keck?"

"I'm a student."

Our individual cover stories had basis in fact and we could document them all to an extent; but if the guards were really looking for something they'd probably find it.

Next, they wanted to know what were our religions. We all replied with various Christian denominations, all true except for Al. We'd rehearsed him many times, even taught him some Protestant prayers and religious theory, but his lip still trembled when he answered, and new sweat moistened his forehead. The officer looked at him closely. In the other countries Al, with his large nose, dark eyes, and olive skin, had been often mistaken for an Arab. He usually nodded modestly when thus addressed, congratulated the speaker on his perceptiveness, and admitted that his father had been born in some other Arab country, usually picking one that was on a friendly footing with the one we were in. But it wasn't going to be so easy this time.

We had been warned that Egypt, being fiercely anti-Israel, and making no distinction between Israelis and Jews, had regulations requiring visitors to carry letters from their home churches declaring that they were members in good standing. I thought it would have been easy to get such a letter for Al before we sailed, from some priest or minister who wanted to help strike a mild blow against religious discrimination, but they had all refused.

"Mr. Keck," the guard asked, "do you have some proof of your religion?"

Woodrow showed his letter.

"And you, Mr. Podell, you also have a letter like——"

I had to distract him away from Al. I started edging toward the door, trying to act suspicious.

"You," he shouted at me. "Come here. Show me your letter." I showed it to him.

"Where are you going?" he asked.

"First to Alexandria, then to Cairo, and across into Jordan," I answered.

"Jordan. How to Jordan?"

I told him we planned to drive from Cairo across the Suez then through the Sinai Peninsula.

"It is impossible!" the guard snapped. "You Americans think you can go anywhere."

"Why is it impossible? Is there no road?"

"You cannot get authorization."

"But why do we need authorization?" Willy jumped in. "We have visas to enter Jordan. They'll let us in."

"It is forbidden to go into the Sinai. No one is allowed. It is a war zone. Do not forget that we are at war with your ally Israel. Next year. You come again next year, and then you can drive to Jordan."

"You are building a road?" Al asked.

"No, next year there will be no Israel."

Finally, and begrudgingly, the officer stamped our passports into Egypt and we were free to move on—twenty yards to the customs office.

We'd been warned that Egyptian customs were tough, but we were hardly prepared for what awaited us. In a blazingly bright room, four clerks behind a wide counter were assiduously searching the luggage and persons of a dozen Arab travelers and workers. They untied knots, opened boxes, poked through tins of tea and cookies, pulled off nailed covers, probed for false bottoms, checked for labels, dumped trunks and suitcases on the floor, searched through pockets and trouser legs and shoes. In a small room to the right, a clerk was exchanging foreign currency for Egyptian pounds at the highly inflated official rate of exchange. Ten American dollars would fetch eight or nine Egyptian pounds on the free market in New York or Beirut, or on the black market inside Egypt, but the Egyptian government was only offering four and a half pounds, and imposing several penalties, including imprisonment, on anyone caught entering or leaving with more foreign money than they had declared. You could double your money by concealing some of your dollars and exchanging them on the black market, but you could also easily double your stay in Egypt—behind bars.

In front of the customs house, in the driveway where we had parked our cars and trailers, two customs officers with lights were searching through the wagon and car ahead of us. They checked the undersides, looked beneath the floor mats, felt behind the seats, emptied the trunk, probed in the gas tank, searched under the hood. In a country where foreign goods are as scarce as in Egypt and where the currency is so weak, smuggling is immensely profitable—and widespread.

For 20 minutes we waited our turn. Almost everyone ahead of us had trouble; half of them had goods confiscated and half of them had to pay customs duties. These were all for minor offenses, like bringing in a can of fruit from Casablanca or carrying a new blanket that was obviously not made in Egypt. What would happen to us if their search uncovered our pistol, our bourbon, and our undeclared American dollars? It was a hot night, and we sweated profusely.

Fortunately for us, it was also a busy night at the customs post, and the tired guard decided to take a chance and search us only halfheartedly. At first I thought he was just reluctant to go plowing through two loaded cars and trailers, but his conversation convinced me that he believed all Americans were so rich they would never attempt to smuggle anything. He handed us a set of temporary Egyptian plates and closed the office.

Outside I breathed deeply and resolved to find a better hiding place for our pistol, drink all our bourbon, and change our undeclared dollars quickly. It takes a certain kind of nerveless constitution to be a smuggler, and I don't have it.

I didn't know it then, but as I was busy making these resolutions and helping wire the Arabic license plates atop our New Jersey ones, Al was busy a few hundred yards away getting us involved in another smuggling project, a real one and a dangerous one.

"Steve," he began when he got back, "there's a man who wants us to carry some stuff to Alexandria tomorrow. He'll pay us two hundred dollars. I told him we'd discuss it with him. He also said he'd treat us to a first class meal, so what do we have to lose?"

We went through the final checkpoint, where our passports were inspected, and entered the dark village of Saloom. It was less a village than a wide, sand-covered street with 20 or 30 shops on either side and a few houses farther back. Al motioned us to stop beside a shop; there was a barber pole outside; a crack of light and the smell of gasoline came from under the door.

"No. No. Don't stop here!" an angry voice whispered from the shadows. "The police will be suspicious. Keep going! Drive farther on! Then walk back. Be sure there are no police."

We left Manu and Woodrow to guard the cars at the end of the village street. The crack of light opened and we quickly entered. Al introduced us to Benny, a gross, nervous Egyptian with the condescending attitude of a man accustomed to dealing with his inferiors.

Benny pushed Willy and me into barber chairs in one part of his shop and whipped soiled aprons around our necks; he pointed for Al to sit at a table in the little restaurant at the other end, "so that no one will suspect we talk business."

Willy reminded Benny that he'd promised to feed us. "Of course, of course, my friends, anything you like. What do you want?"

We suggested meat and vegetables, and Benny hustled over to talk to the thin, pimply Arab dozing on a bench near the door.

"It is a pity, my friends, but there is no meat left today—such good meat it was. Perhaps something else?"

Benny had neither fish nor fowl nor vegetables, and the something else finally turned out to be a pot of cold tea, a stale loaf of dark bread, and one fried egg to be shared by the three of us. Benny strutted around the shop, smug and self-satisfied.

"Eat, eat, my friends. You must be hungry. Then you will rest and tomorrow night leave for Alex."

I asked Benny what he had in mind. In a hushed voice he told us he wanted us to carry a few boxes of watches, nylons, soap, and ballpoint pens to his partners near Alexandria; there were no guns or narcotics in the load, just simple luxuries that brought a good price in Egypt. He couldn't take them himself because there were guards along the road who stopped and searched all cars with Arab drivers. "But they will not bother you," he assured us, "because you are tourists, Americans. They will let you pass—just as they did at the border. They will never search you. It will be easy."

"But what if they *should* stop to search us?" I asked.

"They will never do it. You are tourists—they will not bother tourists."

"But what if they do?" I pressed.

"Tell them you will report them—threaten them—say you will report them to Cairo. Don't let them search you—just drive away. They won't bother you."

If Benny's supper hadn't convinced me that he was a crook, his speech did; I wanted no part of the deal.

Willy broke in. "Look, Steve, we go that way anyway and we have some space. Besides, two hundred dollars is nothing to throw away."

"Yeah, Steve," Al joined him, "and we aren't really *smuggling* anything. What we just brought through the border was worse. Here all we'd be doing is *transporting* some stuff within the country, like a trucking company—there's probably not even a law against it."

I looked at Al wondering if he was serious. Then Benny was on my back with questions about the capacity of the trailer and how much the cars could carry. He appeared distressed that we had so much in our cars. He seemed to look upon us as *his* caravan, expressly sent from New York to take *his* contraband to Alex. How come we'd loaded ourselves down with junk like clothes and stoves and sleeping bags?

Al and Benny entered into an hour of sustained haggling. Al promised to make space in our Land Cruiser if Benny agreed to buy one of our huge spare tires. (We'd been carrying two spares, but the tires were holding up so well, and the spare took up so much space, that we'd been looking for an opportunity to get rid of it.) Benny was happy because he'd gotten the tire for a low price, and we were happy because the tire would have been impossible to sell elsewhere; it was a size especially made for us by Firestone, and Benny might have to wait 50 years to find another car that could use it.

We wearily agreed to rendezvous with Benny as soon as it was dark the next evening and pick up his shipment; Benny suggested we camp until then on the beach at the far edge of Saloom.

We pulled onto the beach, opened the camper, and were asleep in ten minutes, lulled by the gently sighing wind from the sea and the muffled thunder of the waves on the beach. It was Woodrow's turn to stand guard, something we'd been doing regularly since Algiers, so he bundled in the front seat of the Land Cruiser with a reading lamp and grumbled over our expense ledger until morning.

Morning dawned clear, bright, and dry; the sun came up warm against a blue-white and cloudless sky.

The Mediterranean beckoned, a warm and friendly blue. Al and I lost no time in plunging in, and even Manu shrugged off his morning siesta and followed. The warm foaming sea rushed to meet us, washing off the dirt and sweat of days, soothing us, carrying us from the land, taking us into another world. From the roof of the cloudless ceiling of sky to the clear sandy depths of the ocean bottom, it was a world of beauty and contentment. If life was a moment, then ours was unsurpassed.

We were at one and at peace with this world, four bobbing specks in the friendly caress of an eternal sea. But also four hungry specks, and we were soon to find that a camel can more easily pass through the eye of that needle than a hungry speck can get a good meal in Saloom. The town "hotel" was a filthy, weather-beaten old house whose kitchen hands were too busy playing cards to do any more than nod us toward a soft drink chest. If we wanted anything else, they made it clear, we'd have to wait until afternoon. Our buddy Benny hustled us out of his restaurant; he was afraid to be seen with us—and he still didn't have any food. The half dozen food shops in town were hopeless; they had only salt, paper, candles, matches, and some dust-covered packs of Egyptian cigarettes. There wasn't a piece of meat or an egg or anything of substance to be had. After searching the town from end to end we managed to scrounge up our breakfast: a loaf of dry bread, a bottle of honey, and two cans labeled "sliced peaches," which turned out to contain sour kumquats. We added vitamin pills and protein powder.

After breakfast everyone followed his natural inclinations. In five minutes Manu was asleep on the beach under the camper; the only thing Manu liked better than sleeping was reading the newspapers, and since he couldn't find a copy of *Le Monde* in all of Saloom, he did the next best thing. Woodrow went walking off by himself, head bent, discouraged about wasting a day, unhappy over everything. Willy went off to photograph some seashells. I set up my typewriter, coated myself with suntan oil, and began to catch up on our journal. Al started bartering with two young Arabs who came by.

The Arabs had picked our discarded kumquat can out of the sand; it was a major find in metal-shy Egypt. But Al wasn't going to let them get away that easily. He brought out a cigar box filled with junk jewelry he'd found in his mother's basement in Brooklyn, and the haggling began. When an Arab is selling something to a tourist, as is usually the case, the Arab knows his purchase price and his desired profit margin; he won't reveal them, but they certainly set limits for the bargaining. When the situation is reversed, and when the Arab is trying to buy some trinket of uncertain value from a tourist, there are no clear guidelines. The Arab, on uncertain ground, will use every trick to find the seller's lowest price and to determine the intensity of his desire to get rid of the object. An argument over pennies can take hours. In this case it took 40 minutes. Al finally sold a plastic necklace with a broken clasp, a single earring, ten rusty fishhooks, and a candle for three boxes of matches and 20 Egyptian cents. Both sides were happy at the exchange, all the more since it was conducted in grunts and sign language, demonstrating to all that both were skilled international traders.

Just then Benny came puffing up to the camp, shoving everyone away, cursing in Arabic. The men moved off; Benny was a bad man to cross. He glared at us. "You will cause much trouble. The police will come here. You must not talk to these others. You must behave like tourist. Tourist do not associate with these people. You act suspicious. Enjoy the beach! Swim! But don't talk to anyone! Don't sell them anything! Let me see what you were selling."

I showed him Al's box of junk jewelry, and Benny tried to pocket a piece. Al grabbed it back and Benny snapped that it was no way to treat a business partner. Al said the same about Benny and offered to sell him a plastic necklace for a pound. Benny claimed it was outrageous and, besides, he'd need three necklaces since he had three wives.

Then Benny came to the real point of his visit. "I have been thinking about your trailer here. Can air get inside when you're moving?"

I told him it could if the door were left ajar.

"Then I think I will ride inside your trailer when you take the things to Alex. It's not that I don't trust you, but I think it's better that way. I will lie on the floor and no one will see me."

Al lost control. "Look, Benny, you slimy little bastard. We made a deal yesterday, and that deal stands. We've been wasting the whole day waiting for you, and we're going to go through with our original deal. You told us yourself it wasn't safe for an Arab to transport the stuff. Look, if we got stopped we could always say the stuff belonged to us—that we were taking it through Egypt to sell in India or something like that. But if they open the camper and find you hiding there we'll spend the rest of our lives in some Egyptian prison."

"I could explain——"

"Yeah, I'll bet you could. If the guards stopped us you'd probably tell them we were smugglers and you were a loyal citizen who had tried to stop us and we'd kidnapped you. Sorry, Benny, no go. We stick to the original idea. You stay here and we deliver the stuff to your friends in Alex."

"But the shipment is worth thirty thousand American dollars, and——"

Now it was my turn. "Benny, you should have thought of that before you made the deal. This is no time to decide you can't trust us."

He was suddenly glib, friendly Benny again. "Yes, you are right, I can trust you. I come back in afternoon and arrange where to meet you. Everything is okay."

Benny went back to town. Minutes later an old Arab walked shyly up to our camp. He bowed to me, pointed to his old cart by the roadside, went into a pumping pantomime, then imitated the hissing sound of a tire losing air. I lent him our air pump and he brought it back in five minutes with profuse thanks. Five times that day the old man used the pump. Every time he passed our camp on his way to town with a load of withered branches, and everytime he left town with his empty cart, he came by the campsite, went through his hissing pantomime, and borrowed our air pump. I don't know if it was a sign of prestige to use our pump; I don't know if he'd ever heard of a tire patch; I don't know what he'd done the day before or what he'd do the next.

It was afternoon when Manu roused himself. He was in a playful mood (as well he might be after so many hours of sleep) and he began to hawk our suntan oil, shouting in Spanish until he had thirty people around him enjoying the show. Manu is a great performer; he'd once studied for the opera in Spain, and the acting urge was still strong in him. At the end of his five minute spiel he started squirting suntan oil on everybody. He tried to show them it went on the face, but half the people were rubbing it in their hair, and one old guy was rubbing it on his donkey's head. Throughout it all, Al was running around snapping pictures which I imagined he'd tell our sponsor illustrated the universal popularity of Sea and Ski.

While Manu was dispensing the oil, one wrinkled Arab rolled up the sleeve of his tunic to show him a puffy, ugly boil on his arm. It was obviously painful, and he gestured to Manu to ask if the suntan oil would cure it. The crowd clucked their tongues and looked at the ugly boil and then back to Manu.

Al pushed his way through and examined the arm, anxious for an opportunity to put his medical hobby into practice. He went for our first-aid kit, pulled out some aureomycin ointment which he deftly applied to the boil, and wrapped a gauze dressing around it with a flourish. The crowd had a new Messiah, and Al was in his glory.

Everyone came forward with a variety of cuts, scratches, and warts, and Al treated them all with iodine and band-aids, which they displayed as proudly as medals. Not to be treated by the American medicine man was to be a social outcast, and many in the crowd seemed to be inventing ailments for Al to work on. Al returned the compliment and invented cures for them.

One sad man, the keeper of the local war cemetery, pulled me aside. In broken English he explained that his wife seemed ill. She was always very tired and coughed a lot. Would we come to his house and take a look at her? This was something far beyond the treatment of cuts and bruises, and I asked the gravekeeper why he didn't take her to a doctor.

There were no doctors in Saloom, he answered, nor any for 200 miles. His wife was too weak to travel, and even if she could, he couldn't afford to pay for the trip. The few traveling government doctors came through Saloom only once every year or so. He was worried about his young, new wife. Wouldn't we please examine her? Please?

Al agreed to take a look at her, and when he returned he explained that the wife, a pretty girl of eighteen in about her sixth month of pregnancy, was undernourished and had a congestion in her lungs. He gave the gravekeeper two bottles of high-potency vitamins and a package of decongestant tablets. I was relieved. Knowing Al, I was afraid he'd recommend a daily examination.

The gravekeeper was profuse in his thanks, and Al took it all with his customary modesty, beaming like a combination of Mahatma Gandhi and Jonas Salk. The gravekeeper asked to be allowed to show us the cemetery. He was so obviously proud of it that we couldn't refuse.

The cemetery was flat and sandy, a big rectangle filled with several thousand simple headstones. Here and there a tree or a flowering bush —obviously the result of diligent care—gave shade and color. Beyond the walls there were no trees or flowers; just the dead sands of Egypt. The gravekeeper explained that the cemetery was maintained by the Anglo-Egyptian War Monuments Commission. It was one of a dozen that dotted the desert from Tripoli and Tobruk to the grand entombment at El Alamein, and it held the remains of some of the 80,000 Commonwealth soldiers who had died trying to tie the tail of the Desert Fox when Rommel had been sweeping across Africa toward Suez and an attempted link-up with the Japanese in India. The turning of the tide would come at El Alamein; the stemming of the tide had been here.

We walked among the neat rows of identical gravestones, all shining white and pure in the afternoon sun, and we read the inscriptions.

He gave his life that we might live in peace.

We will always remember, when the rest of the world forgets— Mum and Sister.

Tell England, Ye who pass this way, I died for her and rest here content.

If love could have saved, you would never have died.

There were drivers and troopers, flight engineers and artillerymen, privates and sergeants, Canadians and South Africans, all brought from distant lands to die on this uncaring, killing ground.

He gave the greatest gift of all, his own unfinished life.

In alien earth he lies; not for him the last, long slumber under friendly skies.

Into the mosaic of victory I lay this priceless piece, my son.

The desert wind blew mournfully down the hedge of barren hills and across the graves as it swept to meet the sea. The eternal Mediterranean played its funeral sonata on the keyboard of the shore. The sun sank lower over the wasteland.

My mind filled with melancholy thoughts. Of the noble ideals and brave new world for which these men had died. Of what they would feel if they saw what man has made of that world. Of the futility of war, the illogic of hatred, the hopelessness of humanity.

Our heads bowed, with tear-filled eyes, we walked in silence toward the gate. We looked at the last tombstones, and I thought of those who loved these men and would never see their distant resting place: *I shall remember him as he was, a dear son and a good, brave lad.*

We left the cemetery and stood staring with sightless eyes at the barren hills, the encroaching sands, the fruitless earth: *Every soil is a brave man's country.*

It was almost dark when we got back to camp. Woodrow and Willy had closed the camper and hitched it to the Land Cruiser; they were all set to move on. Benny was there, too, glib and expansive, though we were hardly in the mood for him.

"I have it all arranged," Benny greeted us. "You will drive three kilometers on the road to Alex and wait for me there—do not go more than three kilometers. I will leave from my shop with the donkeys when it is dark and I will be there by eight o'clock. I would have come sooner, but it took time to get all the donkeys."

"Why do you need donkeys?" Woodrow asked.

"To bring the things to you. How did you expect me to bring them, in my hands? As it is, I will need 22 donkeys to carry everything. It is very expensive for me."

We all looked at each other, then back at Benny, in silence. To fit the cargo of ten donkeys into our trailer and cars would be a minor miracle; 22 was ridiculous. But why even bother to explain it to Benny? He knew. Of course he knew. And he'd agree—after an argument—he'd agree to let us take just ten, and he'd moan and cut his price accordingly. He'd probably had it planned from the start. But why even bother? Who cared anymore? Did those boys give their lives so we'd be free to traffic with sleazy crooks like Benny? Did they hallow this ground so we could drive through it with a trailer full of contraband watches and cheap nylons? Did we have to mock their sacrifice in their very graveyard?

"Good-bye, Benny, have fun with your donkeys," Al said. "Take them and shove 'em."

The sun was on the far side of the mountain now, well along its nightly journey into the Sahara. Twenty-four hours had passed since we entered Egypt. One day. That day was gone, gone the sun. The wind picked up the somber lament of taps as we headed east toward Alex. One day.

Chapter 8

Weighed Down in Egypt's Land

Benny was either a fool or a liar.

An hour east of Saloom on the road to Alexandria we were stopped by three soldiers with machine guns who wanted to search our car and camper.

"We're American citizens," I told them, trying Benny's advice just to see what would happen.

The soldiers didn't care if we were pregnant camels; they wanted to search the car.

"Yes, we're tourists," Woodrow joined in. "American tourists. You don't have to search us. See, here's my passport."

Woodrow waved his passport. The soldier waved his machine gun. Everything was searched.

By the next morning the road had turned into a jagged torture track of loose white rock against the whiteness of the desert. At one particularly treacherous spot a crew of some 60 *fellaheen* dressed in white robes and turbans, their faces covered with dust like desert apparitions, bent to their labors, kneeling on the harsh, hot roadbed. They struggled without aid of tractor or grader or drill, attacking the reluctant rock with hand and muscle and primitive tools, chopping it with chisels, hitting it with hammers, carting boulders away on their backs, straining and sweating in the desert sun, descendants of the pyramid builders, slaves still after 4,000 years.

To the south, the desert was a wilderness of holes and hills, barren valleys and barren cliffs, a devil's playground. To the north there was an occasional glimpse of the sea.

By afternoon we reached El Alamein, a small village and a large

135

cemetery in the midst of this unhospitable land which had claimed so many lives while giving life to so few. We stopped and walked again through a graveyard, again buried ourselves in the heart of ten thousand tombstones, again grieved over the useless waste of it all.

Nine miles east of El Alamein, where the road swung close to the sea, we stopped and plunged into the beckoning pale water, breaking contact again with the world that was too much with us, washing off the hot dust of the deserts of Egypt and the cold dust of the cemeteries of the world. Then it was on to Alexandria, the Pearl of the Mediterranean.

There is no other city in the world like Alexandria, and the world can be thankful for that. Alexandria is one of a kind, and the kind of one of which one is quite enough. Alexandria is hard to describe, difficult to imagine, and impossible to believe, even if you've been there. But try to envision, if you can, a boisterous Coney Island full of fun-loving crooks . . . a carnival of affable criminals . . . an alumni reunion of ex-cons. . . . Perhaps no metaphors can really capture the carefree and criminal spirit of the place, so let me tell you instead about what happened when the innocent crew of the Trans World Record Expedition met the picaresque denizens of Alexandria, and learned the hard way that the Pearl was only paste.

As we drove in through the outskirts, it was smoky and congested, with steel mills and cement plants in the center of residential sections. Collapsing tenements stood beside caves dug into the hills, and people lived in both. Everything was a mess of overhead wires, trolley tracks, drying wash, muddy streets, belching smokestacks, blowing sand, littered alleys, unabating noise, pushcart vendors, and thousands of ragged children.

The kids swooped down on us when we reached the edge of town, like vultures. In a second they were jumping up and down on the flat top of the camper, climbing onto the canvas roof of the Land Cruiser, hopping on the running boards, crawling across the hood, trying to wriggle their skinny arms into any opening, begging for *baksheesh,* or taking what they could. No sooner did I chase them off than they regrouped and came charging back, heaving pieces of sheep dung, shouting, and then laughing when I took cover. After my shirt had been sufficiently soiled to impress even the press agent for Creslan, I beat a retreat and drove off with a dozen diehards still clinging to the camper.

As we neared the center of Alex our assailants were older, their weapons were verbal, and their interests went beyond bouncing up and down on the camper top.

"Pssst, you want nice girl? Virgin girl?" asked one cross-eyed pimp as he trotted alongside the Land Cruiser.

"Pssst, you want bad girl? Experienced girl?" asked his identical twin who was trotting along the other side of the car.

I speeded up and outdistanced them, but not the tunicked figure who leaped onto the running board and breathed a blast of garlic in my face: "You want change money? Good rate. Five pounds for ten dollars. Best price in Alex. How much you change?"

When I slowed down to push the money changer off, two of his competitors leaped onto the running board and clung to the door as I shifted into second, screaming their prices into my ear, trying to outbid one another, but offering no bargains. Meanwhile, two peddlers were elbowing each other for possession of the other running board, one of them offering to sell us whatever merchandise we might want, and the other offering to buy whatever we might have to sell. Manu introduced them to each other and shoved them off.

When we stopped at a corner for cross traffic we were besieged by another 20 shouting Arabs, all holding up bottles of whiskey, pictures of naked girls, cartons of cigarettes, nylon stockings, Egyptian money, packets of hashish, all excitedly waving their wares and screaming their prices. In a town where everybody instantly knows everything, everybody knew that five foreigners had just arrived in two red Jeeps pulling two loaded trailers; and everybody was anxious to sink his teeth into us before we learned what Alex was all about.

We decided to disassociate ourselves from the cars and trailers, at least until dark when they'd be less conspicuous and when we could look for a campsite without half the town at our heels and the other half at our throats. We parked them along 26th of July Avenue, the most splendid street in Alexandria, a beautiful wide boulevard that curved in a sweeping crescent from the sea. Then we walked over to an attractive outdoor restaurant where we hoped we could a) get a good dinner, b) shake off the entourage of pimps and peddlers, c) keep an eye on the cars so that nothing was stolen, and d) enjoy the sunset over the Mediterranean. We were partly successful: we saw the sunset.

The hawkers did not give up easily, and when the waiter chased them away, new ones took their places. Eventually, we succumbed to their entreaties. Willy bought a dozen colored handkerchiefs for the bargain price of 30 cents. His nose turned green the first time he used one. Woodrow bought a wrist watch for four dollars after checking over the demonstration model. As the peddler handed it to him he palmed the working watch, and all Woodrow got was a face and a back and a lump of dirt where the movement should have been. Manu bought a bathing suit from a man lugging four suitcases of clothing. It was a size 36, as promised, but with a size 24 jock inside.

I got taken, too, though I should have learned my lesson from the others. I bought a pack of Chesterfields at a high price, but still a bargain considering what American cigarettes usually cost abroad. I lit one and choked. My peddler had disappeared, but another one explained that they were "Egyptian Chesterfields."

All this, of course, was going on while we were trying to eat. The peddlers were all around our table with their bags and boxes of merchandise, waving silk underpants in my face and dangling brass bracelets in our soup, though that operation, it must be admitted, did improve its taste, for the food was wretched beyond belief, and that's damn faint praise coming for someone who had had only one full meal in the preceding five days. The soup was indigestible, the salad unchewable, the bread unbreakable, the meat uncutable——and the bill unbelievable. We were charged 50 per cent above the already high prices on the menu because, the waiter explained, it was an indoor menu and we had eaten outdoors. We were charged extra for the bread, extra for the butter, and extra for the sugar and salt. Extra for the tablecloth. And extra for a couple of flowers one of the peddlers had filched from our table. To this were added several taxes which, the manager explained, were for such things as the waiter's old age pension, repainting the kitchen, adjusting Egypt's balance of payments, and widening the Suez Canal.

It was about this time that I think we realized that Alex probably has more con men per acre than any place on earth. But it could have been worse, we agreed, for at least the restaurant had been a good spot for keeping watch on our cars.

As we crossed toward the cars I noticed that the Jeep had a strange tilt to it, that it was leaning at us in an odd way. I ran around to the far side of the car, and there were five young Arabs at work. Three of them had the Jeep jacked up and were removing two tires, a fourth was siphoning the gas out of our tank, and a fifth was trying to jimmy the latch on the camper door. They were so brazen they didn't even try to escape, barely batting an eye when we grabbed them. The leader, a tough kid about fifteen, said they worked for a garage and thought we were the car that had called for assistance. When I asked him how that justified siphoning off our gas he said it was dangerous to work on a car with gas in the tank. I found a policeman, but the gang leader and the cop seemed to be old friends, and in the end I felt fortunate that I wasn't compelled to pay for the "work" they had done.

We were just getting the tires back on when a leering old Arab sidled up to me with a collection of pornographic pictures. When I turned these down he pulled a dozen vials of aphrodisiac out of his pocket—Spanish fly, absinthe, sperm whale extract, pulverized shark fin, pepper extract. I told him I didn't need any.

"Okay. No need aphro. Muneer understands. Then must need this." He winked at me and pulled out from inside his coat an assortment of prophylactics. I pushed him away and told him to go see Al.

Just then Willy ran up, clutching a pile of Egyptian pounds he'd gotten from a money changer who was offering a good rate, seven pounds for ten dollars, almost twice the official government rate. Willy pointed out a fat Arab in an oversized overcoat standing next to a tree a few yards away. The Arab smiled and I caught the gleam of gold teeth. He spread his arms in invitation and opened his coat. Inside, held in place with safety pins, were packets of money—Egyptian pounds, American dollars, Swiss and French francs, British pounds, lire, pesetas, marks, dirham . . .

Woodrow rushed over to him, waving a ten dollar bill.

"What did you get?" Willy asked when he'd returned.

"Seven pounds. I gave him a ten and he gave me—hey, there's only six pounds here. Hey, mister, you only gave me six pounds."

"Yes, certainly," the money changer assured him. "Stamps. It is for stamps. One pound for black market stamps."

"Oh . . . I didn't know about those. Black market stamps. Well, uh, I mean, uh . . ."

By then the money changer had vanished.

And so had Al.

"Pssst. You look for your friend? He send me for you." The whispy voice belonged to a skinny little man in dungarees and tennis sneakers. "Come on. He say you hurry. Follow me."

And before I knew what I was doing, I *was* following him, running across torn-up avenues, trotting down narrow streets, groping my way through inky black alleys until I was utterly lost. We were in a rundown, deserted part of town when my guide demanded a pound for his services. When I gave it to him he led me to a darkened house and pointed upstairs. He told me to wait there for Al.

I walked up the stairs into a combination beerhall-bordello. The windows were boarded up, the floor was painted green, the walls were covered with Arabic graffiti, and the tables looked as though they were on their last legs. As I was looking around for Al, the bartender, who was the Egyptian version of a sumo wrestler, came over to me with a quart of beer, and before I could stop him, had opened it. He demanded immediate payment. I'd barely sat down when two immense, smiling, gold-toothed prostitutes came out of a back room, and the bartender reappeared with two more quarts of beer. I realized I'd been hoaxed. I started to get up, but one of the girls was trying to sit on me. Her friend was finishing the beers. I kept trying to push her off but it isn't easy to dislocate 250 pounds of giggling blubber. I felt as though I were battling the Abominable Jello Woman.

When the bartender switched off the light, both of the girls attacked me. I felt one hand on my wallet and the other reaching for another place. The more attention I devoted to pushing the one away, the more progress the other made. Then my chair collapsed and the two Amazons fell on top of me. I'd rather have been crushed by the camper. Everything was wet with beer, and I squirmed free. I grabbed my wallet, ran for the door, and tumbled down the flight of stairs. My little sneakered friend was waiting for me.

"You want to go back now, look for your friend? I guide you. Only two pounds."

As I followed him down a narrow, dark alley, an Arab in a sailor's hat and pea jacket pulled me into a doorway and whispered, "Good bargain. You buy cheap. Cutty Sark. Just come from ship." It happened so fast I'd given him the pound and been given the bottle before I knew what I was doing.

By the time I got back to the cars, Al was already there, flushed and smiling.

"You know, Steve," he said, "this is a great place if you've got the right attitude. What a wild bunch of crooks. It's my kind of town. I have to come back here some day."

"I'm glad *you* feel that way. Where did you disappear before?"

"I met some guys who wanted to know if we had any watches or foreign perfume to sell."

"Perfume? We don't have any perfume."

"That's right. So I sold them a case of insect repellent instead. And I got rid of that watch Woodrow bought. Hey, what's that in your hand?"

"Scotch."

"Scotch my butt. That's colored water," Al said after he'd examined it.

"How can it be colored water? The seal's intact."

"Sure, and probably so is the press where they printed it. You're lucky you have me along." He took the bottle away from me and put it in with our half case of bourbon in the Land Cruiser. I thought he was nuts. But within fifteen minutes a peddler came along hawking Chevas Regal for one Egyptian pound a bottle.

"Come off it, man," Al said. "You can't sell us any of that colored water junk. We only drink the real stuff. See, a full case of American whiskey we just smuggled in today."

"Real whiskey?" the Arab asked.

"Sure thing, man. Here have a sip." Al poured him a shot of bourbon. The man drank and smiled. "You want to sell some?"

"Sure, I'll let you have a bottle of bourbon for eight pounds."

"No, too much."

"Okay, I'll sell you a bottle of Cutty Sark for three pounds."

And off we drove, Al chuckling to himself that this was his kind of town.

We weren't quite sure where to go. Our plan was to camp outside of town, away from the crooks, and to come back the next morning to visit Pompey's Pillar and the Little Sphinx and the Catacombs of Kamesh-Shuquata. But it wasn't easy to find a place outside of town, because we had entered the delta of the Nile. Gone were the empty desert spaces where we could pitch our tent anywhere. Everything was either under cultivation or under water. It was here that the Nile, in its course to the sea, was channeled into a triangle 100 miles on a side, a lush green delta that provided food and clothing and work and hope for almost all the 27,000,000 people of Egypt. Only 50,000 hardy or hare-brained souls try to live in the other unhospitable 97 per cent of the country. The rest all depend on the Nile. There was little room left for a camp ground.

After blundering down mud lanes and floundering through streams in the dark, we decided to make camp on the wide shoulder of a dirt road beside a stand of date palms next to a cotton field. The mosquitoes, the first we'd encountered in Africa, were fierce and noisy, and the air carried the distinctive aroma of that first night in France, but at least Alexandria's crooks and con men were not likely to find us.

The police found us instead. Just as we had the camper set up and were about to turn in, three policemen popped out of the field and indicated they wanted us to move. They spoke no English, but kept pointing around and saying "*klefti*" while making a knife-like motion across their throats accompanied by a *sscccchhhttt* sound, giving us to understand that there were cutthroats about and that we'd be slaughtered as we slept. At that stage we would have been willing to believe anything anyone told us about Alex, so we broke camp and let the police climb into the cars to show us the way to a better spot. For half an hour we drove along roads a few inches above the water line, crept over creaky bridges, and skidded down muddy lanes until we reached a spot not much different or far removed from the one we'd been in.

We thanked the police for their help, and for being the first honest people we'd met in Alex. They were like friends in an enemy camp, and we missed them when they left. After we had a chance to check our gear we also missed a flashlight, a light meter, a wrench, half a seat belt, and the dashboard ashtray.

Early the next morning one of the policemen was back, banging on the camper door. By sign language he indicated he wanted us to give him a toothbrush, evidently something he'd forgotten to swipe the night before. We were so flabbergasted we let him have it.

We left Alex and cut through the delta of the Nile toward Cairo on a new, paved expressway. The traffic was fast and heavy. The desert was gone, drowned by the river. Irrigated fields, stands of trees, mosques, homes, factories, and restaurants lined the road. It was a wholly new Egypt to us, mechanized and modern, a startling contrast to the rest of that wretched land.

Cairo went by in a rush, a jumble of impressions, a week and a day of work and confusion. I remember isolated things: Three full days spent getting visas for Jordan, Iraq, Lebanon, India and Pakistan. Crowded streets. Getting lost on the wrong side of the river every time we drove anywhere. Mosques and monuments. The ugly Cairo Hilton. The Cairo Museum—the most important collection of archeological objects in the world, stuck in a dark tomb of a building and stacked against each other like flour sacks in a warehouse. Woodrow sick with stomach flu, Willy and Manu with mild cases of "Cairo colon." The Continental Hotel, a grand relic of Old World elegance, with cavernous, thick-carpeted halls and spacious rooms, where we slept between sheets for the first time since Benghazi, the second time in 77 days. I remember a cable Al got from Krinski: CONGRATULATIONS ON YOUR BAR MITZVAH, and Woodrow telling me he was going to quit the expedition and then changing his mind at the last minute. I remember our working for a week to get the cars and equipment in shape for the long, hot haul across the deserts of the Middle East. Answering several dozen letters from friends and sponsors who had not heard of us since Spain and who were giving us up for lost or lazy. I remember the Rex, a wonderful little restaurant near the hotel where, for ten cents, I could get a splendid meal of salad and spaghetti and bread. And there was beer, quarts of iced beer. I ate there twice and sometimes three times a day. But most of all, most of all when I think back to our days in Cairo I remember three things: the oppressive police state atmosphere, the crazy camel drivers, and the wondrous romance of Al and Iftitani.

It was hard to make a move around Cairo without realizing we were in the heart of a police state. On all the approaches to the capital, bridges and factories were marked with signs forbidding the taking of photos. Army camps, military supply depots, and communications installations rimmed the city. When we picked up our mail and cables at the American Express office we found that most of them had been opened by the government censors; and from friends to whom we wrote we later learned that the letters we sent from Cairo had also been opened and then sealed with the censor's stamp. When we checked in at the hotel our passports were confiscated and held for several days while the Egyptian secret police checked us out. When our film came back from the processing lab, several dozen photos showing the poverty of Egypt had mysteriously vanished. When we went to make major purchases, the stores insisted on proof that we had obtained our Egyptian pounds at the vastly distorted official rate, and wherever we went we saw signs warning of the penalties for changing money on the open market. The newspapers and the radio all carried the official government line; we saw no evidence of freedom of the press or speech. When it was reported that President Ben Bella of Algeria, Nasser's main ally in Africa, had been overthrown (and exactly the way we'd been warned he would be), a shock ran through the Egyptian hierarchy and troops were discreetly—but not too discreetly—positioned throughout the city to discourage any spread of kingpin toppling.

But you can't dislike Egypt when it has people like Lamyi—Lamyi Ibrahim Ghoneim—the world's greatest, most wonderful camel driver.

Al and I drove out to the Pyramids late one afternoon to scout locations for some sponsor photos we had to take and to survey a route for our challenge race to the top of the tallest pyramid. As we were looking around, a chubby, grinning, middle-aged Arab in a bright green *galabia* came bounding by on a camel, shouting at us, "Howdy, kids. Dig me baby. It's colossal. Twenty-three skidoo and away we go. Wowie!" He circled us three times on his camel and came trotting back to us yelling, "Wasn't that the most, man. Isn't this camel the living end. Dandy. Dandy. May I present myself. I'm Lamyi and this is Canada Dray." He pronounced it like the soda water. He handed me an engraved business card.

CANADA DRAY

camel for hire

Proprietor:	Pyramids Post
LAMYI IBRAHIM GHONEIM	*Giza, Egypt*

We were still wary after our troubles in Alex, but Lamyi won us over as he enumerated his credentials in what he surely thought was the latest hip Hollywood lingo. "I've been making the tourist scene here for forty years. My daddy-o taught me the trade. There's not another cat in the business who savvies it the way I do, kid. Whenever any big wig pays a visit, the government has me show him around on Canada Dray. He's the most, gentle as a lamb, comfy as a couch. Go ahead, you want to sit on him? Why, the last King and Queen of Sweden said Canada Dray was supercolossal. See, here's a snap of the Queen on him. He's getting old, but he's the best in the business, kiddo. Prime Minister Churchill rode on him once. All those European princesses and counts who come out here ask for him. Even your President Roosevelt said he was the smartest looking camel out here. And you know those tourist posters, the ones with the pyramids and the camel, well, baby, that's us. Everybody takes our picture. I'm very photogenic. Even C.B. DeMille said so. Colossal! C.B. said I was his favorite of all the camel drivers. Oh, certainly I know C.B., and all those other producers too. I made a lot of pictures with old C.B. *Ten Commandments* and dandy stuff like that. I've been in thirty movies, kid, thirty. Now how can I oblige you?"

Lamyi obliged by meeting us the next morning with his brother, two camels, three dogs, and a basketful of props and costumes. He arranged the scene, checked the angle of the sun, adjusted the costumes, posed himself for each picture and, drawing on his extensive cinematic career, even tried to tell Al and Willy how to take the pictures. He was producer, director, star, and press agent all in one.

He was magnificent. He gleefully smeared himself with Sea and Ski suntan oil, exchanged his turban for a Dobbs straw cowboy hat, modeled a Creslan shirt, poured a quart of Macmillan Ring-Free oil into our car, and poured into himself a cup or two of the Bourbon Institute's best, which, he assured me with a wink, doubtless had medicinal value and thus wouldn't conflict with his Islamic beliefs. He also modeled a pair of Thom McAn desert boots, sprayed Canada Dry with Off! insect repellent, lit a cigarette with our Cronco parabolic sunray lighter, posed on the threshold of our Thermos Poptent, and, most important of all, smilingly chomped his way through half a box of Bob Levy's Manischevitz matzos.

After the photo session—which Lamyi said was "such a dandy delight" he wouldn't accept any payment—he brought us to his house for tea and cake. The walls were covered with photos of famous people who had ridden on Canada Dry, and with travel posters on which Lamyi's smiling face gleamed against the now familiar backdrop of the Pyramids. Lamyi showed us letters from his clients, and read favorite passages from them; he discussed his life and the future of his crippled son; expressed his heartfelt hope for peace on earth among men of good will; and pleaded with us to write to him and keep him posted on our trip around the world.

There were tears in his eyes, and ours, when we parted. We'll always remember you, Lamyi. May your days be long and happy, and may your tribe increase.

Which brings us to the romance of Al and Iftitani.

The scene is Cairo, a fantastic place for women. The girls there are, without question, the most beautiful in the Arab world. They've shed the veil and adopted such Western costumes as short skirts, high heels, and low necklines. On the first day there we got stiff necks just looking at them walking by on the streets. Thousands of them. We came in off the desert and there they were—tall, bronzed, statuesque, alluring, graceful, beautiful—and unattainable. Like all good Moslem girls, they just wouldn't mingle with foreigners under any circumstances, even foreigners like Al who can pass for an Arab when he tries. And believe me, he was trying

Enter Iftitani, Al's chambermaid at the hotel. She was about 24, divorced, beautiful, and very, very sexy. She had flashing blue eyes, shiny black hair that fell to her shoulders, a flawless olive skin, long shapely legs, and high firm breasts. Al was captivated by her instantly, as were we all, and he decided to get better acquainted. There was only one problem. Iftitani didn't speak a word of English.

When she came in to straighten up Al's room on the third day of our stay in Cairo, he could contain himself no longer. He had to tell her how he felt. But how? At first Al tried to be subtle. He'd invite her to dinner. Using sign language, he pointed to her, then to himself, and then to his mouth as if he were eating. So what does she do? She calls room service for him.

For fifteen minutes, while Iftitani dusted the room, Al tried every subtle charade he could think of, but he just didn't come across. So why not be blunt? What did he have to lose? He pointed to his bed, then to Iftitani, and then back to himself, and then back to the bed. At last, Iftitani understood. Al was afraid she would be angry, but instead she smiled and nodded her approval. Al was deliriously happy.

Then she almost broke the spell. She asked for *baksheesh.* Now Al is hardly accustomed to giving a girl money for a tumble in the hay, but Iftitani looked so fetching right then, he'd have probably given her the Land Cruiser if she'd asked for it. But all she asked for was one Egyptian pound. She was a bargain at 50 times that price, and Al quickly gave her the pound. Iftitani thanked him and started to walk out of the room. Al ran after her and pointed to the bed. She nodded again and pointed to the calendar on the wall, then to his watch: two o'clock the next afternoon.

Al was excited about his date the entire day. I was just jealous. The next morning I kept sneaking past the maids' room just to get a look at Iftitani. And when I did see her—and thought about her appointment with Al—I became so depressed I went over to Rex and ate three bowls of spaghetti. Later that evening I went to Al's room and, doing my best to sound disinterested, casually inquired about his afternoon's activity.

Al was so reluctant to discuss it I attributed it to some gentlemanly discretion that I had not noticed before. It was only after much effort that I got him to tell me about it:

"By the time Iftitani knocked on the door I was so excited I was practically swinging from the chandelier. And when she came in in that tight blue dress—man, is she built!—didn't you see her today?"

"No, I was over at the museum."

"Well, let me tell you, you missed something. Anyway, she came in and closed the door and went right to the bed. She wasn't wasting any time, and I wasn't going to either. I dashed into the john and tore off my clothing and came charging out like a fighting cock. I bounded into the room stark raving naked."

He became silent.

"Go on, go on. Then what happened?"

"It was pretty embarrassing. She screamed and ran out of the room."

"I thought she'd agreed to do it?"

"I thought so too. I was sure she'd understood."

"How could she *mis*understand?"

"She thought I wanted the sheets changed."

Soon we were back on the road. The vehicles had been serviced, the letters written, the sponsor pictures shot and shipped, the film developed, the supplies laid in, the crew all rested and healed. Ahead lay the parched deserts of the Middle East, now blistering hot in the heat of summer. It was good-bye to Lamyi, and to the beautiful women of Cairo, good-bye to spaghetti at Rex, to the cool hotel rooms, good-bye to Iftitani.

We headed east from Cairo, planning to skirt the Arabian Desert on the north, bridge the Suez Canal, and then cut across the Sinai Peninsula to Jordan. We'd been warned that our plan was impossible, but we were going to try it anyway. In Cairo we'd been told that Egypt had heavily fortified the Sinai against Israel and permitted no foreigners to enter. But we had to give it a go.

Less than halfway to our goal the narrow, desert road was blocked by Egyptian tanks and soldiers. No amount of protests about freedom of travel did us any good. We could not cross the Suez and we could not cross the Sinai. That door to the Middle East was firmly shut. We were forced to retrace our route and return to Cairo where we again petitioned the government for permission to drive across the Sinai and where our request was again rejected. "Next year," we remembered the guard had said, "next year when there is no more Israel."

Finally, an Egyptian official told us that if we were absolutely determined to continue our expedition, there was another way through the Middle East.

"You must take a steamer to Lebanon," he said. "It will be expensive with all your cars, but it is the only way. Though even it is not certain. There is much border trouble between Lebanon and Syria, and the frontier is often closed, so you may not be able to get through. But there is no other way."

"Well, if it's the only way, we'll try it. Where do we get the ship to Lebanon?" I asked.

"Why in Alexandria, of course. Where else?"

Chapter 9

The Holy Land

The S.S. *Lydia* was a floating microcosm of the world we crossed. It was crammed with Egyptians going to visit relatives in Lebanon, Lebanese returning from vacations in Luxor and Aswan, Yugoslavs bound for Belgrade, Cypriots debarking at Limassol, Turks heading for Istanbul. There were Indian girls in saris, Algerian women hidden behind veils, Italians in silk suits, Iraquis in shapeless tunics, Pakistanis in pajamas, and the inescapable summer horde of European students in shorts and beards. There were Chinese and Chadians, Ghanaians, Greeks, and Gibraltarians, Danes and Dutch, and the tri-national crew of the Trans World Record Expedition.

The ship was one of those inexpensive Mediterranean institutions that permit deck passengers, so we had our hands (and our cars) full with curious voyagers, wandering infants, potential pilferers, and tired travelers who understandably preferred the innerspring comfort of our well-padded auto seats to the bare decks and board benches provided for sleeping by the management of the Hellenic-Mediterranean Line. The metal top of our closed camper became home for a family of a dozen Egyptians whose children were dressed in flour sacks that bore the fading marking, "A gift from the people of the United States of America," and who were so comfortable we couldn't bring ourselves to dispossess them during the two-day trip to Beirut.

Lebanon welcomed us. After two months of irrational regulations and unfounded suspicions at every border, it was a relief to enter a country which treated us like tourists rather than enemy agents. The customs search was quick and efficient, the formalities minimal, and the greetings of welcome friendly and sincere.

150

There are many reasons for Lebanon's friendly attitude toward travelers. For one, the Lebanese have a relatively stable government, one which does not feel compelled to hold office by force or to divert attention from internal difficulties to foreign scapegoats. For another, the internal problems of Lebanon are less severe than those of her neighbors. Her lands are fertile and her people well fed; she has none of the barren wastes or grinding poverty of the other Arab nations. (In truth, she is not wholly Arab, or at least not wholly Islamic, for half her people are Christians, sharing many spiritual values with the West.) As a free market, she earns her livelihood from international banking, transshipment of goods, foreign trade and tourism, and has developed an international outlook, considering herself more a member of the world community than the Arab bloc. She knows she can't live without the rest of the world, and she doesn't try.

After having endured for weeks the seldom relieved and always torrid barrenness of the North African deserts, we delighted in this land of fertile plains, snow-speckled mountains, terraced hillside farms, and red-roofed villages set in dark green valleys by the side of rushing rivers. And when we walked along the bustling modern streets and skyscraper-lined avenues of her capital, Beirut, nestled against a low range of hills along the Mediterranean, we felt that—save for the scent of roasting lamb and the intoxicating aroma of *arak*—we could easily have been in San Francisco. Beirut was our last outpost of Western civilization, a final oasis of things familiar in a world that would become ever more foreign and forbidding as we moved eastward—if we could move eastward.

We had reached Lebanon on June 26th, three months and two days after we left New York, and three days after our schedule called for us to be entering Vietnam, half a world away, but now engulfed by war. A schedule, we had come to realize, was meaningless when driving around the world, for it could only take into account such relative certainties as shipping dates and road conditions, geographical features and seasonal changes; it could not hope to predict and evaluate the human factors, the wars and feuds, the distrust and dislikes, the rivalries and revolutions which had blocked our road so many times. When you travel by plane or ship you can sail around or fly over the troubles so effortlessly that you are barely aware of their existence, but by car there is no choice but to drive into the worst and hope for the best.

One of the worst of the worst was right ahead: Syria. Because of her insoluble problems and unstable politics, Syria's relations with the world, and especially with her neighbors, were in constant flux. It was not uncommon for the Syria-Lebanon border, for example, to be closed for weeks, then open to travelers for a month, then suddenly closed again. No one knew what would happen the next week or the next month, and, even more to our distress, no one in Beirut knew what the situation was at the moment, because Lebanon had broken diplomatic relations with Syria and ousted the Syrian legation for conducting activities hostile to the government.

If the Syrian border were closed we would be faced with three unacceptable possibilities: 1) wait until the border reopened (which could take months), 2) ship everything to Greece and drive from there into Turkey and across turbulent Kurdistan into Iran (which might take even more months), and 3) give up and go home.

The Lebanese officials promised a border report within three days. We decided to make the most of them and see Lebanon.

Our first stop was the town of Biblos, which means "book" and which gave the Bible its name. According to our guidebook, it was also "one of the oldest continuously inhabited cities on earth," having been the commercial and religious capital of the Phoenician coast more than 6,000 years ago. At the edge of the sea there are Roman columns and walls, and a small open-air theater. A castle built by Crusaders commands the ground above the city, its ramparts studded with Roman columns they pulled down to build their own monument.

We lunched in Biblos on *mezze,* a Middle-Eastern smorgasbord consisting of grilled garlic chicken, stuffed lamb, *hommos,* shish-kabob, stuffed marrow, *kefta, tobboule, shawerma, kibbe,* and stuffed vine leaves. We then drove inland to the Cedars of Lebanon, the world's most famous forest. Of the thousands of trees that once grew at the foot of the Dahr-el-Kadib slope, only 400 trees remain. Many date back 1,000 years, and the Lebanese claim that one or two are more than 6,000 years old. These are the ones that have seen their brothers taken

*After unloading the Land Cruiser
from the* Queen Elizabeth *at Cherbourg
we began driving the first of the
42,000 land miles that would
take us around the world. We entered
the Pyrenees on a cold and foggy
day and became trapped in a
violent snowstorm near the pass.
Bottom: One of the 300 gas stations we used.*

Near a well on the
edge of the Sahara, Manu (in
white coveralls) accepts
a pigskin filled with water
from an Arab camel
herder. We returned
the kindness by distributing
candy to all
the children.
At left, Steve writes in
his journal at
beach campsite near
Rabat, Morocco. Small tent
behind him is where the three
hitchhiking nurses slept.

Driving by compass across the smooth, unmarred vastness of Tunisia's Chott Djerid, a dried lake larger than Connecticut, we carved tracks in the crusted sand where no automobile had ever gone before. Behind the Land Cruiser is the camper-trailer in which we stored our gear by day and slept by night. Below: Steve laughs as Barbara, one of the New Zealand nurses who accompanied us across North Africa, cracks a joke while cutting his hair. Steve, Al, and Mira eating in Moroccan cafe. When Al wore a fez he easily passed for an Arab.

Photo: Willy Mettler

After we were robbed one night while camped on a beach near Algiers, Steve tried to explain the situation to two Algerian Army detectives, but they were more interested in investigating us than tracking down the robbers. Far right: We reached Sabratha, a once-magnificent Roman metropolis on the Mediterranean coast of Libya, now a graveyard of crumbling limestone pillars.

*On the potholed road across
the Libyan Desert our trailer spindle
snapped (top) so we had to pull
off onto the desert floor (left) and
spend three days making repairs.
Game was scarce in the desert,
and most of our hunting (bottom, left)
was unsuccessful.
Below: Another accident, this time
with the small storage trailer which
broke loose from the Jeep and overturned.
Woodrow (in T-shirt) still had hands bandaged
from his near-fatal accident.*

Photo: Manu Leguineche

*the week before. Above: Al points
to one of the hundreds
of torn-up truck tires
that line the blistering desert road from
Tripoli to Alexandria. Ours survived, and
we became the first ever to drive around the
world on one set of tires.
After we chased the cavalry's camels
out of their watering hole at an
Algerian border camp, we had our first
real bath in twelve days.*

*At the Pyramids we carried out
various oddball assignments
for the expedition's sponsors.
Al shares box of Manischevitz matzos
with Arab camel drivers.
Steve records reaction of
Lamyi Ibrahim Ghoneim
to Tanfastic suntan oil. Al takes
quick ride on Canada Dray for
Creslan clothing commercial, then
exchanges headgear with Lamyi for
Dobbs Hats publicity photo.*

by the Phoenicians to build their ships, by Solomon to build his temple, and by the Pharaohs to build their coffins and treasure chests.

The next day we visited the quiet fishing village of Sidon where Christ once preached and where the Crusaders built their still-standing Castle of the Sea to guard the harbor. Then on to Tyre, "one of the oldest continuously inhabited cities in the world," a town that to the Lebanese symbolizes resistance to oppression, for it once held out for thirteen years against a siege by Nebuchadnezzar, and later resisted the entire army of Alexander the Great.

On the fourth day the word came that the border to Syria was open. The Lebanese officials suggested that, if we really had to leave their paradise for the wretched country beyond the hills, we leave promptly, for no one knew how long the border would stay open. They also reminded us that there was no guarantee Syria would grant us visas and allow us to enter.

It's only about 80 miles, as the crow goes, from Beirut to the border, but what must be the world's biggest mountain stands in between, and for hours we climbed and twisted and hauled our heavy trailers upward. It was evening when we reached the border.

And it was late at night when the Syrians finally let us enter. The visa procedure took hours, and the officials seemed to delight in badgering us with the most ridiculous and irrelevant questions. The guards searched through every page in our passports to make sure we had not been to Israel, because Syria is one of those fanatic Arab countries that won't let anyone in if he has ever visited the Zionist state. Then they spent more hours poking and prying through our luggage, making a list in our passports of every item of value so that when we left Syria the customs police would be able to check whether or not we had sold anything in their country.

The countryside was quite dark and desolate, without a single light, and the few villages we did find had long since gone to sleep. We kept searching the night for a place to camp, but the land on both sides of the road was too hilly and rocky. We were dead tired, and every mile's drive seemed to take hours. Finally, near exhaustion, we came to a flat spot and pulled off the road onto a field. We were opening the camper when two military Jeeps came speeding across the open field and screeched to a halt on either side of us. Four soldiers and an officer leaped out, and we caught the outline of two ugly sub-machine guns. We gave them that dumb tourist look, and in this case it was genuine. The officer, baffled by our presence and unable to make himself understood in Arabic, pointed a flashlight several yards beyond our camp. We were parked at the edge of a military air strip. A low-flying plane would have de-canvased us in one swish. The officer was still shaking his head as we drove off to search for another flat spot.

We were miles along the road and on the outskirts of Damascus before we found one, a huge parking lot filled with trucks. We pulled in, drove past the astonished guard, and pitched our camper in a hurry. It was too late for the policeman to object. In minutes we were fast asleep.

I thought I was having a nightmare, or that we were still at the edge of the airstrip, or that the camper was collapsing. Everything was shaking and jumping. A brilliant yellow eye was coming right at us out of the darkness. Hot red sparks were flying every way and the camper filled with thick smoke. We fell over each other and tumbled out of the camper, soot-covered and shaken up. The guard was doubled over with laughter as he pointed to the narrow-gauge railroad track just behind the camper. He managed to stop laughing long enough to assure us that there'd be no more trains that night. Then he ran off to tell his friends about the crazy Americans and the midnight special.

It seemed we'd just gotten back to sleep when the next disturbance began. It started as a gentle humming, but it soon rose to a roar, and the ground was trembling again. It was only three o'clock in the morning, but the truck drivers were already at it, revving up their engines and preparing to take off early to beat the heat. After half an hour of sound effects they thundered off and let us get back to sleep. For a few minutes.

This time we were roused by music—loud, blasting, ear-splitting music. Loudspeakers were mounted on poles throughout the parking lot, with one directly over our canvas roof, and at the stroke of five they cut loose with Arabic music. Why they played Arabic music—or any music—at five in the morning was more than we could understand.

Damascus, said our guide book, "is one of the oldest continuously inhabited cities on earth." It was not one of the most pleasant we visited, but it had its high points: the ornate Omayyad Mosque where St. John the Baptist is buried; the Al Tekieh Mosque with its soaring twin minarets; the tomb of the conqueror Saladin; a National Museum with relics going back to the very dawn of man; and the best bazaar east of Tangier, where, under a high glass roof, thousands of shops and tiny stalls gave forth their scents of tea and lamb and camphorwood.

What was good in Damascus came from its glorious past; but that past had not proven prologue to an equally glorious future. Trapped in the whirlpool of Arab politics, consumed with hatred for Israel, flirting with the Russians and the Chinese Reds, experimenting with militaristic socialism, feasting on the schism-kabob of Middle Eastern unrest, Damascus was, like its cross-Mediterranean counterpart in Algeria, wracked by poverty, squalor, and discontent. The prophet Mohammed had once declined to enter the then splendid city of Damascus because he claimed that "a man can only enter Paradise once." Today there are better reasons for not making the visit.

We moved on toward Jordan that afternoon, again wasting hours in Syrian customs. It was almost as difficult to get out as to get in.

Jordan was exactly as we had imagined it, unchanged from Biblical times. Only the American-built road was new; all else was eternal. On dry brown hills above the road, shepherds tended small flocks of sheep, as they have for thousands of years, dwelling in the same cliff-hewn buildings and eating the same sparse food that they have since man first moved across this land.

A few miles inside the country we were overtaken by four Jordanian high school teachers in an old Chevrolet. They had seen us at the border post and wanted to talk with us. After a few minutes they fired at us the question we knew they would. Everybody did.

"Why are you making a war in Vietnam?"

"We are helping the South Vietnamese defend their right to live as they wish without coercion from the North," I said.

"The government you help is no good; it is made up of men concerned with their own interests, not those of the people."

"When the war is under control the people can choose the government they want," I replied.

"Will America give aid to any country that is attacked?"

"If they ask us, probably," Al answered.

"Will America aid us when Israel attacks?" they asked.

"Israel is not likely to attack you unless you provoke her. She would be only too happy to live in peace with you," Al told them.

"How can we live in peace with the Jews? They have taken land from our people—and they want to take more. They are building atomic bombs to use against us. We hear on the radio how they will attack. We must crush them first. Drive them into the sea."

"What radio?" I asked.

"All the radio. Radio Moscow, Radio Damascus, Radio Cairo, Radio Peking."

"That's propaganda," I shouted.

"So is your Voice of America. No one believes it. Your government is controlled by the Jewish money lenders and helps Israel. You sold them tanks and jet planes and——"

"That's not true. We sold *you* planes," Al cut in. "Israel bought her planes from France."

"That is not what we heard."

"Perhaps what you hear is wrong."

"And perhaps what *you* hear is wrong. How do you know your leaders tell you the truth? How do you know who sold who planes? How do you know the people of Vietnam want you there?"

"Because our government lets us find out these things for ourselves. We're on our way to Southeast Asia now, and hope to see Vietnam for ourselves," I answered.

"Then do this, when you reach Vietnam, write us about it? We are anxious, and our students want to know. We will believe what you say because you are not like the Americans we hear about. Will you write us?"

"Certainly," I said, "I'll write you in about two months."

But in two months we were trapped in a cellar in Dacca.

This discussion was not an isolated instance; time and again people would ask us about American policies. Yet however heated or hostile those debates became, we almost always parted friends because we understood and respected each other's beliefs. The people to whom we

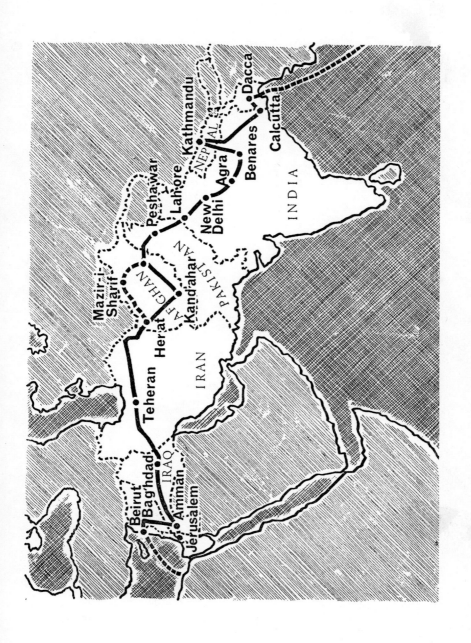

talked went away knowing that Americans, for all their faults, were not the money-grubbing, fat-bellied, race-hating, imperialistic devils they'd heard about on Radio Cairo and Radio Peking. In many places far off the tourist track, and in countries where our diplomats seldom ventured from the capital, we were the first Americans the people had ever seen, and we were not unmindful of the fact that to them we represented the United States and what she stood for. When the people noticed that we ate what they ate, saw humor where they saw humor, felt pain as they felt pain, and found sadness where they found sadness, they realized that we were fellow members of the family of man, brothers under the skin, despite the distances and differences. And when they learned, either from us or from stories about us in their national newspapers, that we had given up good jobs and the comforts of home to find out what their country was like, they developed a new respect for the United States and its people whose unofficial representatives we were.

A young Jordanian plumber—really an intellectual, but a plumber in a land where there is little work for intellectuals—came up to us later that night as we were eating at a small roadside cafe near Jarash. Again it was the same Radio Moscow material, the praise for Cuba, the condemnation for our Vietnam action and, as always, at the bottom, the hatred of Israel.

"They have taken our land and made homeless a million Arabs."

"It was their land two thousand years before there were any Arabs," Al answered.

"We didn't mind the Jews who were there before, but we are against these Jews they bring from Europe. They have no right there," the young man replied.

"Is that the real reason, or is it just that you are envious of what the Israelis have accomplished, how they have taken that barren strip and built thriving cities and prosperous ports and fertile farms? Even now they have a plan for irrigating the Negev Desert and——"

"We will not allow them. We are diverting the water."

"But don't you see, the Jews have done more good to that land in twenty years than your people did in a thousand. Isn't that why you resent them?" Al asked.

"They only could do it because you helped them."

"That's not true. They did most of it on their own. Besides, we helped you. This road, for example, we gave you this, a road as good as any in the Middle East."

"What are roads without factories?" the Arab asked. "Your country does not give us what we want. You give us roads, schools, hospitals. These are all right, but we want to produce. We want factories so we can make things. The Russians say you don't give us factories because you need us for a market for your goods. A factory here would upset your capitalists."

"Why don't you ask the Israelis for help?" I asked. "Why don't you work with them to utilize the rivers and develop the deserts, and——"

"They would not help us. The Jews hate us and we will kill them. Even Mohammed warned us against the Jews, how they would use their wealth against us."

"Look," Al said, "you told us before that all Americans are bad. Do you think we're bad?"

"No, I do not think you are bad. I do not agree with you, but I can see you are good men."

"Then can you still say all Americans are bad?"

"No, I guess there are a few who are good."

"Not a few, but 180,000,000. Americans are the most generous and sympathetic people in the world, but you condemned them before you ever met one. And the same for the Jews. Maybe if you met some personally you would realize that they are as good as anyone else," Al said.

"I have never met a Jew, and if I did I would kill him."

I could see Al's lip twitch as he asked, "But how do you know they are so bad? You say you like us, yet for all you know one of us might be a Jew."

"Then he would be a dead Jew!" the plumber spat, and his friends nodded.

From Jarash the road led to Amman, the ancient capital of Jordan, where we stopped a day to work on the cars and repair an oil-pan leak in the Toyota. From Amman we rolled over barren hills and through deeply shadowed valleys, then across the same desert floor

that Christ and his disciples once trod. The winding road descended
steeply for miles, and suddenly there was a sign in English that said:
SEA LEVEL. The road didn't stop there, but continued downward, down
to the floor of the Jordan River Valley. We had the queer feeling of
driving a submarine, and the heavy, sticky layer of air pressing down
on us confirmed the sensation.

Our first stop was the River Jordan at the spot of Christ's baptism. A
flight of concrete steps intrudes on the tranquil river bank, and a small
cement cross and a Coke stand designate the "traditional place of
Baptism." An Arab gigolo-guide was helping his middle-aged bleached
blonde American patroness down the steps, pawing her familiarly. Two
men were selling bottles of "Holy Jordan River Water" for 50 cents a
pint, and another was hawking rosary beads allegedly made from the
pits of the olives on the Mount of Olives.

Such was the fate of the sacred place where Christ was baptized,
and the fate of the rest of that holy Jordan was no more auspicious.
The river had long been a tragic waste, an untapped resource in a land
where water is as precious as life. The river had been little used for
anything, for centuries drowning itself in the salty graveyard of the
Dead Sea. Yet as soon as Israel announced plans to utilize the river to
irrigate her deserts, the Arab countries countered with a scheme to
prevent it. Syria was preparing to send saboteurs into Israel to blow up
the diversion tunnels, and this would provoke Israel to bomb the Arab
engineers in retaliation. The river which had furnished the water for
the baptism of Christ, the great preacher of tolerance and peace, was
2,000 years later furnishing a focus for intolerance and war.

We followed the muddy trickle of the summer Jordan to where it entered the dismal Dead Sea, the lowest spot on earth, 1,297 feet below sea
level, a ghostly gray lake that looked like a huge empty eye socket. Not
having been able to bathe since Beirut, we seized the opportunity for a
swim, and thus made one of the worst mistakes of our trip. The water
was a frightful shock. It was sticky, viscous, oily, stinging, stinking,
awful. The rocks on the bottom were so slimy we couldn't walk, and
when we tried to swim it was a disaster. The incredibly salty water
stung our eyes, burnt our lips, seared our mouths, and attacked every
orifice of our bodies. It was the most dreadful swim I've ever taken,

and it left us coated with glassy layers of salt that refused to rub off and which cracked and hardened when the air hit them. I have never been so uncomfortable in my life.

In Jerusalem we showered and turned to the city. With guidebook in hand, Al lead the way to "one of the oldest continuously inhabited cities on earth."

We began at the top of the Mount of Olives with a panoramic view of the holy city from the roof of the Chapel of the Ascension. Then down to the Garden of Gethsemane where Judas betrayed Christ, and then farther down to the deep, dark tomb of the Virgin Mary. The sun was especially harsh as we emerged from the tomb to begin the long, arduous climb up the Via Dolorosa, retracing the route along which Jesus carried his cross to Calvary from the Praetorium where he was condemned to death by Pilate and crowned with thorns by the people, to the Church of the Holy Sepulchre beneath which his body was laid to rest.

The people wore the same clothes and sat on the same steps, ate the same food and told the same jokes they did 2,000 years ago. And as we continued our tour of divided Jerusalem, as we visited the war cemetery on Mount Scopus, or saw the Arab soldiers standing guard over the isolated Hebrew University, or looked through the rubble of destroyed buildings and barricades of barbed wire and tank traps into the no man's land leading to Israel, we realized that man himself has not changed very much in those two thousand years.

Leaving Jerusalem on our way to Iraq, we came upon a particularly large refugee camp near the border, one of the many we had seen in the Holy Land, one of the many which hold the million Arabs who fled from Palestine when it became Israel. Their conditions are incredibly wretched. Their tents are torn and filthy, little more than dirty rags really. Their clothes were no better than their tents. The people were all listless and gaunt. The children walked about with swollen bellies. They have no hope—only hatred.

The nation of Jordan, which had 400,000 people when it was established by Great Britain in 1946, now has four times that many because of the influx of the Palestinian refugees, refugees it cannot support, nor even ever provide with the means of supporting themselves on its impoverished soil. Their position is pitiful and, in view of their hatred for the usurping Israelis, potentially explosive, should they decide to resist King Hussein's efforts to keep the delicate peace. Yet to return them to Israel would be to consign them to the status of second-class citizens, and to turn Israel over to them would dispossess the 2,000,000 Jews who have suffered so terribly in other countries and who have struggled so fervently for the right to return to and retain their Promised Land. The Arab refugees pose an enormous problem, one which will neither disappear on its own nor mellow with age, and one which we who saw their haunting faces will never forget—as we will not forget so much that is unholy in the Holy Land.

Chapter 10
The Garden of Eden

Fierce, burning, unremitting and inescapable, the desert sun ruled the road to Baghdad. The heat was unbearable and unbelievable, yet there was little we could do but suffer.

We had hoped that our North African journey would have prepared us for it, but the only valid preparation, save for exceptional men like Lawrence of Arabia, is to be born in the desert. The nomad has so attuned his metabolism to its demands and resources that he can go for three days with but a mouthful of water a day; and to prevent loss of moisture he has learned to endure the unendurable desert heat while completely covered by robes and headdress. We tried to follow his example, but it was hopeless.

Our bodies craved water continuously, so much so that we each needed three gallons a day. And we couldn't always get it. We were crossing the Great Syrian Desert, far less renowned, but far more brutal, than the Sahara. Here there were no water wells or shady oases. Nothing, not a sign of life, not a bush or bit of grass, not a shadow of coolness. Nothing but sand for hundreds of miles and, here and there, fields of big round rocks stretching to the wavering horizon.

We literally began to dehydrate. Our skins became as dry as chalk, and so rough you could strike a match on them. Our throats were too parched to speak. Our eyes were half shut with irritation, and the linings of our nostrils so stiff and dry they cracked when we touched them. We had tried the Arab trick of covering ourselves to curtail evaporation, but it was unbearably uncomfortable, so we drove wearing only our shorts or bathing suits. We put on Arab headdresses and soaked them every fifteen minutes with waste water to keep our temperatures down. It was as bad as the Libyan *ghibli*, but where that fiery blast lasted only hours, this was an eternity. By early morning the temperature was over 110, and before noon it was over 130 degrees and stayed there until sunset. There was not a cloud in the sky nor a breeze. As we drove we searched desperately for a tunnel to rest in, a bridge to crawl under, a cave or a tree to give us shade. But there was nothing. Only the road, and the oil pipelines beside it, and the desert.

Our bodies sought desperately to cope with the strange, harsh environment, but day by day they began to concede defeat. Our temperatures soared. Our pulses raced wildly, sometimes up to 120 beats a minute. Any exertion exhausted us. It was an effort to breathe, a struggle to move, a torture to drive. Even night brought little relief, and mornings found us still exhausted. There was little to eat. It was over a hundred miles from one tiny village to another, and when we reached one we were lucky to get some month-old eggs and some weevil-filled rice. By the third day Al and I were forced to do all the driving, as the others were completely spent.

On the Fourth of July we picked up a BBC news summary and learned that two weeks before, Major Edward H. White II had completed sixty orbits around the earth, and had become a human satellite when he walked outside his capsule. How remote it seemed, how hard to relate to technological accomplishments or dwell on space walks when we were crossing a country 2,000 years behind the world, and struggling for our lives, for a piece of meat and a glass of water. It was difficult to think about men experiencing the sublime freedom of space when we were camped beside people who knew no freedom at all, who would never travel, and whose only contact with technology was the ugly oil pipeline beside the road. To think of Major White required too great an effort; to think even of our friends and families back home was too difficult. We thought instead of that microscopic accident of birth which had caused us to be born in the most prosperous nation on earth, and these other creatures to be born in the most wretched. What if we were they? What if we, like they, had been born never to know a full belly, a day without fear of disease, a carefree love, a rewarding life? What hideous hand had created places like this, bits of hell on earth, and had dared further to mock the image of man by put-

ting him there, limited to sweat and sorrow and a covered mud hole
dug into the ground for a touch of coolness? I had believed existenti-
ally that man can be the master of his fate, that with ambition and
perseverance he can rise and rule; but I realized then that it was not
so, realized that for some men there just are no opportunities, no
hopes, and no comforts except an early grave.

The next day we reached the Valley of the Tigris and the Euphrates,
and camped that night on the shores of the Euphrates, the river that
once watered the Garden of Eden. Just beyond lay Baghdad.

Before we'd been there, the name Baghdad had a magical effect on
us, conjuring up images of caliphs and flying carpets, Ali Baba and the
forty thieves, Aladdin and his magic lamp, Scheherezade and the thousand and one nights. But now we have been to Baghdad and the visions
have been destroyed, destroyed by the heat, a searing, exhausting, unbelievable heat, a heat that comes in shimmering waves, that blisters the
skin, dries the mouth, fevers the brow, and melts the very marrow of the
bones. Heat such as I have never known and hope never to know
again.

We found a palm-treed campsite outside of Baghdad and collapsed
there. For two days we didn't stir from the shade. It was 130 in that
shade, but over 150 out in the brutal July sun. The smallest task became an intolerable exertion that left us spent and panting. We
couldn't walk ten yards in the sun without becoming weak and dizzy.
All along we had dreaded the precious months lost to delays, and now,
in the middle of the Middle East in the middle of summer, the delays
were taking their toll.

After much consideration, we decided to depart from our standard
routine and drive only by night, for the heat of the desert day was no
longer bearable. We knew our decision had its drawbacks. By night it
was easier to get lost, we'd have more traffic to contend with since all
the desert-wise truckers drove at night, and we'd increase our chances
of an accident. This worried us most, for an accident in an Arab country would be disastrous. The Arabs make none of our delicate Western
legal distinctions between murder and manslaughter. To them, if you
hit a man with a car by accident, you might just as well have shot him
with a gun on purpose. Even worse, their code demands an eye for an

eye. Many Arab countries even permit the family of a person killed in an accident to take the life of the driver responsible. But we had to gamble.

Though it was seven in the evening when we broke camp, the air was still heated. The road was thick with cars, carts, buses, trucks, and people. The traffic out of Baghdad crawled along, and our car was swamped with Arab kids begging for *baksheesh*. At the end of one tie-up, which couldn't have lasted more than two minutes and during which we diligently guarded the cars, the kids unscrewed the tail-lights from our trailer.

Al and I led the way in the Land Cruiser as the jam cleared east of Baghdad. The lights of the oncoming traffic were blinding, and the road still shimmered with heat. As we passed a truck parked on the shoulder of the road, Al gave a warning honk on the horn, but it wasn't heeded. A young boy darted out from behind the truck directly into our path. He was less than five yards in front of us.

Al pulled the wheel to the left as hard as he could, plunging across the road through the oncoming traffic, trying desperately to avoid the child. As we swerved I heard the boy scream.

We knew that, though the boy was entirely at fault, and though Al had been driving slowly and carefully and had taken every precaution, he could, under Arab law, be convicted of murder if the boy died. We knew that in situations like this in an Arab country the safest policy was to get away fast. Yet Al stopped the car and rushed back.

The boy was sitting on the road, dazed and shocked. A crowd was around him. His father was comforting him, but his uncle was scolding him for having dashed away from them onto the road. He was apparently unhurt.

When the boy's father saw we were foreigners, he insisted we all go to the police station. I didn't see any reason for it, since our car hadn't hit the boy, but the father and uncle demanded it, and four of their friends climbed on our car to emphasize the point. If I'd known what was going to follow, I would never have consented.

With the father pointing the way, we drove to the West Baghdad police station. From the outside it was a nondescript building with thick walls and no windows. Inside it was so ridiculously sinister that a

Hollywood hack would have rejected it as too corny. The main room was a large, dark, low-ceilinged cavern with a dirt floor, illuminated faintly by a kerosene lantern hung from the ceiling. Several barred doorways led off the main room into the dark back. Off to the right was an office and interrogation room, and to the left a tiny cell into which were jammed some 40 sweating prisoners in their underclothes. A vendor with a tray around his neck was selling them cigarettes and sweetmeats through the bars. Two policemen were sleeping on the dirt floor, and two more were dozing in the office, machine guns cradled between their legs. Beneath the lantern in the main room two men and two women were arguing violently while a policeman yawned nearby. Occasional screams came from the blackened barred rooms in the back.

Nobody spoke English. The father and uncle pushed Al up to a fat policeman in a sweat-soiled undershirt, jabbering in incomprehensible Arabic but making it obvious that they felt Al was the biggest criminal in Baghdad. The policeman nodded, sighed, took one look at Al, and motioned two guards over and told them to strip Al to his underwear and deposit him in the crowded cell. As I pushed in to protest, the police grabbed me and escorted me out to the courtyard, stationing a guard with a carbine to bar my way back. Guards had already been posted around our cars, ostensibly to protect them, but obviously to detain us. What was going on? What were they going to do to Al? How long would we be stuck?

My thoughts were interrupted by the wail of a siren. An ambulance came roaring into the courtyard. Two attendants leaped out and ran into the jail. They came out with a body beneath a blood-stained sheet. I rushed over to the stretcher and flung back the sheet. Under it was a very dead Arab with a dagger in his chest. But what had happened to Al? I brushed aside the carbine and rushed into the jail.

Al was very much alive, jumping up and down in his underwear, waving his passport and some newspaper clippings about our trip, yelling that he had to get to Teheran. On the floor, beneath the flickering lantern, a man lay bleeding from a gaping knife wound in his stomach. Two women were fighting beside him, rolling on the dirt, scratching, spitting, kicking, and tearing their clothes. The policeman would make an occasional perfunctory attempt to separate them, to no avail, and then check on the bleeding man whom the ambulance attendants had strangely left behind.

"What happened?" I asked Al.

"They took my clothes and tried to shove me in that cell and I started yelling I wanted a lawyer. That's what happened."

"No, I mean what happened to them?"

"Oh, they were arguing, and the other guy stabbed this one in the stomach, but this one got the other with a good shot right in the heart, and then their wives started wailing and tearing into each other. One of the prisoners here says it happens all the time. Probably why they have a dirt floor."

Three police with carbines came to escort Al into an old Jeep. One of them threw an old camel blanket over his shoulders.

"Where are they taking you?"

"You got me. But if I'm not back in two days write my mother and tell her to give my stamp collection to Rosalind and my love letters to the Library of Congress. Oh, yes, and you can have my termite collection."

Instead I jumped into the car with Al. The police drove through the dark streets of Baghdad until they came to a large building surrounded by policemen and Army trucks; we were led down several passages into a basement room which served as some kind of court.

At about two in the morning the judge came in, a kindly looking politician in a business suit. He spoke English and was full of praise for the United States and her citizens and their aid to Iraq, and full of understanding for Al and his having been dragged to his chambers at this dreadful hour because some reckless boy had jumped in front of the car. Al assured the judge that he hadn't hit the boy; the judge assured Al the case would be over quickly.

The judge called for the boy to be sent in, and in he came, crawling on his hands and knees, rolling on the floor, kicking his legs in the air, clutching his head and his stomach, and looking like a real basket case. The judge stared at Al. The boy's father insisted that his son's pitiable condition was the result of the accident and demanded Al be made to pay him $1,000 damages; Al insisted that this was a rigged perform-

ance and demanded to be set free. Since someone was obviously lying,
the judge sent the boy to the hospital for an examination. By five in the
morning the results were in: the boy was not hurt. The judge ruled
that Al was free to go—as soon as he paid the father about a hundred
dollars for his troubles. Al refused, and the judge explained it was
customary. Al refused, contending that such matters should be covered
by the accident insurance we'd been compelled to purchase on entering
Iraq; and the judge explained that the insurance wasn't of much use
for anything and that Al would have to pay out of his own pocket. Al
refused, and the judge said he'd have to go back to jail. Al refused, and
phoned the American Embassy where he woke up the First Secretary,
Walter McClelland, who agreed to meet us all back at the West
Baghdad police station.

McClelland was a godsend. He spoke like a native, bargained like an
Arab camel trader, and had behind him experience with similar inci-
dents. After several hours of negotiations, by which time we'd been
awake around the clock and were completely exhausted, McClelland
and the judge and the father and the police came to an agreement
whereby they consented to Al's release and McClelland assured them
that, should the boy turn out to have been hurt and show any delayed
signs of the accident, Al would return from wherever we were to stand
trial. Al left with the Embassy a $50 deposit which would be used to
pay the boy's medical bills, if he had any, or which would be returned
if he didn't.

By then it was afternoon, a blistering hot Baghdad afternoon. We
hadn't slept in thirty hours and we hadn't moved ten miles in three
days. But we headed across the desert. No more night driving for us.

The road from Baghdad to the Iranian border was a blazing inferno,
worse even, if that's possible, than what we'd already been through.
The only thing that kept us going was the knowledge that Iran would
be cooler, that the worst would soon be over. We were starved, dehydrated, exhausted, and more dead than alive when we reached the
frontier. We collapsed in the shade of the immigration shed and slept
for hours.

Iran, at first, seemed little different from Iraq—the same bleak landscape, the same brutal sun, the same unbearable heat. But twenty miles

inside the border we saw a rushing stream that tumbled down from the Zacrost Mountains. Like madmen we rushed for the stream and threw ourselves in. Our parched bodies absorbed the water like dry earth. I could actually feel the water seeping into my skin. I could actually feel my fever subsiding, my strength returning. For two hours we sat in the cool stream as life returned to us, and we knew then with a quiet joy that we had conquered the great deserts of the Middle East. Ahead lay the cool and fertile mountain valleys of Iran and an easy run to Teheran.

Chapter 11

Only Mad Dogs and Englishmen

The Day I Met Lord Jim: The afternoon sun came burning hot and blistered the earth. Life was at a standstill. The land was empty and silent, and even the air was devoid of movement.

We were camped a few miles east of Teheran. The others had gone early that morning into town to buy supplies and service the vehicles before we pushed off across Dasht-i-Kavir Desert. I was sitting on a water can, under the protection of the awning, brewing a pot of coffee when I noticed the lone figure walking across the heat-shimmering field. He came slowly from the direction of the town, stirring up dust as he walked. He was dressed in faded shorts and a blue cotton shirt, wore sandals, and carried a pack over one shoulder. I thought he might follow the trail to the hills and pass the camp, but he left the trail and walked toward me. I leaned back and waited.

He was young, in his early twenties, and bearded. It wasn't a heavy beard but a thin one, pointed at the chin, the kind seamen wear. And indeed, he looked a seaman, with a peaked blue cap and a thin neckerchief tied at the throat. When he spoke the accent was British.

"Name's John Leitch," he said, and we shook hands. "Your mate, Podell, I met him at the Afghan Consulate in town, he said you might sign me on to Kabul."

I poured him a cup of coffee, and he sat down on a gas can.

"Kabul's a long way from the sea," I said.

"It is, but it's a bit closer than from here."

I asked him about himself, and between sipping coffee and swatting flies, he told me that he had been at sea since he was fifteen. In the first years he worked the fishing boats along the English coast, and at eighteen sailed aboard a merchant vessel. He spoke with great knowl-

no mirage, no mirage," he shouted as he leaped into the pool, still laughing as he hit the water. While I parked, Willy and Manu rushed to the pool and threw water over their dusty faces. This wasn't enough for Lord Jim. He reached up, grabbed the unsuspecting Manu by the arm, and pulled him face-first into the pool. Then Manu and Lord Jim pulled Willy into the water with them.

Leaving the cars with Woodrow, who never was too fond of water, Al and I rushed over to the fountain with our cameras. A crowd had already gathered. An Iranian carrying a basket of fruit stood temptingly close to the edge of the pool, watching Jim cavorting like a walrus, when one of his countrymen shoved him into the water. That was it! Other normally respectable citizens of the village began pulling and shoving and throwing one another in. A few, urged on by Lord Jim, dove into the pool of their own accord.

As Al and I were photographing the aquatic melee, we noticed a policeman trying to force his way through the crowd. Unsuccessful, he ran off, and I knew he was going for reinforcements. We warned the others, and we all slipped back to the vehicles and slowly drove off. As we turned down a side street several blocks away, men were still running past us toward the fountain, and we glanced back and saw a truckload of policemen hauling people out of the water.

When we finally made it across the Dasht-i-Kavir it was July 14th— *Le Quatorze Juillet.* It had taken us eight days to drive a miserable six hundred miles. In Paris they were dancing in the streets; in Tahiti the trading schooner *Rotui* was arriving in Papeete from Moorea with the dancing team to compete in the National Fete; and while we had been bumping our way across the desert at ten miles an hour, a U.S. rocket was approaching Mars to shoot the first close photos ever taken of that planet.

We reached Meshed the following morning. After having the generator on the Jeep rewired, we headed southeast toward the frontier. It was dark when we reached the Iranian border town of Talybat. The road beyond became little more than a shifting trail into Afghanistan. We stopped at one of the town's tea shops. The six of us sat around a postage-stamp-sized table and ordered tea and a pot of stew. As always, a crowd gathered. Not a few, but dozens, men and boys, their

faces lit by the glare of oil lamps. Others stared from darkened doorways. Our meal came and we ate, but the audience stayed on, watching with serious faces, curious about our every move. In the past
months we'd become almost oblivious to people staring at us, but now,
for no apparent reason, their curiosity aroused ours. Was this their
excitement for the night? The week? Were they so unaccustomed to
foreigners that they came to see us? What did these people do for
excitement? For amusement? Certainly they had never seen a Shake-
spearean play performed, fine wine with a meal, nor had they ever
been moved by a Renoir. Neither had they read Keats or heard Fran-
cescatti play a Beethoven concerto. But then, what did we know of
the poetry of Sadi and Hafiz and the *dastgahs* of Favabl?

"What these people need is entertainment," Lord Jim said, and without further word stood on a chair and made an announcement in
English, which, of course, none of them understood. After a magnificent build-up, he introduced Manu. He said Manu would sing. Manu
protested, but when we cheered him on, he reluctantly stood up, took a
few deep breaths and began. The darkness of night split open with
"Malaguena." Manu's voice echoed and rang, and, entranced by the
sound of his song, he spread wide his arms and threw back his head;
the notes resounded through the night. Magnificently done. He took
his seat. Not a word had been uttered; not an eyebrow had lifted nor a
face changed its expression. They had listened, but with the same
interest as if Manu had been telling them about the mechanical operation of an electric dishwasher.

We camped that night a few miles from the Afghan border. Although it was hot, ever hot, the prospect of a new country gave us new
spirit. While we sat around the campfire, Lord Jim read the classified
ads in an old London newspaper he had found in Meshed. "Listen to
this," he said excitedly. "Here's a good flat, for five quid. Hey, now
hear this. Here's one overlooking the Thames. Not bad at all." Then
he read on, and suddenly shouted, "Listen, BOAC is looking for airline pilots. What do you know about that? I wonder what they
pay . . ."

Manu was dumbstruck by Lord Jim, and later that night told me
why. "When I met Al in Madrid," he said, "I was very pleased. Al

wanted to see the *New York Times* paper. We go for two hours over
Madrid, looking for *New York Times*. At last, we find—" Manu waved
his arms—"Al is very excited. I feel good. I think Al is a very good
man. Maybe very intelligent, someone good to travel around the world
with. Then—" Manu dropped his hands in disgust—"then Al goes
through the paper very quickly, and then he smiles. He takes two
pages, throws everything else away. He keeps the 'Stock Exchange.' "
Manu sighed: "Crazy foreigners."

The next morning the wind came howling across the plains like a
hurricane at sea, but instead of carrying rain it brought sand and dust.
It obliterated the sun and let pass only a yellow glow of light. The
headlights of the Jeep, which was following a few yards behind the
Land Cruiser, shone dimly through the dust like the eyes of a sea
dragon swimming in a muddy pool.

The Afghan customs house at Islam Qala is an ancient wind-worn
building with cracked mud steps that lead to a veranda. It has a heavy
wooden door studded with iron nails. It was locked. We knocked but
no one came. Al and Lord Jim set off in opposite directions around the
building, and in a few minutes the door creaked open. They had discovered an open window in the rear. I stepped through the archway
and found myself in a cool, dimly lit room. Spread out before me on
an uneven earth floor were thick, richly patterned Persian rugs. As I
walked across the rugs, dust stirred, and when I looked back I saw
that I had left footprints on the patterns. Lord Jim wandered off and
in a back room found two customs officers asleep. The first officer,
wearing a soiled undershirt and pajama trousers, came into the hall-
way rubbing sleep from his eyes. He was joined by the second who
was obviously embarrassed that we'd caught them dozing. They were
friendly, but painstakingly slow. Customs took us three hours.

We drove on into the twilight, past time-worn and abandoned fortresses, through mud villages with mud walls, and past windmills with
rotating blades as high as tall buildings. We drove farther into the past,
on to Herat.

Herat was once the crossroads of great caravan routes linking East
and West. The city was first fortified by Alexander the Great in the
fourth century, but Mongol hordes repeatedly sacked it after that.

There are mosques that date back hundreds of years, but for the most part it is a city of small mud houses and shops, where *ghotis* charge through the dirt streets like Roman chariots, and peddlers hawk their wares in the market square. In the heat of the afternoon, when the city rests, storekeepers ladle water from gutters and throw it onto the street to keep the dust down. As the western gateway to Afghanistan, Herat still rings with adventure and romance.

Four years earlier I had seen Herat for the first time, having reached it by crossing the central desert on a camel caravan from Kabul, a trip that took six weeks. Many changes had taken place since then, among them a modern super highway, built by the Americans and the Russians, that connects Herat with Kabul. Traffic crosses the country in two days.

The new highway, however, had little to do with my plans. I hadn't come to Afghanistan to retrace my steps. I had in mind another route, an almost forgotten trade route across the northern section of the country. It was the route Darius and Marco Polo had followed, and the country through which it went had changed little since then. Our maps showed that a road headed north, followed close to the Soviet border, and crossed the lower Hindu Kush mountains before turning south to Kabul. But no one we talked to in Herat had taken the route the complete distance. Some even doubted that it was possible. We heard that a French expedition had tried to cross a month before but had to turn back after 200 miles.

Still, in spite of the odds, I wanted to take the gamble. Our vehicles could probably withstand the trip, but Al feared that our heavily loaded camper would not make it. Also, the other members of the expedition, exhausted by long months on the road and the drive across the salt wastes of the Dasht-i-Kavir, wanted to reach Kabul quickly via the southern route. Al and I had a conference and agreed that he would lead the expedition in the Land Cruiser to Kabul and I would take the Jeep and meet him there in four or five days, enough time, I figured, to get me through the 800 miles across the north. We spent the day selecting the supplies I would need. I carried only necessities, saving the extra space for fuel cans and water jugs. I laid in a chest of food to see me through. In Herat, I bought a bandoleer and side holster for Blackie's pistol, Afghan clothing, and an extra can for gasoline. As I was loading the Jeep, Lord Jim came up and leaned over the hood. "You know," he began, pushing his cap back on his head, "I can't drive. Somehow in England I never learned to drive."

"You'll have to learn sometime," I said.

"I think so. Everyone should know how to drive. But you see, in the Land Cruiser there are many drivers. It would be rather difficult. Now of course, in the Jeep, there's only you."

I looked at him: "In other words, you want to make the trip with me?"

His face lit up. "As I said, I can't drive, but I can tell you many a good sea story."

"John," I said—it was the first time I had called him John—"I have no idea what's out there. There's the possibility of getting lost, or being robbed by the nomads. Anything can happen. For all we know, there is no road."

"I know," he answered, "but who needs a road?"

I couldn't refuse him.

When Al had everything repacked and was ready to leave for Kabul, he again tried to talk me out of my northern trip, stressing the uncertain nature of the route and the delays and dangers that might await, begging me to abandon my plan and take the easy road to Kabul.

I assured him that I'd be there only a few days after he, and pointed out that he could use the extra time to get everything organized so we'd be ready to push on to India as soon as I arrived, with no time loss. He still asked me to reconsider, and to evaluate the risk. I tried to explain to him, though I could hardly explain it clearly, that I had to go, no matter what seemed reasonable to others.

"I guess that maybe you do," he said sadly. "I guess that's what you meant by the difference between a traveler and an adventurer."

Just before they drove off he took some pictures of me, still gaunt and dusty as I was from our ordeal in Iran. Little did any of us dream that a week later those pictures would be appearing in newspapers around the world with the story about my death in the wilds of northern Afghanistan.

Chapter 12

Xanadu Smith Comes
to Kabul

After a day and a half of easy driving the expedition reached Kabul.

By the third day they had serviced the Land Cruiser, processed our film, and laid in supplies.

On the fifth day, when I was one day overdue, they were told by a geologist they met at the Khyber restaurant that there was a cholera epidemic in the northwest, a particularly violent epidemic that was killing hundreds. "In some small villages," the geologist told them, "they say that up to 80 people a day are dying."

Al and Willy rushed over to the Alien Control Office, but the authorities would neither confirm nor deny the epidemic, and when they went to the newly established Government Tourist Office, they were told that there was no cholera in the north, "just some upset stomachs."

"But our friend has been gone five days," Willy explained. "Maybe the road is not good?"

"All the roads in Afghanistan are good!" the officer shot back.

When Al asked if there was some way they could check if anything had happened to me, the officer suggested Al put his mind on other matters because Afghanistan was a "progressive country where no harm comes to travelers." When Al asked if he would help by reporting me missing to the police, the man dismissed it by saying he was too busy.

On the sixth day, when they were being interviewed by the *Kabul Times* for a story on the expedition and my delay, Al asked the editor about the rumors of a cholera epidemic. The editor turned red.

"There is no cholera in Afghanistan!" he insisted, rushing over to a pile of wire service dispatches on the sideboard. "See, this is what the sickness probably is," he said, waving one of them. "Just *salmonella,* the same kind of trouble you are having in Riverside, California, back in your modern United States. It is not dangerous. So do not say it is cholera."

As they were leaving the office a Peace Corps girl who helped on the newspaper whispered to Woodrow that there was indeed a huge epidemic raging in the north, an epidemic so bad that all her friends in the Peace Corps had been evacuated back to Kabul.

Al rushed over to the American Embassy, where he was told in confidence by an Embassy Officer that the World Health Organization technicians in New Delhi had just positively identified the organism as cholera, a particularly virulent strain of cholera that killed within 48 hours. Al asked how long the epidemic had been in progress, and the officer told him about two weeks.

"Then why didn't the Afghan government warn travelers at the border so that they could protect themselves?"

"You don't understand the problem," the Embassy Officer explained. "An underdeveloped country no more wants to admit that it has cholera than a person publicly admits that he has venereal disease. They feel there's too much stigma attached. These countries take it very personally. But Afghanistan is going to have to confess to this one pretty soon. It's growing every day and it could wipe out the country if they keep quiet about it. They've got to announce it and start giving mass vaccinations. And I imagine they'll close the borders then, too."

"Close the borders?"

The Embassy Officer explained that, under pressure from the World Health Organization, Afghanistan would have to shut her borders to prevent the spread of the disease. No one would be allowed to leave or enter Afghanistan for several months, until the epidemic had run its course.

"They'll probably play it cagey and blame the disease on one of their neighbors," the officer added, "and say they had to close their borders to keep out the cholera that was coming in from Iran or Pakistan or somewhere. But the effect will be the same. You'll be stuck."

Al asked how they could get help finding me, pointing out that I had gone into the heart of the epidemic region and had no cholera shot and was several days overdue in Kabul.

The Embassy Officer regretted that he had no power to order a search for me, and told Al that the Afghans could not launch a search without admitting the backwardness of the interior and the presence of the epidemic, something they were still hoping to hide.

"But if Stephens does get through," the Embassy Officer added, "we'd like to see him. None of us here have ever been up there. I've never even heard of anyone who's crossed Afghanistan by that route. He might be able to tell us some things we'd like to know—if he makes it. Keep us posted."

Later that evening, Al wrote letters and sent my last picture to several of our sponsors reporting that I was missing in the cholera epidemic.

On the seventh day, Xanadu Smith arrived in Kabul. Xanadu is an old friend of mine, an American girl turned international belly dancer. I'd met her six years before in Panama and was intrigued by her, her looks, her grace, and most of all, her romantic desire to see the world. "It's hard for the average girl to see the world the way I dreamed of seeing it," she said the first time I met her, "but not for an entertainer." After that initial encounter, Xanadu and I rendezvoused several times, always somewhere along one of my trips. Once it was South America, another time Tahiti, before that, Spain. This time I'd cabled her before I left Teheran and she'd flown to Kabul from Singapore. When she located Al at the Hotel Kabul he told her I was lost in the north.

"Lost! Not Steve. Not if I know him. I'll bet he's shacked up with some nomad girl in the hills."

"We'll find out soon enough," Al replied. He explained that he and Willy were leaving to search for me as soon as they could get cholera shots and police clearance permits. They got them that afternoon, and so did Xanadu. The next morning they set out from Kabul, driving along the northern road, heading back to Herat. Xanadu sat tense and erect up front, dressed in white from head to toe—white stretch pants, white blouse, a white scarf and even white shoulder-length gloves to protect her from the sun. They drove due north at first, along a stretch of asphalt laid by the Russians, then westward through the foothills of the Hindu Kush, past the impenetrable high snow-peaks soaring 14,000 feet into the clouds. All day they wound through the foothills, and by nightfall emerged from them and made camp by a rushing river swollen with melting snow.

All the next morning they plowed westward, traversing now dry and dusty country, the big river gone, the road gone, the earth lifeless, until they saw a trail of dust against the glare of the high noon sky. Al shot the Land Cruiser forward, racing toward it, and soon the dust trail revealed a car—a Land Rover driven by two naturalists from the Field Museum Afghanistan Expedition. The men were returning to Kabul from their camp near Pul-i-Khumri because of the cholera. They told Al they had not seen any other foreigners in that region—especially ones in a red Jeep.

The search party pushed on as the day died and the land grew ever more parched and barren. Gone now were even the smallest streams. No villages, no shops, not even a nomad encampment. Now there was nothing. Just a wasteland of scrub grass and a gravel track through it that vanished short of the horizon.

Chapter 13

The Noonday Sun

After the main body of the expedition swung south toward Kabul, Lord Jim and I made final preparations for our journey across northern Afghanistan. The most important item was fuel. At the edge of Herat we located a gasoline depot and filled the tank and six spare cans. At the depot we heard an alarming rumor about cholera in the north, and there was also mention that the roads might be closed. No one knew for certain, and they said the only people who might be able to answer our questions were the medical authorities. We drove to the Herat infirmary.

"We are not sure it is cholera," the medic told us when we arrived, "and we won't know definitely until a medical team investigates. We have called in doctors and in a few days we should know."

"Are the roads open?" I asked.

"There's a road block at Karukh, 40 miles to the northeast, but beyond that I don't know."

The news was discouraging, but there was always the chance that it might not be cholera. If I had to wait for the results, I preferred waiting in Karukh rather than Herat. It would be a 40-mile start, and if we had to turn back, we would have at least made the attempt.

Since neither Lord Jim nor I had recent cholera shots, I asked the medic if he would vaccinate us. "Certainly," he said, leading us into a small, dark room, "but there is no assurance it will protect you." He then sterilized a syringe and two needles by placing them in the lid of a small metal box and holding it over an alcohol flame a few seconds. I was certain that if we didn't die from cholera we would from an infection from the needle.

184

We left Herat the following morning, loaded with fuel and food. A few miles from town the road all but disappeared. The ruts were deep and filled with dust, and the best we could do was ten miles an hour. By mid-morning we entered a wide valley dotted by clusters of gypsy tents. Small villages with steep footpaths leading to them nestled in the far-off hills. We left the valley through a pass at the eastern end and began a steep ascent up the Siah Bubak Range. The road, although difficult to negotiate, was passable, and by afternoon we were in Karukh. It had taken us eight hours of constant driving to do 40 miles.

The medic in Herat was right. The military had a road block at the entrance to Karukh. A heavy log lay across our path. As we approached, two soldiers who had been squatting in front of their tent near the road leaped to their feet and rushed to roll back the log. They waved us past. It was strange that they hadn't stopped us, but we weren't staying around to let them change their minds.

The main street of Karukh was unpaved and dusty, with one-story buildings flanking it. There were a few shops with hitching posts in front, and tethered to the warped poles were pack horses, strings of camels, and donkeys with heavy loads strapped to their thin flanks. In the afternoon heat only a few men moved in the street, tall, gaunt men like those we had seen in Herat. They were dressed in baggy pantaloons, knee-length shirts, and intricately patterned vests. Their turbans were white, with trailing ends that fell down over one shoulder. There were no vehicles anywhere.

As we drove down the street, horses reared up and camels pulled at their ropes. Faces from the dark interiors of shops watched us pass, while a few young boys clad in rags ran after us shouting in Pushtu. We were halfway down the street when two soldiers stepped in front of us and made us stop.

The taller one of the two motioned for us to follow him. We offered him a seat in the Jeep but he refused. He insisted that we drive behind him as he walked at a snail's pace through the town. He led us to a military barracks where he ordered us to wait, and vanished into the building flying the Afghan flag. Presently he returned with an officer at his side.

The officer stepped up to us smartly and saluted. Lord Jim returned the salute. The man then asked something in Pushtu and pointed to the north. "Yes, yes," Lord Jim answered, "we are heading north." The officer nodded, took our passports and went back to his building. Fifteen minutes later he returned, handed back our passports, and then, most unexpectedly, rolled up his sleeve to reveal an ugly, festering boil. He grimaced, and in sign language asked if we had anything to heal his wound. I took out our first-aid kit, applied antiseptic salve to a piece of gauze, and taped it to his arm. He bowed and thanked us. Just as we were about to leave I caught the only word in his vocabulary which I understood—*doctor*. Lord Jim and I looked at each other in surprise. "The blokes think we're doctors," Lord Jim said. "Imagine— doctors."

The town was waiting for the medical team and had obviously mistaken us for them. Out of sight of the barracks, we checked our passports and found that special notations in Pushtu had been inserted. What they said we didn't know, but when we showed them to the guards at the roadblock at the northern end of the town, they saluted and motioned for us to pass. All of northern Afghanistan lay before us. We let out wild shouts of joy as we drove on.

We did not see another vehicle that day, only mounted pack animals and horsemen, and by dusk even they had disappeared. We reached an impoverished village, just four lonely mud houses, but the only place around for us to spend our first night. As I knew from past experience in Afghanistan, safety lay either in numbers or within the confines of a village. Lawless bands still make raids on solitary travelers. Peaceful nomads by day turn into marauding renegades by night. The unwritten law that applies is as primitive as the land itself. Once you are accepted as a member of a caravan, or are allowed to spend the night in a village, you have full guarantee of protection by everyone within that group. Similarly, you are expected to defend that caravan or village against whatever dangers confront it while you are part of it.

But whether we would be permitted to stay in the village was another thing. In front of one of the houses, on a bank of hard mud, three men sat drinking tea. We stopped and greeted the leader of the group.

He motioned for us to join them in tea. Now all we had to do was make friends.

We sat cross-legged on Persian rugs that covered the bank. Our host gave us a pot of tea, two glasses, and a bowl of lump sugar. He then went through a low door covered with a sack, and returned with a plate of *pilau* and four slabs of *nan,* a hard flat bread. We nodded several times to show our appreciation. I don't know whether they had been talking before we arrived, but now no words passed among them. They sat motionless, watching as we ate.

Darkness fell over the valley. The night was deathly still. We finished our meal and stretched out, with our heads and backs resting against the building. The elder still extended no invitation for us to remain. I thought of offering him money, but that might have offended him. Then an idea came to me. I went to the Jeep, removed our shortwave radio from its plastic bag, and brought it back. After turning it on and fiddling with the dial, I handed it to the old man. He beamed with pleasure. He tuned in a station in Peking. It was Chinese music, all clanging and clashing and complete discord. He turned up the volume full, and soon others—all men, of course—appeared and knelt around the radio. The old man, perhaps fearful now that we might leave, sent a young boy for mats and blankets. My scheme had worked. We were invited for the night. I was half asleep when he switched stations and found Kabul. Years before I had never even heard the name Kabul, but at that moment it meant as much to me as it did to these people. Washington and New York were only memories, distant and unreal.

I awoke slowly the next morning, aware of clean dawn and fresh silence. I propped myself up on my elbows. From a nomad camp in the valley far below, spiraled columns of blue smoke rose skyward. Horses and sheep grazed near black goatskin tents. It is in moments like these that one feels most deeply the great beauty of life. With my legs warm beneath the blankets, I sat up and drank the tea the old man served. When we finished, we collected the radio, thanked him, and drove off.

We had traveled 30 miles over difficult roads when we decided to have lunch in the cool shade of an undercut cliff. Lord Jim set to work gathering wood for a fire, and I went to get the food chest. It was gone! I tore the car apart but it was nowhere. It must have bounced out of the Jeep, or else it had been stolen. We would have to drive on and hope to buy our food in the villages or from the nomads.

We drove from valley to valley, across unmarked trails, foot by foot, sometimes inch by inch. Many valleys were barren, but in others, always close to the hills, were great nomad camps of the tribes who came from central Afghanistan. During the summer months they migrate north to the forbidden reaches of Turkmen and Uzbek, and when winter comes with cold winds from the steppes, they move southward in a wide sweep as far as the fringes of Pakistan.

Often we passed within yards of nomad camps where naked children came bounding out of the tents, always stopping short before they reached us, and then running behind us after we passed. In the dark interior of the tents, the women halted their work to watch us. Most of the nomad women had strong, handsome features, with tattoos about the chin. Unlike the other women of the Moslem world, they go unveiled.

At noon the second day we reached Qala-i-Naw. At the entrance to town, soldiers flagged us down, but let us through when they checked our passports. We had high hopes of finding a large, thriving city, for Qala-i-Naw on our map showed up big. It wasn't. It looked more like an abandoned mining town in Nevada. Shops and public buildings were boarded up, private homes were locked. Only one tea shop was open, and there a few old men sat idly, lost in thought. Lord Jim and I joined them and drank two pots of tea. When we asked for food the proprietor only shrugged his shoulders. We drove up and down the street several times, but there was no food to be had.

As we were leaving Qala-i-Naw we noticed a Russian-made Jeep parked in a side street. There was writing on its side. We drove over to get a better look: WORLD HEALTH ORGANIZATION. "Hello, there," someone shouted, and we saw the medic from Herat standing in the shadow of the building. His hair and clothing were covered with dust. "We drove through the night. Saw you parked in the village back there," he said, pointing westward. He mentioned nothing about our posing as doctors or getting through the barricades. We asked him where we could buy food.

"Not possible," he said, "and if it were, I wouldn't. Several dozen cases of cholera broke out here in the past 24 hours."

"But we're starved."

"Stick to melons," he said, walking over to his Jeep. From behind the rear seat he pulled out a ripe yellow one. He handed it to me and wished us a good journey.

A mile from town we saw a cemetery. Moslem cemeteries look much like Christian cemeteries. There are mounds above the graves and stone markers at the head. We watched two gravediggers swing crude picks at the hard, stony earth. We counted more than twenty graves freshly covered over.

That night we met a platoon of soldiers bivouacked on an open plain. We sought the warmness of their fire, and when I used the radio routine, it again brought us an invitation for the night. We bedded down in security. The next morning we thanked them and left.

The heat during the day was becoming unbearable. We longed for the cool mountains, but the Hindu Kush were a long way off. Thirst began to become a problem. After seeing cholera-abandoned towns and the many fresh graves, we stopped drinking river water indiscriminately. But we didn't stop bathing in the rivers. In fact, we seldom passed one into which we didn't run and leap, clothing and all. One afternoon when the sun was burning brightest, we came out of the hills and saw a deep, swift river before us. According to our map it was the Murghab, which flows north into the Soviet Union. We followed it until it widened, and then parked on its western bank. With a roar like a wild beast, Lord Jim took off at full run toward the water, across a mire of bluish mud. Suddenly one of his sandals stuck in the mud, then his foot itself. The mud was sucking him down like quicksand. It was up to his knees. When he tried to lift one leg, the other sank deeper. I had to act fast. I tore off my shirt, threw an end to him, and pulled him slowly to safety.

We followed the river northward, and an hour before sunset reached the town of Murghab on the Afghan-Soviet border. It was a large town and surprisingly untouched by the cholera. We found a tea shop. They had food. At last! We ordered a meal. The very thought of food, after so many days without, made us wild with hunger.

As we waited to be served, I felt someone studying us. I turned to see a man in Western clothes. Odd. He was clean shaven and wore an expensive karakul cap of gray Persian lamb. When he saw me looking at him, he either lowered his eyes or quickly glanced away. When tea arrived I momentarily forgot about him. When I looked again he was gone.

A few minutes later, just as our food arrived, the man with the karakul cap returned. Following close behind him were two armed soldiers. They came right up to us. What they were looking for I don't know, but after checking our passports and papers they escorted us back to the Jeep and led us out of the village.

"It's not the first time I've been kicked out of town," Lord Jim said, as we left dusty tracks between us and Murghab, "but they could at least have let us eat."

Our map showed no other towns or villages for 50 miles or more. We were at the mercy of the night. It came pressing in on us. The darkness was incredible, and we felt as if we were driving in a void. The country was hilly, with deep canyons. As we came out of a pass our headlights picked up the glare of green eyes on the ridges above us. At first we thought they might be sheep, but they did not run away as sheep would. Instead these creatures followed us, unknown forms in an alien land. Then one crossed our trail and halted a few dozen yards ahead. I laid a heavy hand on the horn and Lord Jim shouted at the top of his voice. No mistaking, it was a wolf, thin-ribbed, with yellow matted fur. The beast snarled and moved off the road to join the others on the ridge. Although the trail was rutted, I speeded up to a pace that could have easily broken an axle. The wolves fell back, but when we had to slow down again, they closed in. I shot ahead. After an hour's run they grew weary of trailing us.

By midnight we were just too beat to continue. We found a towering cliff and pulled the Jeep in close to its base. We unrolled our sleeping bags and I took the first watch. At 2:00 A.M. I woke Lord Jim and handed him the pistol.

An hour hadn't passed when I felt Lord Jim shaking me. I sat up with a start. He whispered that he thought he heard noises nearby. We waited, staring into the darkness for what seemed an interminable time. Nothing. Not a sound except the wind in the hills above. "I know something is out there," Lord Jim said. "I can feel it." Since he was not one to be easily alarmed, I took the pistol and fired it skyward. The shot vibrated through the gorge, echoing and re-echoing. The stillness of night, like the breaking of a spell, was shattered. Below us, not 30 yards distant, I caught the sound of feet slipping on the loose gravel. Then silence fell to the valley. Whatever it had been, man or beast, neither Lord Jim nor I slept the rest of the night.

The first light of dawn came in slow-moving patterns. Hills of soft grays with shadowed ridges appear intimate in the early hours, but soon under an Afghan sun they turn to harsh glares. We finally slept some, a few hours, until hunger forced us on.

Lord Jim was proving a valuable companion. It was true he couldn't drive, nor, for some reason—like Manu—could he even master the basic principles. He could navigate a ship, sail a sloop in a gale, and tie any knot from a double sheet bend to a running bowline. But drive, never. So instead, he talked. He talked incessantly. About everything. But mostly he talked about food; and when it really got hot, he talked about beer. Buckets of beer, barrels of beer. And the hotter it became, the wilder his visions ran. "Imagine if we found a jet airstrip right here in the middle of the desert," he would say. "Right up there by the rise." I would find myself staring hard at the horizon, visualizing a jet airstrip. "There's a big super airliner there, all warmed up. We stumble aboard, and off we go thundering through the skies. And do you know where to, you know where?"

"Where?" I asked.

"To Germany. Right straight to Munich. Mind you now, you are on the plane, half dead of thirst. This pretty hostess offers you drinks, food, anything you want, but you say, 'Nah, I can wait.' And then maybe ten hours later with your tongue hanging a yard out you arrive in Munich. Where do you go? Hah, hah, that's it, right straight to The Hofbrau. You order two pints—no, four pints—of suds. Then you say, 'You know, mate, I just stepped off the Afghan desert.' Then you know what happens? I'll tell you. They kick you out. 'He's touched,' they'll say."

Lord Jim might be quiet for ten minutes, then he would begin talking about food. In loving detail he would describe each course, from Chinese soup in Singapore to pheasant under glass in Buckingham. And always when he finished, after an hour's discourse, he'd ask what I'd most like to eat, and I'd find myself, often against my will at first, describing the most elegant meal I could possibly imagine.

Sometimes when Lord Jim was talking we didn't think thoughts, only pictures; other times we just drove in silence, mesmerized by the empty plains and desert. Seldom did our speed exceed ten miles an hour, for if I tried to go faster, the vibration threatened to shake us apart.

Often darkness came before we could find a village. Once we were searching the night when we saw a glimmer of light in the distance. We approached cautiously and found a group of soldiers camped near the trail. They were huddled around a small oil lamp, and beyond them, in front of an abandoned house, sat four men. On seeing our Jeep, one of the men approached and asked us in broken English if we would sit and have tea with them. Between sips of tea he told us he'd learned his English working for the Americans building the road in the south. He explained that he lived in the village of Qaisar, a few miles beyond, but that it was now sealed off. "Much sickness," he said.

When we asked him where we could buy food, he answered, "Nomad people. Friend. Give eat you give dollar. People my village there . . ." He indicated that a nomad camp was beyond his village. I unfolded our map and asked him to point out the location. He studied the map for a long time and finally put a finger on a dot east of Kandahar, a city in southern Afghanistan, perhaps 600 miles away. It was apparent he couldn't read. Before refolding the map I studied it for a moment. We had only made a dent across the country.

The man insisted we spend the night and start off for the encampment in the morning. By morning we were famished. We didn't even wait for tea, but thanked the man, threw our bags into the Jeep, and headed for the nomad camp to buy food. The road into Qaisar was closed, so rather than spend time explaining to the guards that we only wanted to pass through, we circled the town by crossing a river. Ten minutes later we saw the camp.

The goatskin tents, with their side flaps open, caught the first rays of the morning sun. We left the trail and turned toward the first group of tents. The children were the first to see us, then the women. As we approached, the boys didn't move to greet us but stood their ground. Lord Jim was about to hop out of the slow-moving Jeep when I caught his arm. Each child, even the youngest, held firmly in his hand a smooth round stone, and when I looked beyond the children I noticed the women were busily picking up stones. We didn't stop, but continued on past them in second gear, and it was well we did, for riding after us at full gallop were three mounted horsemen. They caught up with us as we reached the main trail. Two riders pulled their steeds to a halt while the third charged past us and didn't stop until he was a hundred yards ahead. He waited until we had driven to within a few yards of him, and then spurred his horse into full gallop, only to halt again a hundred yards ahead. Each time we approached he did the same, until we were out of the valley; only then did he leave us and ride back to his camp. I put the pistol on safety and slid it back under the seat. "Fine creatures," Jim said, and pulled his cap down over his eyes to take a nap.

We entered another valley and as far as we could see there were clusters of tents. As we passed from one camp to another, huge sheep dogs came charging after us. Their masters seldom called them back, and to prevent their leaping into the Jeep, we had to speed up and zigzag back and forth. We could not get close enough to any camp to explain to anyone that all we wanted was to buy food.

At dusk we reached the village of Sheerin Tagab and parked in front of a tea shop. I ordered tea while Lord Jim went shopping in the street. He returned with two melons and a kilo of grapes, the only food available. We ate heartily, drank our sweetened tea, and fell asleep with our heads on the table. We would have slept that way all night had the shopkeeper not awakened us. The shop was quiet and empty, except for a young boy sweeping the mud floor with a short-handled broom. I explained in sign language that we wanted to stay for the night. The man nodded his approval, but when he went out to look over the Jeep he came back and insisted that we lock it. We explained that the Jeep had no doors and was impossible to lock. He pondered over this for a long time, looking at the front of the shop, the Jeep, and the street where the villagers passed by. Then he motioned for the boy to follow him into the house. Presently they returned, carrying a heavy wooden bed with side boards. They placed the bed flush against the Jeep on the side facing the street. I was astonished to discover that two infants were asleep in the bed. Anyone who tried to rob the Jeep in the night would first have to remove his children.

It was dawn when we awoke. I lay zipped up in my sleeping bag and watched two donkeys come to drink from a water hole behind the shop. The shopkeeper had removed the bed, and now people passing in the street stopped to inspect the two foreigners who had spent the night in their village. Every few minutes the shopkeeper came out shouting and sent the people hurrying off to their own business. We had two pots of tea and a slab of *nan* and set off just as the sun was coming over the hilltops.

The days turned into a week. Time seemed to have passed us and gone ahead. We were two days overdue in Kabul, and certainly by now Al and the others would be concerned. And there was Xanadu. I remembered the cable from Teheran. She would be waiting. But we were less than halfway, and worst of all, the lack of food and the endless driving were beginning to take their toll. I found it ever harder to get back into the Jeep once I got out. And the roads did not improve. In one valley we found sand dunes as large as those we'd seen in the Sahara. In others, powder-fine dust was axle deep; only low gear could pull us through. In another valley we found strange mounds of earth which, we discovered, were marmot diggings. We spent the morning hunting and that night dined on baked marmot. The meat was edible but far from enjoyable. Lord Jim no longer talked about food. He sat sullen and silent, his face peeling from sunburn, his lips cracked, holding on with one hand as we thumped over the rutted trail. Most likely he was thinking about the sea, but I never asked him any more.

Many times I found my mind wandering. Once we reached a village and followed a protecting stone wall ten feet high that led to a gate.

The wall, the gate, and the structure of the entire village reminded me of China. *The war is over, and I am riding a coal-burning train across the Gobi Desert. Ahead, rising out of the dust of the desert, appear the walls of Peking. The train passes through a narrow opening in the massive, thirty-foot thick wall and we enter a strange and fascinating city where we are greeted by unfamiliar sounds and smells and an explosion of color. The restaurants and shops are filled with food; meats and delicacies hang in windows, vendors sell food on street corners, peddlers push carts laden with vegetables.* There was food to be had, inside the walled city, and I pounded on the wooden gate until my knuckles turned red. But the gate was locked, and again I knew I was in Afghanistan.

Our maps showed another large town, Sheberghan, 50 miles beyond the walled city. There was certain to be food there. We drove through the night and reached Sheberghan a few hours before dawn. We located an inn, aroused the keeper, and persuaded him to give us a room for the night. He lit a candle and led us into a large room with thick walls. The windows were cracked and broken. Sand covered the sills, and the beds were wooden pallets without mattresses. But we had no complaints; to us it could have been the Hilton. We slept well.

I awoke dreaming of food. "Six eggs I shall have," I told Lord Jim.

"With muffins and jam," he added.

"And hot coffee with cream—and no tea."

We called the roomboy and explained what we wanted. Twenty minutes later he returned with two glasses of tea. "Our food," we shouted, "where's our food?" He only shrugged his shoulders. I stormed out of the room in search of the kitchen. In a large sitting room I noticed a man drinking tea. He was clean shaven and wore a Western sports shirt. It turned out he was an Afghan doctor, educated in England, and sent to Sheberghan from Kabul to fight the cholera epidemic. "Don't drink the water," he warned.

"Okay, we won't drink the water. But why won't they serve us eggs?"

"Definitely not. The eggs are bad. They can carry cholera."

"But we haven't eaten anything but melons in a week."

"Drink the tea. You'll survive." He explained that five people had died there during the night, and that every village in the north was suffering heavy losses. "Do you know that a man can die two days after drinking bad water?" he asked. He saw that his threat didn't move me. "Then come with me and see for yourself," he said. "But no camera." I agreed, no camera.

Outside the hotel the doctor and I climbed into a Russian-made Jeep. The driver shot off with alarming speed through a maze of twisted, winding streets, without regard for pedestrians or passengers. Finally we slid to a halt in front of a low wooden door with a heavy iron knocker. We got out, and the driver knocked while the doctor and I stood back. Presently the door creaked open. A black-turbaned man in white livery bowed as we entered. Through an empty, unlit corridor we followed the doorman, who, on reaching an open courtyard, stepped aside and vanished.

The courtyard had been turned into a hospital ward. The stench of disease and death hung in the air. I hadn't realized that cholera could be such a foul disease. Diarrhea and vomiting are its first symptoms, and the doctor explained that an infected person can pass off gallons of liquid in a few short hours. Dehydration follows, and it becomes impossible for the body to replenish itself rapidly enough. In most cases, death is inevitable.

The dying watched with passive eyes as we moved among them. The courtyard smelled of death. Hands reached up and grabbed the doctor's arm, and when they missed, they reached for his trouser leg. In five minutes I'd had enough. The doctor led me back to the street and sunlight. He gave instructions to the driver and we shook hands in parting. "And remember," he said, "no water."

"No water," I replied.

The following afternoon we were driving through a small village when a man approached us carrying a child, a girl about seven. Her right ankle was swarming with flies. The man held her out for me to look at her leg. "I'm not a doctor," I said. "No doctor." He pushed the child closer to me. His eyes were wet and he seemed to be suffering as much as the child. I had to do what I could. I brushed away the flies and found an infection so severe that it had eaten away the flesh down to the bone. Lord Jim took out the first-aid kit and together we tried our best to cleanse the wound. The pain must have been excruciating, but the child didn't whimper. She only looked up at us with big round eyes. I applied antiseptic salve and bandaged her leg. I gave the man the tube and explained that he had to keep the flies away.

Immediately we were besieged by others who wanted us to treat their ailments. A merchant came from his shop and pulled up his shirt and wanted me to feel a lump in his abdomen. Another man dragged his frightened son through the crowd and showed me a growth between the boy's thumb and forefinger. Others showed me swollen glands, rotted teeth, and smashed fingers. In the end Lord Jim and I gave away every pill and every tube and bottle of medicine we had, until finally, with people running after the Jeep, pleading with us, we left town. We drove in silence the rest of the day.

At sunset we were 50 miles from Mazar-i-Sharif. We decided to push on through the night. The night led us into a wide valley that brought unprecedented difficulties. Flash floods from the mountains had carved a deep gorge across the road. We back-tracked and began again. And again. At one dry river bed we found a crude log bridge held together with straw and mud. We drove slowly onto it. It held our weight. We had reached the center when the rear wheels suddenly broke through. The Jeep dropped down to its axle. We tried four-wheel drive but it couldn't pull us out. To free the Jeep we had no alternative but to pull down the bridge. We began hacking away at the supports, log by log, until finally the whole structure came crashing down and fell four feet to the river bed below. The Jeep was undamaged and we drove off.

At midnight we passed through Balkh, which Marco Polo called the Mother of Oriental Cities. Her mosques were as beautiful as those he had found in Samarkand, and within her walls were the great tombs of kings and religious leaders, including Zoroaster. Marco Polo mentions in his *Travels* how Balkh fell into Genghis Khan's disfavor, and how in a rage Khan marched everyone onto the plain—men, women, and children, totalling some 50,000—and with his army of mounted horsemen, slaughtered them all.

It was dawn when we reached Mazar-i-Sharif. There were signs of fear of the cholera epidemic. Shops and buildings were boarded up, and there were no people on the streets. There was no food to be had.

We decided not to waste any time, but to push on through the city and try to reach the Hindu Kush where we could join the new Russian-built road to Kabul.

We began to lose track of time. We drove, following the trail or the sun, joining with a road when we found one. We camped in the open now, too exhausted to stand watch. We arrived at one small village and found a gaunt English-speaking school teacher. He proudly informed us that at Pul-i-Khumri, only 50 miles distant, we would find a good road. "We have magnificent roads in Afghanistan now," he said. "We are such a poor country my people are lucky if they have a donkey. Now suddenly we have roads, given to us by America and Russia. Why? Because the Russians were very clever. For 200 years they wanted a road through our country. So they decided to announce to the world that they were going to give us aid. They will build roads for the underdeveloped Afghanistan nation. Of course, you Americans could not let them outdo you, so you make the same announcement, and you help to build the road that the Russians have always wanted. For two centuries Great Britain had deliberately kept Afghanistan backward—without roads. Britain knew that Afghanistan was Russia's block to India. Now there is a superhighway, built by Americans for Russians."

News of the new road that led over the Hindu Kush to Kabul was like hearing that the Garden of Eden was over the next hill. We left immediately, and Lord Jim was his talkative self again, rambling on about food and hot showers and buckets of beer.

But when we arrived in Pul-i-Khumri our hopes were dashed. There was no road there. We heard it began at Doshi, farther to the south. We crawled back into the Jeep and set out again.

We passed the spot where Marco Polo had turned to the northeast and crossed the upper Oxus through the Wakhan corridor to the Pamir plateau, where the present-day borders of Afghanistan, Pakistan, Kashmir, Red China and the Soviet Union meet.

After driving many hours we lost hope of finding a road at Doshi, so as evening came on we began to scout for a place to camp for the night. It took all my failing strength to hold onto the wheel and to keep from falling out of the Jeep. I tied myself in. Then, in the far distance, I saw a thin line of dust. It was a truck—but it was moving faster than a truck. I began to imagine things, for when it came closer, I thought it looked like our Land Cruiser. Its top was off and people were standing up.

I even thought they were waving. I stopped the Jeep and tried to step out, but I forgot I was tied in. I fumbled with the knots. The vehicle stopped now, a few yards away. At that moment I passed beyond dreams, beyond feelings and emotions. I was beyond life itself. I was in another place, another world. Coming toward me, through swirling clouds of dust, was a beautiful creature in white, all in white. It had to be an angel. Her arms were stretched out and she called to me, by name—"Steve, Steve."

Chapter 14
A Tale of the Khyber Pass

"Do you want a cup of tea, mister?"

For that brief sleepy instant, when I heard the mention of tea, I was back in a dusty village in northern Afghanistan, but when I opened my eyes and saw cream-colored walls and curtained windows and Xanadu standing behind the roomboy, I remembered stumbling dust-covered and dead tired into the Kabul Hotel the night before. And now I was being awakened by the roomboy—asking if I wanted tea! I sent him flying out, with instructions never to mention that beverage in my presence again.

Under Xanadu's care I had little to ask for, except perhaps that my convalescence could continue indefinitely. From the Khyber Restaurant she brought trays of food—charcoal broiled steaks, baked potatoes, bowls of chilled fruit, ice cream, and quarts of cold beer—all of which she tenderly fed me. I was finding out what it felt like to be a pampered lap dog, and enjoying it, until Al came into the room. "Look at our great adventurer," he chuckled. "Pretty soft while the rest of the troops are up to their elbows in grease and living on camel meat." That afternoon I went out into the streets of Kabul.

Kabul had changed much since the last time I had seen it. The main streets had been paved and several new though not modern buildings erected, and there were now even homes with refrigerators, and shops that carried Coca-Cola. But for the most part, it still has the air of a city clinging to the past while being pushed into the present. Nomad traders still walk the streets in sleeveless sheepskin jackets, and in the old section of the city—separated from the new by the Kabul River, which also serves at its sewerage system—craftsmen still sit in openfront cubicles where, with skills that have been passed down from father to son for centuries, they work in bronze and sheet metal, make Afghan jackets with thick fur cuffs and collars, weave multicolored wool rugs, pound designs into leather. Farther down the dirt street behind the shops it's still possible to sign up for a camel caravan through the central desert via Kandahar.

Since I had to recuperate in Kabul for a few days, Xanadu signed a contract with the cultural attaché of the Afghan government to do three performances at the Kabul Nandary, a theater run by the government. She would then ride with us through the Khyber Pass to Lahore in Pakistan, and from there fly to Kathmandu, where she had bookings for August. In the meantime, in the enclosed lot behind the Kabul Hotel, the others worked on our battered Jeep and small trailer, getting them into shape for our push across Pakistan and India.

Our expedition was the subject of much speculation in the city. Despite the articles in the *Kabul Times*, they didn't believe that we were driving around the world, and they certainly didn't believe I'd made the northern crossing just because I'd wanted to follow Marco Polo's trail. Our expedition, they were sure, was only a cover story. We were three Americans, one Spaniard, and one Swiss, in two red Jeeps loaded with sophisticated cameras and tape recorders, escorting a dark-eyed, exotic-looking belly dancer. That could mean only one thing: we were C.I.A. agents.

When I looked around Kabul, and especially the hotel, I could understand their suspicions. Neutral Afghanistan, and especially its capital, had become a Cold War center of intrigue, much as Lisbon and Madrid had been in World War II. Nationals from a dozen countries whipped through the lobby—Yugoslavs, East Germans, Indonesians, British, Egyptians, Pakistanis, Poles—all on mysterious missions. There were Russians too, all over the hotel, all in dark business suits with wide lapels. They never smiled, talked only with one another, and followed in single file behind their delegation leader wherever he went, whether to the front desk, the restaurant, or the men's room. And Red Chinese also, sharp-eyed little men in conservative Western dress who always smiled and didn't follow anyone, who scurried across the lobby and down the halls like drafts of warm air. And Americans, crew-cut AID personnel, sitting around the lobby talking, wearing Bermuda

shorts and sports shirts and loafers, resting in the heat of the day
(which in Kabul is most of the day), sipping tall drinks and chewing
salted nuts. And an attractive French girl, allegedly an actress, who
evinced an interest in Al but who quickly switched to one of the
Chinese when she found we really were driving around the world.

I was sitting in the lobby, resting and taking in this James Bond
scene, when a phone call came from the American Embassy. It was
the Embassy Officer with whom Al had discussed my trip across the
north. He was upset about something, something that could not be
discussed on the phone, and he asked that I come over to the embassy.

When I walked into his office he handed me a State Department dispatch. It was several pages long, and the gist of it was that the *New
York Times*, the wire services, and newspapers across the United
States had published the news—taken Al's letters to our sponsors—that
I was missing in a cholera epidemic in northern Afghanistan. The
State Department had received some twenty telegrams inquiring
about my safety, and hundreds inquiring about the cholera epidemic,
the very thing the Afghan authorities had wanted to keep quiet. My
trip had touched off a bomb, and the Afghan authorities were angered
at the news getting out the way it had. Neighboring countries were
demanding information from the Afghan government and threatening
to close their borders to contain the epidemic.

The Embassy Officer suggested that Al, who had broken the news
and with whom the Afghanis were especially angry, leave the country
immediately, and that I follow as soon as I was able, certainly before
the borders shut. Back at the hotel, we decided that Al would leave
immediately for Lahore in the Land Cruiser with Woodrow, Manu,
and Lord Jim, who now wanted to continue on to Pakistan, and
Willy, Xanadu and I would follow in a few days. Al would wait for
us in Lahore and pick up the mail and supplies that had been sent
to us there. That night they loaded up the Land Cruiser and took
off. I went back to my room to rest. And Xanadu opened at the
Kabul Nandary.

I was asleep when Xanadu came storming into my room, crying and
angry. Her agreement with the cultural attaché called for the management of the Nandary to give her a percentage of the house after

each show. When she went to collect her fee the manager told her that only 120 tickets had been sold. Xanadu pointed out that the house was full, but the manager insisted that only the first few rows had been occupied. There followed a heated argument, and she left in a fury. I promised her that Willy and I would go to her performance the following evening and count heads.

We took seats in the last row. The hall filled rapidly, and well before show time every seat—400 of them—had been taken. By the time the show began more than 100 men were standing along the wall.

The lights dimmed slowly until the auditorium was black. The crowd settled down. Slowly, ever so softly, a drum begins to beat in the magic of total darkness. It increases in tempo, very quickly, and stops abruptly on a solid beat. A dim, orange light above the platform breaks the darkness to reveal, like an arrow notched in a taut bow string, Xanadu standing ready and motionless, with heavily painted eyes and masses of hair tumbling wildly down her chest. She drops a hand and a drum begins. Another drummer joins in, then another, and another. The sound becomes deafening and the mood intoxicating. It is wild and savage and beautiful.

Willy and I could still hear the audience clamoring for more as we worked our way backstage to compliment Xanadu. The manager was also complimenting her, sheepishly, with eyes that never left the floor, and holding out a receipt for her to sign.

"I won't sign it," she shouted. Then turning to me: "Steve, he said there were 160 in the audience. I know there were more. Tell him, Steve, that the house was filled. I could see."

Willy and I told the manager that we had counted more than 500 men, but, joined now by two assistants, he insisted we were mistaken. In exasperation we demanded that he ring up the cultural attaché. When we got through, the attaché said he wanted nothing to do with the matter. I told the attaché and the manager that Xanadu would never again perform in Kabul. We went back to the hotel and prepared to leave the next morning. I was asleep when the phone rang.

"My government is very sensitive," the caller began. He refused to identify himself, but he spoke with authority. "Your friend has insulted us. She says we cheat her and she says she will not dance for us. She has a contract for a performance tomorrow and she will dance tomorrow."

"No, she won't," I replied.

"I tell you she *will* dance, and she will stop making statements about our government. And you, Mr. Stephens, have caused us problems and embarrassment enough by your trip through the north. We will tolerate no more. Do you understand? Your friend will dance tomorrow." The phone went dead.

I didn't mention the threatening call to Xanadu, not wanting to upset her further, and the next morning we nonchalantly checked out of the hotel and drove off in the Jeep, heading toward the border. I kept looking back over my shoulder to see if the Afghans were following us, but the road was empty—completely empty—and I began to fear that the border had already been closed by the epidemic.

When we reached Jahalabad, the city near the entrance to the Khyber Pass, we learned that the border was closed—for the evening.

No one is allowed to drive through the Khyber after sunset, allegedly in deference to its dangerous twists and narrow roadbed, but actually in deference to the lawless Pathan warriors who rule the high mountains surrounding the pass and who attack unwary travelers for sport or spoils. It was a tense overnight delay for us, but it could have been far worse if we'd tried to cross 30 years before when there was a treaty in effect between the British and the Afghans by which the latter agreed not to rob or raid travelers only on Tuesdays and Fridays.

We camped that night in the main square of Jahalabad, getting our tents pitched just in time to beat the streaks of rain which swept in over the mountain barrier, the first rain we had had since Morocco, our first rain in 84 days.

The next morning we were up early and at the Afghan police post the hour the border opened. We held our breath as we laid our passports and car documents on the inspector's desk. If the authorities in Kabul were trying to catch us, they knew we had to go through the Khyber Pass. The police inspector looked at Xanadu, then at Willy, and then at me. He opened the passports slowly, and then carefully, ever so carefully, checked the names and photographs. I thought I caught a half-smile on his face as he did. He rose to his full height, motioned for us to be seated and, with our passports in hand, walked to the back room. I could see beautiful Xanadu in chains on an auction block and Willy and myself making little stones out of big stones along some road in the Hindu Kush. The inspector returned, followed by a thin, stern officer in a short-sleeved uniform.

"You are Mr. Stephens?" he asked Willy.

"No, he is," Willy said, pointing to me.

"This is your passport?"

"It is. Why, is something wrong?" I asked.

He studied me and then the photograph. It had been taken in Paris when I renewed my passport four months before, and there were obvious changes. I was now heavily bearded, twenty pounds lighter, and ten shades darker after months on the desert. The officer finally caught the resemblance and directed me to wait.

Without saying a word, he went to the filing cabinet, rummaged through a folder, and withdrew a paper. He turned and looked at me: "Your friend left this for you two days ago."

It was a map of Pakistan with a heavy red line drawn across it from the Khyber Pass to Lahore. Al's note with it said: "Please follow line. Search party retiring."

As we drove toward the Pakistan frontier post Xanadu said, "I don't know what you were so nervous about. You'd think you'd never crossed a border before." I told her about the threatening phone call, and threw in a few comments about its being a man's world and my duty to protect her. But she turned a shoulder, assuring us she could take care of herself no matter what happened. A few hours later she would change her mind.

DRIVE ON THE LEFT. The huge sign, in several languages, marked the entrance into Pakistan. From that point until we reached Central America, half a world away, we would have to discard our most basic driving habits and alter all our customary reactions and responses. They can be hard habits to break, and I found myself constantly swinging back to the right side of the road, only to discover turbaned Sikh drivers bearing down on us in huge trucks while I wondered what *they* were doing on the wrong side. After enough close calls, however, one learns.

At first approach the Khyber Pass was unexceptional, just a long climb like so many other mountain passes we had negotiated, distinguished from the others only by the big signs DRIVE ON THE LEFT and ABSOLUTELY NO PHOTOGRAPHS. But by the time we were a few hundred yards into it, its character had changed completely, and the reason for the picture-taking prohibitions was apparent. It was no longer a simple avenue of transportation, but an awesome instrument of defense. Massive concrete pillboxes dominated the road, strategically situated above it and capable of pouring withering streams of machine gun fire onto it. Concealed sentry posts were carved into the mountainside, their rifle slits barely visible; beside them, jagged tank traps stood silently waiting, ready at first alarm to be thrown into place to block the gateway to Asia.

For 23 miles the road snaked and twisted and bent back upon itself. A steep rock wall defined one side, a sheer drop the other. The mountains above, the gorge below, the fortresses, the road, the rocks, and even the sky overhead, were all bleak and lifeless; but it was not for its beauty that the Khyber had gained its fame.

To reach India from the west, the traveler, and the would-be conqueror as well, has to cut through the Khyber Pass. Farther north, the entry to India is decisively blocked by the world's most impenetrable mountain ranges, the Hindu Kush, the Pamirs, and Karakoram. To the south, the deserts of Persia and Registan and Baluchistan present a formidable barrier, capped by the Kirthar and Sulaiman Mountains. In a frontier of 1,000 miles from the shores of the Arabian Sea to the 28,000-foot peaks of the Karakoram, only two passes, the Khyber and the Bolan, offer entry into the subcontinent, with the Bolan dropping the traveler smack in the middle of the Great Indian Desert. It is almost as if nature had singled out the Khyber for the historic role it would play, and it is through it that almost all the invaders of India have marched over the centuries, the Aryans and the White Huns, the armies of Darius the Great and the armies of Alexander the Great, the Tartars and the Mongols, the Moghals and the Parthians. The British were the last on the scene, and the many battle-scarred regimental crests that line the walls of the pass give testimony to their bravery and military accomplishments. The last crest honors the most famous regiment of all, the Khyber Rifles.

We had gone only a few miles beyond the eastern end of the pass when we came to a fresh water spring. At a water catch nearby, several women in bright nomad dress were washing clothes. We were low on water and I decided to fill our Thermos and canteens. I warned Xanadu not to mingle with the women, but she paid no attention and wandered over and sat down with them and began chatting in sign language. Almost immediately a man came running across the field. When he stopped to pick up a stone, I could see rage in his eyes.

He rushed up to me, knocked a canteen from my hands, and turned on Xanadu, grabbing her by the arm, snapping her to her feet. He drew back his hand to strike her with the stone. I leaped and caught his arm as it came down and knocked him to the ground, breaking his grip on Xanadu, who ran back to the Jeep. The man had brute strength, and I realized that if I remained within his reach I could well be the loser, especially in my weakened condition.

In the scuffle I'd kicked his stone away, and he went running for another one. Meanwhile two more nomads came rushing across the field to help him. I ran back to the Jeep, where Xanadu was near hysterics—and Willy was taking pictures. By now the two men had reached their friend and had armed themselves with stones, one of which slammed into the side of the Jeep as I started the engine. We sped off down the road, Xanadu clinging to me tightly, no longer telling me how well she could take care of herself.

In Peshawar, the first big city beyond the pass, we stopped at a roadside stand to eat and rest. On the way out of town, I bought a newspaper, the *Khyber Mail*, "The Frontier's Only English Daily." The shortwave set was in the Land Cruiser, so it had been several days since we'd heard any news. What was happening around us, we wondered. As I drove, Xanadu read the headlines. UNITED STATES INCREASES BOMBING OF NORTH VIETNAM. . . . RIOTS IN MAJOR PAKISTAN CITIES OVER U.S. POSTPONEMENT OF AID. . . . TENSION GROWING IN KASHMIR. . . . A GROUP OF FOREIGN JOURNALISTS ROBBED IN THE

KHYBER PASS. . . . . A group of foreign journalists! Xanadu read
on:

>   The delight of the local pressmen in welcoming men of their
> profession from abroad was marred by a sense of shame afflicted
> by the sad story described to them by the group of globetrotters.
> The three journalists were robbed of articles worth Rs. 3,000 on
> Thursday night while camping on Jamrud Road, near the unpoliced
> tribal territories. The journalists said their camper's trailer had
> broken down on Thursday evening due to which they had to camp
> at the dangerous place. At about midnight some people came in a
> truck and made good with bags of camera lenses and tools and
> other things and also the jacks on which the trailer was standing.
> The matter was reported to the police who are investigating. The
> journalists were part of an expedition attempting to set a record
> for the longest . . . After getting their camper's trailer re-
> paired the touring journalists left for Lahore last evening.

As Xanadu read, my foot pressed ever more heavily on the accelerator, and we were soon flying along the road to Lahore, desperately
anxious to rejoin the others and find out what had happened. But the
fates were against us. Thirty miles out of Peshawar, the monsoon rains,
of which we'd had a hint the night before, struck with all their fury. It
was much as if some celestial battery of water cannons were blasting
away at us. Down and down the rain drummed, relentlessly, until it
threatened to wash away the earth itself. The skies turned black and
made the afternoon darker than night. Lightning tore through the
heavens. In twenty minutes the road was awash; in an hour the water
was so high it threatened to flood out the engine.

Even without the rain, the road was deadly enough. It was typical
of the roads throughout Pakistan and India, a narrow asphalt one-
laner with a four-inch drop onto the mud or rock shoulders on either
side. They are poorly maintained remnants of the British Raj, built in
the days before there was much auto traffic, and so narrow that two
cars cannot pass abreast, forcing one of them to put a wheel on the
shoulder.

We'd been warned by other motorists that the Pakistani truckers
would willfully smash into an oncoming car rather than slow down or
take to the shoulder, but we couldn't believe it. Believe it! Courtesy
as we know it in the West plays no part in a situation in which a
worn tire or a broken spring can mean economic disaster for a trucker's family. It's become a law of survival for the Pak trucker to hold

the road, using every manner of highway bullying, from honking horns to blinking lights, to make the other man take to the ditch. Our little Jeep was no match for the ten-ton trucks and the blinding rain, so when we reached a town we made camp for the night.

We were in Lahore the next afternoon, and at the American Consulate found a note from Al telling us where he was camped. We arrived there a few minutes before the monsoons struck, and as the rains beat down on the camper, they told us their tale of the Khyber Pass.

They had just cleared the pass and were a few miles beyond Jamrud Fort, which guards the eastern approach, when the right spindle on the camper snapped off. Al skidded 30 yards before he could get the bucking camper under control and come to a complete stop.

They were in a mess. They had ended up on the approach to a bridge over a dry river. They couldn't move with a wheel missing, yet they couldn't block the bridge. They had no choice but to drag the camper onto the shoulder, though it was only three feet wide and had a steep thirty-foot embankment down the side. The rear of the camper was dug deep into the mud and the front end jutted out over space. They used everything they could—jacks, rocks, boulders, tent braces, gas cans—to prop it up and to prevent it from sliding down the embankment.

For most of the afternoon they labored underneath the camper trying to unbolt and remove the axle, a delicate operation where a slight mistake could crush them beneath the camper, or else send it hurtling down the hill. When they finally had the axle off, Al and Lord Jim loaded it into the Land Cruiser and headed to Peshawar to find a welding shop. Woodrow and Manu remained behind to guard the crippled camper. It was evening by the time Al and Lord Jim had the spindle welded into place in Peshawar, and the monsoons had already begun as they headed back.

They had gone only half way when they came to a roadblock manned by four Pakistani soldiers who told them that the rivers had jumped their banks and were flooding the road ahead. They said that it was extremely dangerous and that no cars were being allowed through. Only after Al explained that they had to get back to the camper before it was washed away did the guards reluctantly agree to let them pass. By the time they were a mile beyond the roadblock it was completely dark, and with the driving rain it was impossible to see. The road was now covered with two feet of rushing, muddy water.

They feared they might drive off the road and go completely under water so Lord Jim suggested that he go in front and scout a path. Al gave him a flashlight to mark the way, and tied a life line from the car bumper to his waist. In this way, with Lord Jim half walking and half swimming ahead, they made their way back to the camper.

"I don't know what took them so long," Woodrow interrupted. "After they left, Manu and I didn't know what to do, so we took our sleeping bags and hid beneath the bridge. The river was absolutely dry and it was comfortable under the bridge. I was trying to get some sleep when the monsoons hit. We just got out in time. When the water came I thought we were going to drown."

I was about to tell him that only a fool would have camped in a river bed, but I could see the experience was traumatic enough. I thought back to the day I had interviewed him in Washington, when I told him of the many hazards that lay ahead of the expedition. He hadn't paid attention to me then, but it's a lot harder not to pay attention to a flooded river that's rushing down on top of you. I was sure that if Woodrow had the chance to do it over again, he'd have stayed in Decatur.

"A huge wall of water four feet high came at us," he continued, "pushing branches and trees and boulders that big." He stretched out his arms to full length. "It swept over our spot in a minute. It was horrible. Horrible."

In the meantime, the neglected camper was about ready to topple down the embankment. Al and Lord Jim arrived just in time to install new supports, but these were washed away as fast as they could get them into place. It was nearly midnight when the rains finally stopped and they could brace up the camper with jacks and gas cans. But it was too dark and much too dangerous for anyone to crawl under the camper to bolt the axle back into place; so they decided to pitch the Poptent below and wait until morning. They parked the Land Cruiser next to the camper, and Manu volunteered to sit inside and keep watch.

"But what about the robbery?" I asked.

"It happened after midnight," Al answered. "I heard noises above and stuck my head out of the tent. Two trucks were parked on the road. I thought they must be curious passersby, and was about to go back to sleep when I heard someone knocking a gas can from under the trailer. I grabbed the flashlight and zipped open the tent. I shined the light and caught three men pulling the jacks from under the trailer. Lord Jim grabbed the entrenching tool and we started up the embankment but it was hard going. By the time we made it to the road the men were in their trucks and driving off. They had taken both jacks, all the gas cans, and had unzipped the rear curtain on the Land Cruiser and stolen the bag of lenses."

"Weren't you in the Land Cruiser?" I said to Manu.

"I was," he nodded, "but these *banditos,* they very quiet."

"Quiet," Al shouted. "It sounded like an avalanche coming down the side of a mountain when they pulled out the jacks."

"And you didn't hear them?" I asked Manu.

"No," he answered.

When I looked around and didn't see Lord Jim, Al broke the news to me. After the camper had been repaired and the expedition had reached Peshawar and reported the theft to the police, Lord Jim had met several Pathan tribesmen who were heading north to the Valley of Kafirs, where the great Gilgit and Baltistan met to form the Karakorum Range. There was adventure. With his pack and his savings of ten dollars, Lord Jim set off, walking behind half a dozen gun-bearing Pathans.

We decided to leave Pakistan the next day. Several days before, the U.S. Congress had postponed approval of foreign aid funds in retaliation against Pakistan's warming relations with Red China. There were violent riots throughout Pakistan. Students paraded through the streets carrying placards and banners, and in both Karachi and Lahore, demonstrators had tried to sack the USIS buildings. Then in Kashmir, just north of Pakistan, guerrilla warfare had begun on a large scale. For the past 20 years the fairytale land of snowcapped mountains and deep blue lakes had been a bone of contention between India and Pakistan, and now both sides were ready to battle over the disputed area.

We saw Xanadu off at the airport and reached the Indian border at

7:05 P.M., five minutes after it had closed. Nothing could get us through. The military on both sides were tightening regulations. No one passed. We spent our last night in West Pakistan camped near the border. The night was black, and low-hanging rain clouds blanked out the stars. Somewhere in the distance, a drum beat ruefully. Its steady, unceasing beat lent an eerie mood to the night. Curious, I set off to investigate: an elder in a village had died and the mourners were praying over his body. The drum continued until the rains of the monsoon washed the air clear of its sound. It was toward morning.

Chapter 15

Where the Road Freezes Before the Bridge

Crossing the border into India was, to us, like opening the pages of Kipling and being greeted by turbaned soldiers wearing long coats and bright sashes. The great subcontinent of India, land of fabled color contrasts, lyric sweetness, and jeweled temples, land of 480,000,000 people and 250,000,000 sacred cows, stretched before us on 2,000 miles of broken roads, under torrential monsoon rains.

Our first stop was Amritsar, the Sikh capital and religious center. It was my second visit and I was anxious to show the others one of India's Seven Wonders, the Golden Temple. We parked beside the outer walls and left the vehicles under the watchful eyes of saber-carrying Sikh guards. At the entrance we removed our shoes, washed our feet in a special pool, and put on turbans provided by the keeper. We then entered the most sacred of all Sikh holy places.

That first view of the Golden Temple is startling. It stands in the center of a vast pool, dazzling under the bright summer sun. The sparkling gold-covered dome and the marble-inlaid walls catch the sun's rays and reflect in the still waters. There is an arcaded walk along the outer walls with low hanging trees, where pilgrims sit or stroll, as soft and silent as shadows. Here certainly all is peaceful and serene and set off from the outside world of confusion and despair.

To reach the temple we had to cross a long and narrow wooden bridge over the Pool of Immortality, a path of sun-heated boards that burned the soles of our bare feet and sent us scurrying into the protection of the temple. Once inside we forgot the sun and heat, for we were greeted by the fascinating sound of Indian music. Under the dome of the temple, sitting cross-legged on velvet cushions, a half dozen Sikh

213

musicians strummed *tamburas*, four-stringed lutes, and *vinas*, the seven-stringed harps of ancient India. The music flowed like a current to the people as they sat on the cool marble floor, their heads swaying to the unchanging melody. We joined them, listening, watching, smelling the strong scent of burning incense. We passed an hour, or maybe it was two, but finally had to leave and return to the world waiting outside.

Al had gone back to the vehicles earlier than the rest of us, and when we arrived we found him surrounded by Sikh children. "Steve," he said when he saw me, "look at her, isn't she beautiful." He pointed to a child of thirteen or fourteen.

"Hey, Al, listen——" I said.

"I know, I know. She can't be more than fifteen. But look at those eyes, aren't they sexy? And you know, I can tell she likes me."

"But, Al——"

"In fact, I even think she wants to——"

"Damn it, Al," I said, "that's not a girl; she's a *boy*."

Al looked at me, startled, unbelieving. I explained that no male Sikh ever cuts his hair. It is one of the five symbols of the Sikh religion. When Sikh boys are young, before they wear turbans, they simply roll their hair in a knot and tie it on top of their heads. As a rule, the boys are extremely handsome, almost to the point of being beautiful. They invariably have big brown eyes and long eyelashes. It was understandable how Al had made his mistake, and when I convinced him of it he climbed into the Land Cruiser grumbling, "And I thought I was a good judge of women."

As we were driving out of Armitsar, Al turned to me. "If that was really a boy back there, how come he had a comb stuck in his hair?"

I explained that it was one of the other four symbols of the Sikhs; they all wear a comb in their hair as a symbol of cleanliness. They also wear a steel wrist band that denotes brotherhood; wear underpants at all times, even when bathing, as a sign of purity and continence; and always carry a knife or dagger as a symbol of strength and manliness.

In New Delhi we discovered that the Burmese Embassy in Washington had done nothing about processing our visa applications, and the Burmese attaché would only suggest that we apply again with the Burmese consul in Calcutta.

The newspaper reports of my adventure in Afghanistan had brought stacks of letters and cables which we found waiting at the American Express office in New Delhi, including one from our agent, Jerry Klein, that *Life* Magazine wanted a story on it, and another from Krinski:

I TOLD YOU NOT TO DRINK THE WATER.

From New Delhi we turned south to Agra, the home of the Taj Mahal. Our first view of the Taj was through a cane field and across the muddy Jumna River. Bathed in the afternoon downpour of sunlight, the white marble dome and sparkling minarets stood before us in awe-inspiring beauty; but there is more to the Taj than sheer beauty alone, for it stands as the greatest monument ever built to love. When Princess Mumtazal-Mahal, the beautiful wife of the Mongul Emperor Shah Jehan, died, the grief-stricken Shah had the mausoleum built in her memory. Her body was laid in carved marble beneath the dome, where, on the night of the full moon, pencil-thin shafts of light fall upon their resting place—for the Shah too, upon his death, asked to be laid beside her.

But there is also another story, one seldom told. To build the Taj Mahal, Emperor Shah Jehan halted all building throughout India for 22 years and used 22,000 forced laborers and $230,000,000 to build his monument to love.

That afternoon I sat in the cool interior upon the marble floor in a far corner, and in my journal I jotted down my impressions as they came to me:

> Three hours, and I've watched a thousand people pass, mostly pilgrims, and considering this one day of one month of one year, and multiplying this by four hundred, I think of the many millions who have come to gaze upon the two marble tombs where Shah Jehan and his wife lie. They come in hushed voices, in bare feet with gentle footsteps, with bent shoulders, in the human flow of life, mighty as any great river. Time passes yet we cannot comprehend time. We do not see time passing, nor a child growing, we only know that a child becomes an adult, a hand is wrinkled, an eye no longer sees as well. Nor does the Taj know the passing of time, except, perhaps, for the chatter marks from footsteps worn in the hard marble stairs.

That evening I walked in the moonlight, along the reflecting pools, up the marble stairs, and gazed at the dome silhouetted against the soft night sky. The sound of a harp came from a group of boys seated in a circle, and somewhere beyond them I could hear a flute playing. I felt the splendor of an Indian night. It was all too short, for time stood toward morning, the flute faded, and night grew old.

We took our noon meal in Agra in a small open stall along the river. The food was hot and spicy, and as we ate, holy men and mystics passed. A snake charmer in a white turban played his flute, and his fat cobra swayed to and fro on the straw cover of his basket. Soon a crowd gathered around us, as it inevitably did, and it grew until we could no longer see our Land Cruiser.

Of all the people we met in our journey, those in India and Pakistan were the most inquisitive. Perhaps it is the very poverty and drabness of their own lives, where days follow dreary days without change or hope, that makes them so curious about the lives of others. Perhaps as we were telling them about our travels they escaped for a few minutes from the hopeless villages where they had been born and where they would most likely die. A dozen times a day we were stopped by Indians who asked, "From what country are you coming?" and a dozen times a night, when we tried to camp, Indians would peer into the camper to ask, "From what country are you coming?" It was impossible to eat, sleep, buy gas, brush our teeth, or even answer a call of nature in a seemingly empty field without having some *dhoutied* Indian pop up to ask, "From what country are you coming?"

Along the roads east from Agra we saw the *sadhus*, the holy men. Naked they walk across the face of India, carrying a small brass bowl for begging, a staff, sometimes an umbrella. They wear a string of large brown beads about their necks, and sometimes a loin cloth. They walk straight and proud, their matted and tangled hair down to their shoulders, their beards down to their chests. They belong to no caste. They are men who have renounced all worldly possessions and all worldly values, for the *sadhu* believes that in so doing he rises above mankind and that his last acts will leave no marks. When this happens he will not be reborn, the tiresome cycle of reincarnation will be finally broken, and the *sadhu* will achieve nirvana, the passionless peace of inperturbability attained through the annihilation of disturbing desires.

It is well said that a man who can drive across India can drive anywhere. The roads were as narrow, the shoulders as steep, and the truckers as rude as those in Pakistan. Huge carts, drawn by oxen, blocked the roads in front of us. When the monsoon rains struck, as they did almost every afternoon, they obliterated the road and made driving treacherous. After three days, the pounding force of the rains had washed away the letters painted on the rear of the camper: Trade Winds Around the World.

Our biggest problem was avoiding an accident with the villagers and the cattle on the road. Most of India's 480,000,000 people and 250,000,000 cows wander around with little to do, and all of them seem to prefer the highway, above all other places, for meeting, walking, sleeping and even defecating. The cows were everywhere. They walk the city streets, they sleep in the doorways of shops and homes, they wander along the roads. In a country where they are regarded as the repository of someone's soul, and consequently never killed or restrained, and rarely even chased out of the grain fields, they have grown defiant. No amount of honking or hollering would get them out of our path, and they'd stay there until the spirit moved them.

The people of India, 83 per cent of whom live in villages, use the roads for footpaths between the villages and as meeting places within the villages, and only with the greatest reluctance would they interrupt their conversation long enough to let us pass.

But worst of all were the people who slept on the road. They used it for a bed at night because it was warmer and dryer than the ground around it, and because, like so many poor Indians, they had no real home or bed of their own. Ten or twenty times a night we'd come to a harrowing stop inches from some recumbent form who'd awaken to blink in the glare of our headlights and slowly shuffle off the road to let us pass.

Taken together, these conditions slowed us to under a hundred miles a day. They also weighed heavily on us, for they summed up, in a sense, the deep problems of India, a deplorably backward nation that seems destined—one is tempted to say determined—to remain that way for years to come. Even those who love her most are forced to admit that her prospects for joining the march of progress are slim indeed, that hope of improving the conditions of her starving millions is fast fading, that nothing short of a miracle will solve the problems which have turned her into a cauldron of misery for so many.

Three days after leaving Agra we reached Khajuraho, and since it was impossible to find privacy while camping in India, we moved into a circuit house. The circuit house is a common sight in India and Pakistan, designated by various names as "dak bungalow," "circuit house," "inspection house," or just plain "rest house," but whatever the name, it means one thing: a public place for the traveler to rest for the night. In the days before the automobile, travelers in India had to rely on horses for transportation; and though it was possible for a rider on horse to travel more than twenty miles a day, the bullock carts carrying his luggage could do no more, so the British built rest houses every twenty miles. Though somewhat in disrepair, they are grand buildings, usually with spacious rooms and high ceilings. There are verandas and wide corridors and great unused dining rooms with heavy oak furniture. And most important, from our point of view, they are surrounded by high walls with heavy steel gates.

In the age of automobiles and airplanes, few travelers use the rest houses anymore, but they still remain for those who want to use them, and we often did. We relied on them not so much for their comfort, though they were admittedly drier than our tents or camper in the middle of a monsoon downpour, but for the privacy and protection offered by the surrounding walls. Once the caretaker had closed the gates, we had no need to unload our vehicles or post guards through the night as we would otherwise. We sat on the veranda, watching night close in, listening to the strange sounds of the forest beyond. Al read aloud about the ruins of Khajuraho, built by the Chandels, a mysterious dynasty which ruled middle India over 900 years ago. Of the 85 temples they built, only 20 remain. Every inch of the temples, the columns, steps, balconies and archways is richly decorated with exquisite carvings. As we found out the next morning, the carvings are of erotic motif, giving a full dissertation on love in which all forms of love play are depicted by Hindu gods and goddesses. None of the carvings is more than two feet high. They are sculptured in simple but imposing lines. The figures look Oriental, with narrow, slanted eyes and long noses. The bodies are graceful. Although they are completely frank, they do not offend. Nowhere in the world have I seen works in stone that so revealingly captured the physical emotions of man. We spent hours climbing through the temples and learning much, but we were uncertain how we would ever be able to show our color slides back home.

But why is eroticism enshrined in Hindu temples of worship? In Hindu philosophy the ecstasy of love is held to be the closest approach to supreme happiness. To the Hindu the sexual act has a double purpose of immediate satisfaction and procreation, and he refuses to exalt the one above the other. Since all nature is religious, the deity creates the world through human love, and from it receives pleasure. Thus the erotic temples of Khajuraho.

The next afternoon we reached Benares on the Ganges, India's holiest city, some 3,000 years old. What Mecca is to the Arab, Benares is to the Hindu, for it is to Benares that he must make at least one pilgrimage in his lifetime. He comes there to descend the steps (*ghats*) to the Ganges, and with the sacred water of the river wash away his sins. And there also the pious Hindus come to burn their dead.

After we had set up camp, we hired a skiff to take us out on the river. We pushed off from the stone steps and let the current carry us downstream. Hindus by the thousands lined the banks, many standing waist deep in the turbid water, others immersing themselves completely. Some took the water into their mouths, swished it around, and then blew it out through cupped hands as though in offering.

Sitting on the steps above the worshippers were the holy men, many completely naked, with penetrating black eyes and painted faces. And beyond the steps was the skyline of Benares, with 15,000 shrines and temples. We continued to drift, toward columns of blue smoke twisting skyward. Here were the burning *ghats* of Manikarnika, the holiest cremation site of India. As we drifted closer we watched two men prepare a pyre by piling logs in even rows. A corpse wrapped in a bright orange sari waited its turn. A few yards away four men carried a body wrapped in white silk on a bamboo stretcher down to the river for its final cleansing. At another *ghat* a man with a long pole poked into the ashes at the base of the pyre and lifted a charred leg which he threw back into the flames. At another *ghat* an old man with white hair, naked to the waist, prepared to light a pyre which held the body of his wife. He stuffed straw between the logs and walked seven times around the corpse, as is the custom. He then set fire to the straw, and soon his wife's body was engulfed in smoke and flame. As the sari burned away he heaped more wood upon her naked body, while from the steps above, disinterested faces watched the solemn ritual.

We saw no tears, no wailing, no displays of emotion. Children ran along the banks of the river, playing hide-and-seek among the burning *ghats*. Holy men sat on the steps, inured to the stench of burning flesh. Cows and goats walked among the pyres. A dog gnawed on a burned leg he had pulled from the ashes.

As we turned to head upstream, a boat rowed across our bow carrying an uncremated body wrapped in a sari. When it reached the middle of the river, the corpse was dropped overboard. Our oarsman explained that not all Hindus are cremated. He said that many of the Brahmin priests are not, nor are children who die before they are three; others considered unfit for cremation are those who die of smallpox or leprosy. They are merely dumped into the river.

The practice may seem bizarre, but it was not so remarkable in comparison with a Parsee funeral I had seen near Bombay. The members of the Parsee sect believe that earth, air, fire, and water are the four sacred elements of which the world is made, and that they must not be contaminated; thus, they can neither bury their dead in the ground, nor submerge them in the rivers, nor cremate them. When a Parsee dies his body is carried to a large open-air arena where it is laid to rest on a stone step. Thousands of vultures roost atop the arena, and in minutes they pick the body clean to the bones. This practice is frowned on by Indian Hindus who consider cremation the most purifying and desirable disposition of the dead.

The Hindu also firmly believes in the transmigration of the soul, of the soul being reborn in other bodies. For this reason, as is well known, no Hindu will kill any animal or eat flesh out of respect for the human soul it may contain. But the philosophy is followed to what the Westerner can only regard as ridiculous extremes. No animal, however badly off, is killed. The maimed and the crippled go on living. Suffering cows lie dying in the gutters. Cattle with broken limbs hobble pitifully through the streets. A few of the more fortunate ones are taken to one of the 43 old-age homes India maintains for dying cows.

On the road to Patna we saw dozens of cattle trampling the fields of young rice shoots while the farmers stood by unwilling to drive them out. At the villages nearby, children with swollen bellies came out to beg. This is India. But then, as we were told by Indian scholars, India is much older and wiser than the rest of the world.

From Patna we had to ferry across the Ganges to reach the northern border of India and the road to Kathmandu. The ferry was a leaking old paddlewheeler with two decks. There was no dock, so it was tied up to the river bank. To enable us to drive aboard, the crew placed two heavy planks from the top of the bank to the side of the boat six feet below. They were just wide enough for the wheels, so if I made one slight turn the car would go plummeting off into the Ganges. I felt I was walking a tightrope. After an eternity, the front wheels touched the deck, but the car would go no farther.

When I looked out I could see that the top of the Land Cruiser was wedged against the base of the upper deck. The steep angle of the planks did not provide enough room for the car to pass through the opening. I tried to back up, but it was impossible on the wet planks. We had to decrease the angle, which meant that we either waited for the river to rise or we lowered the planks. I quickly enlisted a dozen laborers to dig away the bank beneath the planks. Inch by inch the planks dropped, but by now we had aroused the curiosity of every passenger aboard the ferry, and as they came to the starboard side to watch us, that side of the ship sank lower into the river, making our conditions worse. I shouted to Willy and Manu to push everyone back, and when they had, there was enough clearance for the Land Cruiser to pass. But the moment I started the engine, 200 barefooted Indians rushed back to see if I could make it, almost knocking Willy and Manu overboard, and again the ship sank deeper into the water.

Several times more, Manu and Willy pushed them back, but each time I started to drive aboard, they rushed forward. It took some angry words from the captain and crew to keep the passengers back; then I was able to drive on with ease.

The crossing took two hours. The Ganges was as wide as a lake and as choppy as the ocean. A delay at the Indian border cost us another two hours, and it would be dark when we reached Kathmandu. Leaving the border town of Roxall, we crossed a flat plain before reaching the start of Tribhuwan Rajpath, the highest highway in Asia.

The Rajpath is an extremely narrow dirt road, one lane in width, which in places becomes axle-deep in mud. It begins its ascent through a rain forest of trees and underbrush as dense as the Amazon. We drove slowly, climbing and twisting, past slide areas that threatened to topple down upon us if we as much as spoke too loudly. When we entered a blind curve we dared not sound our horns. After several hours we found ourselves driving through banks of clouds, the road often following the rim of a precipice thousands of feet above deep valleys. Once we stopped to admire the view, only to discover that the road beneath us was supported by thin logs. The temperature, after the hot plains of India, turned brisk, and when the winds blew away the clouds, we had a sweeping view of the eternal snow-capped Himalayas.

At dusk we reached Sinbhanjan Pass at 9,000 feet. From here the road dropped down into the Valley of Kathmandu. It was dark when we entered the capital. We drove to the Snow View Hotel where Xanadu had told us she'd be staying. She was thrilled to see us and immediately began talking excitedly about Kathmandu. To us it was a disappointment, just another town we had driven through in the dark. But the next morning, when we threw open our windows, we changed our minds completely. We had awakened in a land of fairytales. We had found Shangri-La.

The beauty of Kathmandu is unsurpassed; it belongs to another world. Most of Nepal's art and architecture are indigenous, and what impressed me most about the city was that these treasures are all in use. Buildings that in other countries would have been chained off, with guards selling tickets to tourists for a hurried view, are being used by the people. In ancient temples, built centuries before America was discovered, bells ring as they always have; and massive doors with heavy iron hinges, constructed when the armies of Genghis Khan marched across Asia, still swing closed each night and open with the first light of dawn.

Perhaps the unique nature of Nepal is a result of her never having been colonized or exploited by foreign powers. It was the Rana family —the ruling aristocracy who had usurped the powers of the kings, and turned Nepal into their private estate—who forbade visitors to enter the country. The mountainous terrain made it easy to enforce the ban.

Only when India achieved her independence after World War II were the King's supporters able to secure aid from the sympathetic Indian government. When the King's revolution succeeded, the Rana prime minister resigned, and the country began to emerge from obscurity. In 1951 King Tribhuvana regained power, to be succeeded in 1955 by his son Mahendra. In 1956 the first road connecting Nepal with the outside world was completed.

After breakfast we hurried off to see the old section of Kathmandu, a city within a city, encircled by a high wall with narrow openings for gates, where the streets are cobbled and narrow and overhung by carved wooden balconies. In dimly lighted shops craftsmen sit cross-legged and practice their ancient arts and sell their wares. By mid-morning the streets are crowded. From the highlands come men and women in colorful costumes. The men wear strips of cloth wrapped around their waists, from which hangs the *khukuri*, the Nepalese scimitar. The women wear ankle-length robes, and adorn themselves with bangles around the wrists and heavy jewelry about their necks.

Since there are no beasts of burden in Nepal the task of transporting supplies is left to porters. They hurry through the streets in never-ending streams, jogging along in single file, carrying their heavy loads in baskets held in place by straps around their heads. And since the Kathmandu Valley is predominately Hindu, the sacred cows wander freely through the streets. In fact, in Nepal it is a capital offense to kill a cow. That night as we were sitting around after dinner, Mr. Mendies, the proprietor of the Snow View Hotel, told us a story about the sacred cows of Nepal. It seems a friend of his was driving his automobile into the city late one night when a bull crossed suddenly in front of him. The collision was unavoidable. Both the bull and the driver were injured. An ambulance was summoned, but when it arrived, it took away the bull instead of the injured man. We burst into laughter. But Mr. Mendies raised his hand; the story wasn't over. "My friend had to make it on his own to the hospital," he continued, "and after he was patched up, he was arrested and placed in jail, where he had to remain until the bull fully recovered. Not only that, but he had to pay a fine and all the hospital expenses for the bull."

"Holy hell," Willy said, standing up, "I'm good for a week in jail. I kicked one this afternoon."

I then had to tell of Xanadu's experiences in the old section that afternoon. We had driven the Land Cruiser through the narrow streets to a small courtyard surrounded by shops and filled with street vendors who sold various fruits. Xanadu never could resist sampling the fruit wherever she went, and she filled a paper sack with a half dozen varieties. Nor could she resist animals. She loves them all, and at the risk of her own safety she always stops to pet strange dogs, monkeys, goats, cows, and even an elephant once. She would never heed my warnings. As we were walking across the courtyard, she threw the peelings of the fruit she was eating to several goats that followed her. She stopped now and then to pet one. Onto the scene came a great black bull, as mean as any I've seen anywhere, and that includes the *plazas de toros* of Spain and Mexico. The bull sniffed the air, and when he saw the goats having a feast, he came forth like a locomotive. Everyone rushed out of the way, except Xanadu. "Oh, look at the nice cow," she said and fed him a banana peel. I expected to see her tossed and trampled at that very moment, but she wasn't. The bull kept sniffing at the bag she carried, moving closer and closer to her. Finally it became obvious that he wasn't about to settle for mere peelings; he wanted the bag and everything in it.

Xanadu, somewhat concerned now, sidled back to the parked Land Cruiser and squeezed into the front seat, thinking it might deter the bull. It didn't, of course. He pushed his nose in after her, and she was unable to close the door. She slid across to the driver's side. The bull was climbing into the Land Cruiser, so Xanadu leaped out onto the pavement. The bull was angered now, and Xanadu, still clutching the bag, kept backing away, while the bull, with his body half through the car, came after her, pushing the vehicle like a small tinker toy. The Land Cruiser was well on its way to being completely demolished, and it might have been if not for two porters from the highlands—certainly not Hindus—who dropped their loads and beat the beast off with sticks.

"And where were you?" Xanadu angrily asked me when it was over.

"Watching."

"Why didn't you do something?"

"I didn't want to go to jail," I said, and only after Mr. Mendies told his story after dinner did she talk to me.

Ever since we'd arrived in the capital, people had been approaching me to ask if I wanted to sell the cars. Nepal was one of the few countries in the world which permit a visitor to sell his automobile in it without having to pay a tariff. I decided it was the best chance I had to get rid of the Jeep. We had needed it mostly as a support vehicle to carry supplies, but these were now largely used up. The Land Cruiser had ample room for us all, and with Southeast Asia and the Australian Outback ahead of us, I was not too certain the Jeep could make it. I sold it to Prince Kumar Sumsher J. B. Rana.

The day before we left Kathmandu I made a final visit to the old section. The streets were exceptionally crowded and I stopped the car often to let porters, Tibetan refugees, Buddhists monks, and two young and pretty Indian girls with waist-length pigtails pass. It was when I stopped to let the girls pass that I thought I saw a familiar face in the distance. I did a double take and looked again. I then let out such a loud shout that Xanadu, who was sitting next to me, jumped a foot high off her seat. The person I saw was bearded; he wore an Afghan shirt opened at the throat, faded blue shorts, and a blue seaman's cap. He carried a pack over his shoulder. There was no mistaking him—it was Lord Jim.

When he saw me, he threw off his pack and came rushing up exclaiming, "I knew I'd meet you again. I just knew it." And in the next excited breath he was telling us about the wilds of northern Pakistan and Swat, about living with a tribe of Pathans, of barely escaping from a landslide, of fighting his way through Kashmir and crossing India.

Then, with his chest puffed out, he said, "I made it, skipper. I got my stake."

"You mean you came into money?"

"You know it. I'm fixed." Xanadu and I both congratulated him. It seemed like one of those things that could only happen to Lord Jim, one of those unbelievable episodes in life, where the wealthy old uncle passes away and leaves a fortune to a wayward nephew.

"If you don't mind," I asked, "how much?"

"Fifty quid."

"How much?"

"In Yankee dollars about one hundred and forty."

Xanadu and I burst into laughter. This great fortune came from his share in a fishing boat his brother had sold. But Lord Jim was happy, and nothing else, I guess, really mattered. We carried him off to find a cheap hotel.

The next morning, as we were preparing to leave Kathmandu, I went to see Lord Jim and asked if he wanted to come with us. "I can't," he said. "I want to see Nepal first. I might even try to get into Tibet." Somehow I was envious. I was looking at Lord Jim, but seeing myself when I was a young man in China. I saw my youth before me, and what I wanted to say to him was, "Fine, I'll go with you." But I could only shake his hand and wish him luck.

At the Snow View, Xanadu was waiting to see us off, with a basket of fruit. I left with promises to see her in Singapore in a month, but in a month we were a long way from Singapore. We were trapped in Dacca.

The last leg of our Indian journey took us across the state of Bihar. The monsoon in Bihar had come late, and the rains that did fall were light, so that crops were withering and dying in the fields. Each year India must rely upon the unreliable monsoons. One year there may be too much rain, causing floods, and the next year, too little rain, causing famine. There are few dikes or dams to harness the water when it threatens to overrun the land, and few catches or reservoirs to store the water when it is plentiful. There are only small communal water holes near each village, and in these the people wash their clothing, and bathe, and urinate, and water their cattle, and then collect water for drinking and cooking.

When we looked across the fields—where one man farms only half an acre while one man in the United States farms 350 acres—we saw a system of cultivation that is almost exactly as it was in India 4,000 years ago. The crops are the same, the shallow-draft plows are identical, and the yield is no better than it was then. But India can no longer feed herself using the old methods. Her growing population and her stagnant agricultural production have made it necessary for her to depend upon other nations for food. The month we were there she asked the United States for 8,000,000 tons of wheat to prevent mass starvation in the year ahead. Yet each year India's huge rat population —which the Hindus refuse to kill because of their beliefs—consumes 12,000,000 tons.

By late afternoon we passed through the big mining and industrial complex northwest of Calcutta, India's hope for the future, a region that could potentially be as prosperous as the Ruhr of Europe. We crossed the Howrah Bridge over the Hooghly River, one of the many tributaries of the Ganges, and drove into Calcutta, to be swept into the currents of a human river of ever-moving life——moving, but going nowhere.

Three hundred years ago, Calcutta was just a small fishing village. From this she has grown to become the second largest city on the mainland of Asia. Her problems have grown with her. People came to Calcutta from all over India to find work in the new factories, and when famine struck their rural areas they came to beg and steal food. During the great famine of 1943 they came by the millions to the city. Garrisons of soldiers blockaded the roads, and those starving people who didn't die in the streets of Calcutta, died in the big camps outside.

Calcutta was also the scene of the worst communal rioting between Hindus and Moslems. On the afternoon of August 9, 1947, 16,000 people were killed in the streets. Corpses blocked drains and choked back alleys. It was believed that the matter could only be settled by the partition of India. The partition took place, and Pakistan was created for the Moslems, but nothing really was settled, for the disorganized rioters of 1946 became the organized armies of 1966. What is so tragic about the affair is that the Pakistanis and Indians are ethnically of the same stock, of one inheritance, and once all Hindu. Their differences are solely religious, and both sides, once brothers, are now prepared to die for their beliefs. And the Trans World Record Expedition was going to be caught in the middle.

In Calcutta, we moved into the Lytton Hotel which had an enclosed courtyard where we could store our camper and equipment, and then went directly to the Burmese Consulate. Our applications for visas to drive through Burma were promptly rejected: no one could enter Burma, they told us, except by plane, and then only for a 24-hour stopover. Al waved his Operation Termite letter, but the Museum of Natural History was going to have to get its Burmese specimens some other way. Everything we tried failed. Al had written to a dozen people who he thought could help us, but none of the replies which reached us in Calcutta were the least bit encouraging.

Mr. Sway Tin, the president of the Automobile Association of Burma, wrote him that: "Entry into and exit from the territory of Burma by way of road or overland passage is prohibited."

The United States Embassy in Rangoon wrote: "Reference is made to your letter of July 6th. As a matter of firm policy, the Burmese government does not permit foreigners to enter Burma by land route. Therefore, it is considered by this office . . ."

Al had even tried the Japanese Embassy, since Japan had strong trade relations with Burma and we were testing our Land Cruiser for a major Japanese company. The Japanese Consul wrote from Rangoon that, "It is also very impossible for a foreigner to obtain permit to cross the road due to security reasons and because these reasons unknown to us I advise that you give up your expedition in this country. So sorry."

Everyone we spoke to in Calcutta had the same words: "Impossible, it can't be done." They further pointed out that it was not only impossible to enter Burma, but that it might soon be impossible to enter East Pakistan because of the growing tensions with India. Perhaps they were right, and there was every reason to think they were, but we still had to try it. Had I listened to all the warnings people gave me in the past, I might never have gotten around the world the first time, certainly not four times.

Eight years ago I had decided to drive the still-uncompleted Inter-American highway from Texas to Panama. "Foolish. Impossible. Suicide," they said. I did drive the highway, all the way, and had no great difficulty. "Great. Sounds like an interesting trip. I knew you could do it," they then said. Several years later I decided to cross Russia by Jeep. The Soviet Embassy in Washington told me it was impossible. Our State Department told me it was impossible. Even Intourist, the official Russian tourist bureau, said it was impossible. But I was determined to find a way. In Paris I sought out a back-alley travel agent who claimed he could arrange anything, even trips to the moon, if anyone wanted to go there. I worked through him, and in three weeks had my Soviet visa and necessary car documents.

Somehow, although everything now looked hopeless, I knew from experience that nothing was hopeless until you tried. Woodrow, Willy, and Manu didn't want to take the risk, so Al and I would have to try alone. This was our plan: Al and I would drive from Calcutta through East Pakistan to Burma, and hopefully through Burma. After we left, the others would ship the camper and equipment from Calcutta to Singapore, then fly to meet us in Bangkok on the other side of Burma. In the event that Al and I could not get through Burma, we would return to Calcutta, ship the Land Cruiser around Burma, and rejoin the others in Bangkok. Everything was arranged, and on Saturday morning, September 4th, Al and I left Calcutta and headed northeast toward the border of East Pakistan.

Chapter 16

"You Are No Longer Our Friends"

The country northeast of Calcutta is a vast alluvial plain where, during the monsoon, jute grows in endless waves in the flooded fields. Every now and then the flat contour of the land is broken by lone, wide-rooted trees and thick clusters of bamboo. Along the elevated roads, built atop enbankments of hardened mud, heavy, slow-moving ox carts haul loads of freshly cut bamboo or dried jute. The villages appear as they do throughout India: mud houses with pounded earth out front where withered old women stuff twigs and leaves beneath blackened pots on mud hearths to heat their tea water.

Twenty miles from the border we saw two soldiers, carrying rifles, leaning against a tree. We gave little thought to them until we drove a few miles farther and passed several more soldiers. Then we entered a small village and saw half a dozen Jeeps filled with armed troops. In the next village we found the streets all patrolled by soldiers. They were no longer in pairs or small groups, but in platoons and companies, and the Jeeps gave way to armored cars and tanks.

Five miles from the border we made a wrong turn in a village and became hopelessly disoriented. Trying to get out, we turned down a mud road and came to a clearing where army trucks and tanks were parked. Two soldiers, both carrying submachine guns, rushed up to us. I stopped and Al leaned out the door to ask for directions. "You are under arrest," the sergeant shouted.

"We are what?" Al exclaimed, stepping out of the Land Cruiser. He had a camera over his shoulder, and the sergeant immediately placed his hand over the lens, barking instructions to the private, who hurried off. The private returned in a few minutes with an officer, a Sikh lieutenant who wore an olive-colored uniform and a matching turban.

Dacca to see *Gone With the Wind*, their first movie and visit to the capital in almost a year. To make the overnight trip from their mission they had to take three ferries and drive many miles across monsoon-drenched roads. They were excited to be going to the big city, and to be talking to other Americans. As we stood at the rail Reverend Teel answered many of our questions about life in East Pakistan.

"Poverty and population are synonymous," he said. "There are over 60,000,000 people in East Pakistan. It's the most over-populated area in the world, except possibly Java. But they want to learn, and this is the hope of the nation, the people's willingness to learn."

For his mission it was a good omen, he explained, but it also made life for the missionaries difficult. The missionaries had absolutely no privacy. "There's no escaping the people," he said. People came to the mission to learn, but also to see how Americans lived, what they ate, how they passed their time—everything they did. "It is often hard for us to distinguish between those who are just curious and those who have a sincere desire to learn."

"They all love books," he went on, "especially if they have pictures or photographs." Then he smiled. "Give them a Sears catalog and it replaces the Bible. They cut out the pictures and paste them on their walls. The women copy the dresses; the men make furniture from the pictures—toys, tables, everything."

The trip lasted nearly three hours. Hundreds of black-hulled ships, their triangular sails filled with wind, were a striking sight on the river. I leaned against the rail and watched a convoy of large double-masted sailing vessels cross our starboard bow. Their gunwales were high off the water, and their bowsprits turned upwards like huge ramrods. They looked like eighteenth-century pirate vessels, with bellying square sails and seamen guarding the forward decks. Farther down the river there were smaller, red-sailed boats. Silhouetted against the glare of the morning sun, near-naked seamen with outstretched arms stood along the decks, tending the sails and tiller.

A network of canals serve East Pakistan as water roads for the smallest sailing boats. When the wind fails a score of men leap off and walk along the sides of the canals, pulling the boats by long lines fastened to the bows. And every so often, usually where two canals converge, there will be a gigantic fishing net worked by half a dozen men.

When we docked and said good-bye to the Teels, we promised to visit their other mission on the road to Burma. They sped ahead in their Land Rover to see *Gone With the Wind.*

We caught two more ferries and drove into Dacca a little past noon. Dacca is not an impressive town. There is little to see and nothing to do. The State Department personnel office classifies it as a hardship post. Of all the capital cities of the East, Dacca is the least known, and the least attractive. Yet it governs more than 60,000,000 people. Even more important, ever since the city was established in 1608 as the seat of the Imperial Mogul Viceroys, it has been the Far Eastern center for the teaching of Islam.

We located the Government Tourist Bureau, from which we hoped to get a letter of introduction to facilitate our trip across East Pakistan. Mr. S. Huda Chaudhury, the deputy director, was cordial and listened with keen interest to the story of our travels across Africa and the Middle East. Finally, when we explained our intention to drive to Chittagong in the southeast part of his country and from there on to Burma, he leaned back in his chair. "Gentlemen, I doubt if you can do it," he said.

"We realize it's difficult," I admitted. "We know Burma has been closed to foreigners for years. All we want to do is give it a try."

He paused before speaking. "I don't believe you understand. Haven't you heard the latest news?"

Al and I looked at each other.

"The situation with India has reached a crisis. The Indians have just bombed Lahore. There is no telling what will happen. You had better register immediately with the police."

We went directly to police headquarters. In the Foreigner's Registration Office we found half a dozen police officials huddled around an old radio. They interrupted their excited conversation only long enough to put our names in the registration book, the only entries, I noticed, in many days. The officer turning the dials of the radio nervously glanced up at a clock on the opposite wall; the President of

Pakistan, Field Marshal Mohammed Ayub Khan, was to address the nation at 1:00 P.M. It was 12:55, so we decided to wait.

The President's voice came over the radio, slow, deep, forceful. The office was now packed. All heads leaned toward the radio.

"The hour of trial for the hundred million people of Pakistan has struck. Today the Indians have given final proof of the evil intentions they have always harbored against Pakistan. The Indian rulers were never reconciled to the establishment of an independent Pakistan where Muslims could build a homeland of their own.

"They secured massive arms assistance from some of our friends in the West who permitted themselves to be taken in. We always knew that these arms would be used against us. Now that the Indian rulers have ordered their armies to march into the sacred territory of Pakistan, the time has come to give them a crushing reply. The hundred million people of Pakistan will not rest till India's guns are silenced forever. A state of emergency has been declared. *We are at war!*"

War between India and Pakistan! There was no going back to Calcutta. We had to get through Burma now.

We left the office dismayed. Crowds were gathering in the streets. Newsboys screamed the headlines: LAHORE BOMBED. EMERGENCY DECLARED. A squadron of Pakistani jets roared overhead. We drove to a gas station to fill our tank and spare cans. Lines of cars and trucks were ahead of us, waiting to buy gasoline before it was rationed. As we waited in line the manager of the station came over to us.

"We helped arm India so she could defend herself against China," I said.

"India used you. We told you then that it was only a trick so India could get your guns to use against us."

"But look at your own army," Al said. "Every gun and tank and plane you have is American. India has British planes and German rifles, and only a few American weapons. But everything you have is American. Every one of your pilots and officers has been trained by America."

He could not see the point. We were traitors to Pakistan, and that settled it. The Pakistani truck driver behind us came up and voiced the same sentiments. "Americans are no longer our friends," he said, waving a clenched fist. "But even though the Indians have your guns, we will crush them anyway."

"But you're outnumbered four to one. There are 500,000,000 Indians, and their soldiers may well be crossing your borders now."

"We are not worried. Indians are moral cowards. We are Moslems. We have moral courage. This is important. We will win. We will crush them."

We gassed up and headed for the first of the three ferries we would have to take to reach Chittagong. At the ferry landing, near Narayanganj, ten miles east of Dacca, we handed our papers to the guard. Without looking at them the guard handed them back, shaking his head. "No ferry," he said.

"But we must take the ferry," I insisted.

"There are no ferries," he repeated. "The government has taken them all into service. You might try the steamer in Narayanganj."

We drove directly to Narayanganj and through its narrow streets to the waterfront. Luck was with us. A steamer was loading cargo. We parked the car and ran up the gangplank to speak to the captain. The mate informed us that the captain was not aboard, and that if we wanted to book passage we would have to go to the shipping office. We copied down the address and after a half hour's search found the office.

"Sorry," a clerk said, "but the *Harappa* is not leaving Narayanganj."

"But she's loading now. We saw it."

"Maybe so, but we have just received orders from the commanding general of the port that no ships are to leave until orders come from the high command in Dacca." The head shipping agent gave us the same story.

We finally located the captain of the *Harappa*. "The best thing you can do," he advised, "is to return to Dacca and find yourself a hotel and wait. Even if you did get authorization to board, and even if we did get authorization to sail, you couldn't pass beyond Chandipur. The military has the road blocked."

We took his advice and went to the American Consulate in Dacca to register. We parked in front of the Adamjee Building and took the elevator to the fifth floor. After checking our passports, a guard led us into a front office where a young foreign service officer was talking excitedly into the telephone: "All Americans are to report to the Consulate . . . No, we'll try to keep you posted . . . No, we have no official word . . . No . . . All communications have been cut . . . Sorry."

When the young man hung up we introduced ourselves and explained that we'd just arrived in East Pakistan. He was startled. He asked us to wait, rose quickly and ducked into an office marked CONSULATE GENERAL. In a moment he was back. "Mr. Bowling, the Consul General, would like to see you," he said.

Consul General Bowling sat behind a polished but cluttered desk, flanked by the flags of the United States and the State Department. Three officials were poring over the latest newspapers, and a secretary was taking notes. The men were dressed in sports clothes, and then I remembered that it was Labor Day back home.

"You've picked a very unlikely time to be driving through East Pakistan," the Consul said. "And my assistant tells me you're journalists. I don't think the Paks will be too pleased when they find out. You're the only two foreign journalists in the country."

"But we didn't come here to write about the war."

"Tell that to them. I advise you to keep out of sight until this whole thing has ended. I wish you luck," he said, and we left.

The next morning we read the headline: CHITTAGONG BOMBED. I read on: "Indian Air Force planes launched unprovoked, cowardly attacks on civilian targets in Karachi, Chittagong . . ."

I glanced at the next column, headlined, RESPONSE FROM EAST PAKISTAN: "President Ayub's call to his countrymen to crush the Indian aggression on our sacred territory met with an immediate, spontaneous response from East Pakistan. The 60,000,000 people of the province now stand as one man behind Ayub to protect the sovereignty and sanctity of every inch of our soil. . . . The students held meetings and took vows to defend the country, even if that means shedding of the last drop of their blood. . . ."

East Pakistan was going mad, and it was apparent that the government's propaganda machine was trying to stir up the people, and for good reason. All the actual fighting was in West Pakistan near Kashmir, 1,500 miles away and completely separated by Indian territory. President Ayub's government needed the support of East Pakistan to furnish soldiers and equipment and to put pressure on India's eastern flank, so he was involving them through the press and radio. But for the aroused people of East Pakistan there was no visible enemy, no invading troops, no one to release their wrath upon, except for those who aroused suspicion. And who else were those but the foreigners? It was unsafe for foreigners to walk the streets. Several Americans were even pulled from their cars and beaten. The newspapers and radio warned the citizens to be on the watch for suspicious looking people and to report them. The military asked the citizens to arm themselves and to shoot enemy guerrillas on sight; this request soon had to be modified, for several Pakistani pilots were shot by their own people while bailing out of their planes.

Most menacing was the government's appeal to the students. They were encouraged to set themselves up as vigilantes, enforcers of the emergency defense laws. When a curfew was placed on the city, they patrolled the streets looking for offenders. To us, they were the biggest offenders. And during air raid blackouts they combed the residential sections searching for glimmers of light, beating on fences and doors with sticks as a warning.

By the third day other nations were taking sides. Moslem Indonesia offered to send troops to help Pakistan. Iran and Turkey promised support. Castro announced he was going to help. China leaped to the side of Pakistan; Peking accused India of crossing the Assam frontier into Chinese territory and of erecting new fortifications on her borders. It looked as if China were going to attack India, perhaps using East Pakistan as a military corridor.

Al and I were in a particularly bad situation. We did not have any diplomatic immunity or legitimate function in Dacca, as the other Americans did. We had no friends in Dacca. Nor did we have a plausible excuse for being in East Pakistan. Who would believe that we were driving around the world in the middle of a war? It also looked as though we would no longer even have a place to stay, for already the hotel staff was casting suspicious eyes at us, and any night we expected our doors to come crashing down and vigilantes to drag us out into the street. There was not only no means of escape, but we could not even communicate with the outside world. All the postal, telephone, and cable services had been discontinued. We decided to go to the USIS to see if there was some means of getting word to the other members of the expedition.

When we reached the USIS the men were busy boarding up the windows. We learned that the university students were going to demonstrate in front of the building in protest against America's aid to India. There were rumors that they might even attempt to sack the library. We weren't in East Pakistan to cover the war, but we weren't going to let them get away with sacking our library, either. If we could do nothing else, we would at least get photographs of them doing it. Al dashed across the street and into a four-story office building whose open balconies offered a perfect vantage point for taking pictures. I positioned myself in a parked bus.

I soon heard the shouts of the marchers moving down Topkhana Road. I checked and saw Al kneeling on the third-floor balcony, adjusting his camera. Suddenly two soldiers came up behind him and dragged him into the building. I jumped out of the bus and rushed into the building. A sign above the entrance read CIVIL DEFENSE HEAD-QUARTERS AND OFFICE OF THE COMMISSIONER OF DACCA. It didn't sound like the ideal place in which to be running around with a camera.

I hurried up to the third floor. Down the corridor I saw a crowd in front of one of the rooms, all trying to peer in. I pushed my way through. Six army officers were standing in the center of the room. Two of them were holding Al down in a chair while the others were firing questions at him. A few feet away a civilian was pulling the film out of his camera. I heard the words "Indian spy."

"What's happening here? What are you doing to my friend?" I shouted.

They all turned to me.

"This Indian spy is your friend?"

"I told you, I'm not a spy," Al cut in.

"He's an American journalist. And so am I," I said.

"It is forbidden to take photographs here," the soldier answered, and demanded my identification.

"But we are reporting on the unity and morale of the people of East Pakistan," I said, handing him my passport. "We are not spies."

He studied it carefully, then walked across the room to make a phone call. When he hung up he turned to us. "We shall see," he said.

Half an hour later the door opened and in walked the American Vice Consul. He'd been summoned to vouch for our identity. "I thought the Consul General told you two to stay out of trouble," he said.

The entire city was becoming hysterical. Hindus and Moslems, even old friends, were beginning to fight with one another, and there were fears that communal riots like those of 1947, which claimed nearly a million lives, might occur again. An emergency proclamation required all automobiles driving on the streets of Dacca—even during the daylight hours—to have their headlights blackened with paint or covered with tape. At night it was impossible for drivers to see, and there were many accidents. Many took it upon themselves to camouflage their cars with tree branches and leaves. But instead of being disguised, the vehicles were all the more obvious, masses of green moving through a brown landscape. And even more ridiculous were the gas station owners who covered their pumps with foliage. When we stopped at one such station to get the one-gallon daily ration of gasoline, Al began to photograph the jungle-covered gas pumps, but the attendant started screaming for the police, and we had to drive off without the photographs or the gasoline. The government next passed a rule making it a crime to carry a camera; anyone doing so was accused of spying.

Then one afternoon we discovered we were being followed. Wherever we drove a small yellow Renault kept close behind us, and when we returned to our hotel rooms, we found that our bags had been searched.

That evening we decided to try to find a safer place to stay. Reverend Teel had given us the address of his missionary friends in Dacca, and we went to see if they knew anyone who could put us up. We drove out to Dhaumondai, the section of Dacca where the members of the foreign community live—the suburb the Pakistanis call the "Golden Ghetto"—and located their house. They weren't home. Their *chaukidar* looked at us suspiciously and told us we'd have to come back later that night.

As we climbed into the Land Cruiser, the air-raid sirens began howling. The quiet residential street soon filled with noise and confusion. People ducked out of their houses to scan the skies for enemy planes, while those caught on the streets ran for cover. The *chaukidar* impatiently gestured for us to hurry and leave so he could lock the gates behind us. But by now vigilante bands were running down the streets, chasing foreigners to cover, shouting and banging on the fences with clubs and sticks. Despite the protests of the *chaukidar*, I drove the Land Cruiser into the yard behind the house and parked it where it couldn't be seen from the street, and Al slammed the gates shut just as the mob was on us. We ran into the house, followed by the *chaukidar*. Having little other choice but to give us shelter, he led us into a small pantry adjoining the kitchen, lifted a trap door in the floor, and pointed down into a cellar. We descended a dark stairway and he closed the door above us.

Time seemed to have stopped in that cellar. It was like a prison, but it was also our refuge from the crazed world outside. We waited.

When the sirens faded away the *chaukidar* opened the trap door and led us back into the house. The missionaries returned an hour later, and when we explained that we had had to leave our hotel and needed a safe place to stay, they put us in touch with Bill Maillefert, the acting Chief Information Officer at USIS, and a man who knew as much about what was going on in East Pakistan as any American there.

We spent the next day at the Mailleferts' home in Dhaumondai, discussing the war in general and our problems in particular, and by the time we left Mr. Maillefert had arranged for us to move in with Mike Schneider, an audio-visual specialist at USIS, who lived alone in a large house near the Mailleferts'.

We had plenty of company there, for Mike's house was the nightly gathering place for a group of other unfortunate foreigners, mostly Americans, who'd been caught in the middle of the hostilities. There was Peter Brescia, who worked for USIS. Just a few months before, when the war in South Vietnam had really opened up, he and his wife had been evacuated from Saigon to Bangkok. They had just been posted at Dacca. There was Ken Wimmel, also USIS, and his new Indian bride, Arati, a girl he'd married in Calcutta. She was traveling under an Indian passport and lived in mortal fear that she would be arrested by the Pakistan police.

"I remember the communal riots back home when I was a child," she said. "Our newspapers reported that every Hindu living in Pakistan had been murdered by the Moslems, and later, when the riots were over, our Hindu friends in Pakistan told us they had been told that all Moslems in India had been murdered. People were killing one another for no good reason, just killing. The same thing is happening now. All the Indians in Dacca have been arrested, the High Commissioner, everyone."

Then there were a few of Mike's friends from the British legation who stopped by to swap information, and every now and then a missionary or AID engineer who got caught when the air-raid sirens sounded. There were also Peace Corps volunteers, many with beards, who'd been ordered back to Dacca from the countryside when the emergency began. And there were others who popped in and out with the latest rumors and directives.

When we weren't listening to the rumors, we listened to the short-wave set, perhaps the biggest rumor monger of all. First we would tune in to Radio Pakistan and hear that, "The brave Pak armies are advancing and inflicting heavy blows upon the aggressor in all sectors. Our brave jawans have destroyed 63 American-made Indian tanks in the Sialkot-Jammu section in the last 24 hours. Our gallant airmen shot down 21 enemy planes in today's action. We have lost only one aircraft." We would then turn the dial and pick up All-India Radio to learn that, "The Indian Army is advancing. In a fierce battle in the Waggha-Attari section we have smashed 56 enemy tanks while losing only two of our own. Indian Air Force jets have brought down 42 Pakistani planes today, with no losses." By the eighth day of the fighting our running tabulations of the tanks supposedly lost by both sides exceeded the combined losses of the Allied Forces in World War II.

On our second day at Mike's house we saw a directive from Consul General Bowling.

NOTICE TO AMERICANS IN EAST PAKISTAN

East Pakistan has become an area of hostilities . . . the Consul General has therefore determined to evacuate from East Pakistan (all Americans) in the near future, using aircraft chartered by the U.S. Government if such aircraft can be brought into Dacca. We hope to have aircraft in Dacca on Saturday, September 11. All Americans should report to the American Consulate General for processing as soon as it is convenient. They should bring their passports or other proof of U.S. citizenship.

Ken Wimmel and his Indian wife were in despair at the implications that directive had for her. The rest of us just filled out the forms, wondered what would happen, and waited. A few people started packing and preparing to close their houses. September 11th came and went. September 12th came and went. And September 13th. And September 14th. There were no planes and there was no evacuation, only more directives and rumors.

The Consul General had no guarantee that the evacuation could be arranged, and his request had been met with three days of stony silence from the Pakistan officials. They then told the Consul General that there were no planes available for charter inside Pakistan, since they had all been turned over to the military; and when he explained he wanted to bring in U.S. Air Force planes from Bangkok or Manila, the Paks still refused approval, claiming they could not authorize American planes to land in Dacca as long as the airfield was being bombed by India. When the Consul General pointed out that there hadn't really been any Indian attacks on the airfield, the Pakistanis said that, in any case, the airfield was reserved for their own planes and restricted to foreigners.

When word that the Americans were trying to evacuate reached the citizens of Dacca, there was an angry uproar. The government helped it along, trying to channel the people's frustration at its inability to quickly defeat the Indians into an outburst against the Americans. Thousands marched through the streets of Dacca to the USIS and the American Consulate General protesting America's aid to India and her refusal to help Pakistan in her hour of trial. Rocks were thrown

through the windows and people beaten up. Pakistanis severed all
social relationships with Americans, and even the closest friendships
were broken. No American could walk or drive through Dacca without
fear of being attacked. The *Holiday,* the newspaper published by the
son-in-law of President Ayub Khan, ran the following editorial in bold-
face type on its front page when it learned of the Americans' attempt
to evacuate.

> "Yankee go home." It seems as if the oft expressed wish of people
> resenting the "Ugly Americans' " presence on Pakistan's soil is
> going to be fulfilled at last. The warmongers with the Bible in one
> hand and Stengun in another preaching their weird doctrines to
> unreceptive audiences, and "tough guys" always spoiling for a
> good "lynch" of hapless Negroes or "egg heads" seem to scare
> easily in more exotic lands.
> Alarmed by the recent developments in the Pakistan-India con-
> flict, Americans in Dacca are preparing themselves for a mass exo-
> dus to the dreamland that is America. They are gonna build the
> "great society" there. LBJ is calling them. We are told they fear
> a mass uprising of Daccaites angered by their criminal negligence
> in arming Indians against Pakistanis.

On September 16th, it appeared that the Pakistan government might
give the green light, for they presented the Consul General with a long
list of items—gold, jewelry, cameras, radios, Pakistani money—that
were declared war contraband and could not be taken out in an evacuation. Consul General Bowling promptly issued a directive listing these
restrictions, and it gave heart to the American community, because it
was the first sign that the Paks were even considering the evacuation
proposal in a serious way.

The hopes aroused by the directive were quickly dashed the next
night by new rumors that ran through the foreign community. I was
sorting out our equipment at Mike Schneider's house, and Al was carefully concealing our film behind the linings of our suitcases, when
a friend of Mike's from the British Consulate came rushing in. (No
foreigners communicated anything important to each other by phone
anymore because all phones were tapped by the Pakistani secret police.)
He reported that the Pakistanis had definitely decided to forbid the
evacuation because they said they had learned that the Indians were
planning to bomb Dacca in force as soon as the Americans left. The

Paks were going to hold the Americans as hostages to ensure the safety of the city.

The next morning there were still no evacuation planes, and still more rumors. Peter Brescia came in and reported the latest gossip: "The Paks might allow Bowling to get the women and children out of the city. But all men, whether private citizens or U.S. government personnel, will have to remain behind."

There were still no planes.

The next morning a friend of Mike's from the USIS came running in, waving a consular envelope of the kind we'd become quite familiar with by now. "The latest directive," he shouted, "the latest directive on the evacuation." He left to deliver other envelopes to other anxious would-be evacuees, and we tore it open and began to read.

NOTICE TO AMERICANS IN EAST PAKISTAN

Subject: Operation Icarus

1. Due to the delay in obtaining official evacuation transportation, the following preparations should be made.
    a. Beeswax—this material should be collected by all persons and stored in an air-conditioned room. Beeswax will be delivered by Jeep to official homes. Private citizens must appear in person.
    b. Feathers—this will be distributed according to the length of each individual's arms, and will not exceed. . . .

A few of us laughed, but only a few.

Chapter 17

Remove Blanket for Access to MLG Torque Shaft

All through the hot monsoon morning the Pakistani jet fighter-bombers roared over us, winging their way toward enemy India with loads of bombs and bullets, returning proudly to their Dacca base with their toll of tanks and trucks and temples and children. It was Sunday, September 19th, and the war which had inflamed the subcontinent was burning into its third terrible week.

But for us, September 19th would be the last day in Dacca—we hoped. We were getting out, according to a directive issued the night before, and we were waiting with the other evacuees in front of the building that housed the U.S. Consulate General, waiting to see if this, too, wasn't another rumor.

A few diplomats who were staying behind—consular workers and AID officials—put their arms around their wives' shoulders and reassured them that they would get out, and themselves looked around for assurance. They got none from the sullen Pakistanis across the road who were looking on with unconcealed scorn, except for a few—servants or assistants of those who were leaving—whose faces reflected bewilderment and a sense of loss. Fat drops of rain began to fall. We waited tensely for some definite sign that the evacuation was finally under way.

That sign was a silence. Shortly after noon the air grew quiet save for the rain. The incessant drone of the Pakistani warplanes had stopped.

The roar of plane engines returned an hour later, but this time it was a C-130 bearing the markings of the United States Air Force, a great gray ark that lumbered in low over the rooftops of Dacca and headed northeast toward the airport. A minute later another C-130 flew over us, then another, and another, each accompanied by our silent cheers, until seven of the big birds had landed.

Pakistani soldiers herded the evacuees down the street to an abandoned office where our passports were checked and our luggage searched to make sure that we weren't trying to take out any items on the prohibited list. Half of these prohibitions were just harassments, spiteful attempts to force the departing Americans to leave behind all their valuables; the other half were the products of a war hysteria which saw a spy behind every camera and an enemy agent beside every radio.

Particularly hurt by these harsh restrictions were those individuals who had become so discouraged by the hopeless waste of the war and the sudden hostility of the people they had journeyed halfway around the world to help that they had decided, though reluctantly, never to return. For them the evacuation would be permanent. Most of them had seen years of their work consumed in a few weeks as the meager resources of East Pakistan were marshaled for killing—farms they had supervised untended, doctors they had trained drafted, factories they had helped build converted for war production, flood control projects they had surveyed postponed indefinitely, ideals they had preached abandoned in the heat of the conflict. When they tried to take their few possessions with them, the Pakistanis refused, insisting they leave behind everything they owned, as if the loss of their love's labor had not been great enough.

The regulations also hit us hard, for we had brought into the country almost everything that was now on the prohibited list, including two radios, two tape recorders, $3,000 worth of cameras, a pistol, photos, and film. All this, and our car and heavy equipment as well, we had to leave behind. After I had pointed out to Consul General Bowling that we had no house in Dacca, he had agreed to let us store our car and equipment in the Consulate's parking lot. There was a good chance, we knew, that should the situation get out of hand, as it seemed more likely to every day, and should the Pakistanis' dissatisfaction with their inability to win the war be channeled by their leaders into more violent anti-American actions, the Consulate would be sacked and our equipment seized or destroyed. A good chance, we knew, that the Trans

World Record Expedition would see its last day in Dacca, its goal unattained, its struggles for naught, its dreams destroyed.

The evacuation flight will not be soon forgotten by those of us who were on it, cramped together on the metal paratroopers' benches in the belly of the huge transport, pondering the metaphysical implications of a sign that said REMOVE BLANKET FOR ACCESS TO MLG TORQUE SHAFT, and cracking feeble jokes while we tried not to think about how close we'd really come. The airmen were so self-assured and so completely in control—the first of our countrymen we'd seen in control of anything for a long time—that we gradually relaxed and breathed easy, also for the first time in a long time.

A young doctor told us how this, his first assignment, had turned out so different from his dreams, and his wife passed out homebaked cookies. A man on the other side of us, a well-traveled representative of a fertilizer firm, told us about his other close calls in Asia and the Middle East, and the problems of selling phosphates when nations wanted napalm.

Up front in the plane, we saw Mrs. Maillefert, too far away to talk to us but not far enough to hide the tears that hung in her eyes because she'd been ordered to leave while her husband had to stay behind. Mrs. Teel, the reverend's wife, was comforting her. Her husband also had chosen to stay behind, to keep his mission in Faridpur open to preach peace and tolerance. Next to them, Ken Wimmel and his Indian wife, Arati, who'd come closer than anyone to not making it, held hands in silence throughout the flight.

The evacuation planes were heading back to their base in Manila, but when they landed in Bangkok to refuel, Al and I got off, for we wanted to stay as close to the action as possible so we could rush back to claim our equipment when the war stopped.

Yet that day might be a long way off. The Bangkok papers, which ran front-page stories on our arrival, also reported that the fighting had intensified all along the Lahore and Sialkut sectors, and that Pakistanis protesting American aid to India had burned the USIS libraries and attacked the U.S. consulates in Karachi, Rawalpindi, and Dacca.

Our more immediate concern was with the other members of our expedition. We had seen them last in Calcutta and had told them to meet us in Bangkok, yet we found no message and began to wonder if perhaps they had been stranded in India as we had been in Dacca.

We spent two days searching for them, and then I remembered once having told Woodrow about the Thai Song Greet, an inexpensive Chinese hotel near the Hualompong Railroad Station. We decided to look for him there. I'd stayed at the Thai Song Greet six years before, and when I walked in I saw it hadn't changed. The rates were still 33 cents a night, and the rooms were still filled with unshaven bohemians and impoverished hitchhikers. The hotel's downstairs entrance is also a restaurant of sorts, with sawdust-covered cement floors, initial-carved wooden tables, and a charcoal-fed cooking stove that burns 18 hours a day. One *baht* (five cents) buys a steaming bowl of the most glorious Chinese noodle soup in the Orient, and two *baht* brings a heaping plate of sweet and sour pork or a dish of fried shrimp and greens. Sandal-shod travelers sit around the tables all days, seldom eating, conserving their stake, nursing a bottle of Coke or a cup of tea or a glass of Mekong whiskey for hours, exchanging the latest lowdown on the black market in India, the cheapest way to get to Angkor Wat, the job situation in Australia, the cholera epidemic in Afghanistan, and the Red Cross center down the street where one can get free treatments for VD.

Many of the travelers at the Thai Song Greet are no more than runners, long distance runners who chase madly around the globe, running away from discipline, responsibility, respectability, and the square world. But others sitting around the time-worn tables—and it is hard to tell which ones until you hear them speak, until you hear how they lovingly caress the sounds of Jaipur and Jahalabad, Matsuyama and Miyajimaguchi, until you understand they are journeying toward rather than from—these are the true travelers, the ones to whom the world is a way of life rather than an escape from life, the ones to whom travel is a full-time love rather than a part-time affair. They know the world as well as most people know their home towns, and love it far more. They are the restless, the adventurous, the insatiably curious, much like Lord Jim, in many ways much like me.

You'll find them in Bangkok because the atmosphere is permissive, the prices cheap, the sights unsurpassed, and the women accommodating; and you'll find them at the Thai Song Greet because it's their special spot in Thailand, as they have their special spots all over the world, the Globe Restaurant in Kathmandu, the YMCA in New Delhi, the Sikh temples in Singapore and Kuala Lumpur, the Red Shield in Calcutta, the Ichigaya Hostel in Tokyo, the Khyber Restaurant in Kabul.

We were sitting among the travelers at the tables, exchanging information, when Woodrow walked in. He was dressed in his baggy shorts and a soiled T-shirt. He was trying to grow a beard and to adopt the appearance of the others at the Thai Song Greet. He was startled to see us and explained that he and the others had given us up for lost and assumed the expedition was finished. Manu had gone to cover the fighting in Kashmir for his news agency and Willy had flown back to Zurich. They had taken their belongings out of the camper and had left it in Calcutta, despite our agreement that they ship it to Singapore.

"So you've given up then," I said to Woodrow.

"Well, I don't know. I mean it looks pretty hopeless. You let me know when you get the car out. I've got a nice job selling vitamin pills to the natives. The guy in charge takes me to a small village and gives me a bunch of bottles and I yell for about five minutes about anything I want. Those people don't understand English anyway, so it doesn't matter what I tell them. Then my boss translates into Thai. He tells them I'm an American doctor and that I recommend the pills for curing everything. The people buy them like mad and I get six dollars a day."

Though Woodrow's hotel was the cheapest place in town, and though such considerations were beginning to loom ever more important now that we faced an indeterminate delay and large shipping charges thereafter, neither Al nor I felt up to staying with the mosquitoes, the heat, the noise, and the crowds at the Thai Song Greet. We were both knocked out from our ordeal in East Pakistan, so we decided to convalesce in the moderate comfort of the Europe, a quiet old hotel with window-screens and ceiling fans. For three days we stayed in our rooms, just resting and trying to regain our strength, but we made little progress in the humid summer heat of Bangkok. We had little appetite, little energy. Our only desire was to sleep, often most of the day. We sometimes ran fevers and sweated profusely; at other times we shivered in the heat.

I'm sure that, had these symptoms hit us suddenly, we would have rushed to a doctor, but they had crept up on us so gradually over a period of so many weeks that when we finally did notice them, we assumed they were nothing more than the effects of the Asian heat and humidity and the lack of nourishing food in East Pakistan.

Since we were not noticeably improved by the fourth day, we decided there was little to be gained by remaining idle. Somehow we had to get the expedition back on the road. Al stayed in Bangkok to negotiate through the embassies for the release of our equipment, and I left for Singapore, the nearest port from which I could arrange to have our camper shipped out of Calcutta.

The coal-burning, clickety-clackety Singapore Express took 48 hours, during which I sat on a hard bench and looked out at the thick Malay jungle. The heat was oppressive and my eyes ached from the harsh glare. I bought food from vendors at the stations, but could eat little.

A warm surprise met me at Singapore. Pushing through the crowd, waving excitedly, was Xanadu, full of smiles and cheer. She threw her arms around me and kissed me—then pushed me away. Her smile was gone.

"Do you feel well?" she asked.

"Not exactly like a roaring tiger, but you try that train for two days. How did you know I was coming?"

"Al cabled me. Have you looked in a mirror lately?"

"No, what's wrong?"

"You're completely yellow, even your eyes."

I humored her about being able to fit in with the populace, and while she checked me into a little Chinese hotel, I set out for the shipping offices along the Raffles Quay. The harbor of Singapore, the busiest in Asia, was filled with ocean liners and tramp steamers waiting to load or unload their cargoes, some lying at anchor out beyond the basin, others tied up beside the huge godowns. I crossed the Anderson Bridge over the Singapore River where hundreds of sampans rested on the bank. Barefoot Chinese laborers wobbled up and down the narrow planks between the ships and the stone quay, sweating profusely in the burning sun and high humidity which have always made Singapore, for all its charms, an intolerable place to live.

All day I dragged myself through the steaming streets of the city, climbing up or down to the shipping offices, and all day I got the same story: "Sorry, we can't arrange for shipping out of Calcutta." Because of India's stringent export regulations, it would be necessary to have a special permit to ship our camper out of Calcutta, and they told me I could only get that permit by going back to Calcutta.

"Even if you do," one agent warned me, "there's no guarantee our ships will be going there. There's a war on, you know."

I solicited the help of an old friend, Keith Fatt Tan, an influential businessman, but even with his connections there was nothing that could be done.

"How long will we have to wait, Keith?" I asked.

"It's hard to say. The Indians and the Pakistanis each claim to have the other's port blockaded, and the merchants are afraid to send their ships in. All the schedules are disrupted. Even some of the American grain shipments are in danger." I noticed he was looking at me strangely. "I think you should forget about that now and see a doctor."

I thanked him and left and went to three more shipping agents and got the same story. That evening I collapsed in Xanadu's room.

Thin shafts of sunset came through the drawn window blinds, and I felt a firm hand pulling back my eyelid. Slowly the room came into focus, and I saw a man in a light suit leaning over me, English, with gray hair, a thin moustache. Behind him I dimly saw Xanadu, and beside her Keith Fatt. The doctor poked and probed and took a blood and urine sample. I was asleep before he left.

He returned the next afternoon to tell me I had yellow jaundice and hepatitis, possibly from the water in India or Pakistan, he said, maybe even from my unsterilized cholera shot in Afghanistan. Whichever, it wasn't important. What was important was that the doctor said I needed to spend two months in bed and another four months convalescing. It would be six months before I could get back on my feet. Six months!

I had Xanadu cable the news to Al in Bangkok and tell him to see a doctor since he had the same symptoms. Three days later I got a letter from Al: "If misery wants company, you've got it. I don't have any of your bugs, but I have something called *giardia lamblia*. It's very interesting. It's some kind of insidious tropical parasite that sets up house in your guts and eats up all your vitamins. It's a cute little thing, looks like a monkey under the microscope, but it sure leaves you weak. The doctor here says I won't die from it, but he can't guarantee he can get rid of it, especially since I've got such a thriving and well-established colony. He's got me on atabrine pills, and we should know in two weeks."

The Trans World Record Expedition was stranded, scattered, almost impoverished, and flat on its back. Yet we had to get back on the road. So when Xanadu told me that Keith Fatt had a possibility for a rapid cure, I listened intently, and when Keith Fatt came up with a Chinese herb doctor, I agreed to submit to anything. Our Western doctors have no treatment for yellow jaundice and hepatitis other than a long rest, and there was no time for a long rest, so I decided to gamble with the bearded old herb specialist, even though so many authorities put them down as quacks and fakers.

The Chinese herb doctors are highly respected throughout the Orient, and the one who worked on me used techniques that have been passed down for 2,500 years. They believe that all the organs of the body—heart, lungs, liver, kidneys, and so on—have vital nerves that affect their well being. These nerves lead to specific areas of the skin into which, depending on the ailment, the doctors stick surgical needles and apply heated suction cups in various manners to effectuate a cure. They used this acupuncture treatment on me, along with a dozen strange medications, so that I soon felt like a cross between a human pin cushion and a human garbage disposal. Five times a day I swallowed two dozen green objects that looked like slugs. Three times a day I swallowed one dozen large red pills that must have been vitamins. Twice a day I chewed a handful of stuff that looked and tasted like sawdust. Then there were the meals. Breakfast was a huge bowl of bitter berries, and lunch and dinner were high-protein mixtures that looked like toad bellies and shark's eyes. When I asked Xanadu what they really were she jokingly said they were fried baby mice and boiled blowfish brain. At least I think she was joking.

The most obnoxious, but also most important, part of my regimen was a two-gallon bucket of liquid that I had to consume every day. Xanadu had the Chinese cooks in the kitchen prepare it each morning, and they took unhappy turns bringing it to my room, holding the boiling pot with one hand and their noses with the other. I could smell the cook coming along the hall well before I heard him, and when Xanadu removed the lid, the odor was enough to peel the paint from the walls. Yet, miraculous as it seems, each day that I drank it, more of my normal color and strength returned.

In ten days I was back on my feet and ready to return to Bangkok. Xanadu and I had a tearful parting, and she left to belly-dance for the troops in Vietnam.

By the time I got back to Bangkok, Al was back on his feet and his *giardia lamblia* were gone, but little else had improved. The camper was still in India, Manu was still in Kashmir, and Woodrow was still hustling pills. The Indo-Pak war was still going full force, and neither side seemed willing to make a move toward peace. Nor were they even able to, for the dispute was, as are so many of the problems between foreign countries which from the distant perspective of the United States appear to be easily settled trifles, a matter on which neither side could dare concede anything, a matter of national life or death.

If Pakistan's President Ayub Khan backed down on his demands for a plebiscite in Kashmir, it would have outraged his fanatic Moslem countrymen who ever since partition have sought a union with their religious brethren in the disputed regions. The war was one Khan had not wanted, but one from which, once committed, he could not back out. He could either execute the will of the hawks in his administration, or those hawks would execute their own. He knew he could never win the war against India's superior resources, yet he had to keep on fighting. His only hope was that some powerful third country would intervene and compel a face-saving cease-fire, but the only one that had shown an inclination for intervention was Red China, and she was pouring gasoline, not water, on the flames.

The maneuvering room of India's Prime Minister Shastri was equally restricted. Belittled as a weak and ineffectual successor to Pandit Nehru, "the great Banyan tree in whose shadow nothing grew," Shastri could ill afford to halt the conflict short of a victory that would enable India to maintain her hold on Kashmir. To accede to the Pakistani demands for a plebiscite would establish a precedent that within a decade would see the utter dissolution of India as a political entity. Kashmir's importance to India lay in neither its apple orchards nor its tourist attractions, nor even in its water resources or its strategic location, but in its role as a symbol of Indian unity. If the Kashmiris were permitted to hold a plebiscite to determine whether they wanted continued union with India, or union with Pakistan, or complete independence, the floodgates would be opened, whatever the outcome. The dissatisfied people of Bihar would renew their demands for a separate state of their own. Communist leaders of Keralia could seek to sever their tenuous ties to New Delhi. The long-persecuted Sikhs in East Punjab would certainly increase their demands for an autonomous nation. So, too, would the Tamil-speaking people who resented the government's attempts to establish Hindi as the national language. All the diverse forces which had been threatening to pull India asunder would have been given free rein. Within a few years the largest democracy in Asia, and the great brown hope of the Western world for the growth and survival of democratic institutions in the unhospitable soil of the Orient, would be a mass of splinter states, each inadequately equipped and ill-prepared for self-government, each with its own policies, intrigues, distrusts, hatreds, prejudices, and potential for making war on its neighbors. Out of Kashmir could come chaos on the subcontinent. No, the war would not easily be settled, and the Trans World Record Expedition would not easily get back on the road.

Even the road we hoped to get back on was getting worse every day that October of 1965. The stepped-up war in South Vietnam had bracketed the country with bombs and engulfed it in burning napalm. It would be suicide for us to try to cross it. Cambodia, after breaking relations with the United States, seemed bent on breaking its avowed neutrality by serving as a supply line for Vietcong munitions and provisions, a staging area for raids, and a sanctuary from which the VC could conduct their war. It was still possible for American tourists to enter Cambodia, but even that might not be possible much longer because the Thais and the Cambodians had renewed their centuries-old animosity and were shooting and raiding along the frontier and threatening to close the border and halt travel. In Thailand itself, Communist guerrilla units in the guise of a liberation movement had established control in several of the northeast provinces and had resisted all Bangkok's attempts to oust them, a frightening parallel to the situation in Vietnam, and one which was to keep growing. The guerrillas had also sent units into the provinces along the Malayan border in southern Thailand, where the scope of their operations was expanding to include the killing and robbing of travelers on the road from Bangkok to Singapore. In Malaya, many of Sukarno's "Crush Malaysia" terrorists were still at large, still bombing bridges and murdering officials and attacking travelers. The situation between Malaya and Singapore was also tense and uncertain, for Singapore had been heaping criticism on the government in Kuala Lumpur and following independent policies since leaving the federation three months previously.

Perhaps worst of all was Indonesia, our stepping stone from Singapore to Australia. She was bathed in blood. The week after our evacuation from Dacca, a Communist-led revolt in Indonesia had taken the lives of six top generals and shattered Sukarno's *nasakom* (coexistence) policy. The military had assumed control, and the counter-revolution was one of the bloodiest in history, with more than 200,000 Communist Party members put to death and thousands more put in prison, throwing Indonesia into a turmoil for months. There were no bright spots, no hopeful signs, no peaceful places anywhere along our route. Every country around us was a loaded chamber in our worldwide game of Russian roulette.

But before we could get back in the game we had to extricate our car and equipment from East Pakistan, and to this end I began writing letters to our contacts in Washington and Dacca. Al booked passage on a ship for Japan where he would seek to enlist the aid of the Toyota Motor Company, the major sponsor of our expedition and one of the most powerful corporations in Japan. As an ever-growing force in Asia, Japan pulled a lot of weight with Pakistan, and Al hoped he could convince Toyota to persuade the Japanese Foreign Office to ask Pakistan to let us take our car and equipment out so we could get on with our trip. If nothing else, I thought Al would be out of the trouble zone for a while, in the one nation in Asia where everything was peaceful.

Two days after his arrival in Tokyo, Al was roughed up when he got caught in the middle of a violent riot protesting the ratification of a treaty with Korea. The riots spread to the National Diet the next day, and for a brief moment of history Japan seemed to totter on the brink of a revolution. Our jinx hadn't let us down.

Three days later I received a note from Al in Nagoya: "Situation negative. Toyota had 20 Land Cruisers of its own in Dacca. The Pak Army grabbed them all, painted them green, and sent them to the front lines. Toyota wishes us luck with ours. What do we do now?"

Chapter 18

"What Took You So Long?"

Whatever we were going to do, we weren't going to wait any longer. Six weeks had passed since our evacuation from Dacca, and the war still raged with passionate intensity. No one we approached offered any hope for either its quick solution or the recovery of our car and equipment. We'd have to help ourselves. For a start, I'd fly to Calcutta and ship the camper out to Singapore. Al would go from Japan to Hong Kong where he'd try to line up some writing assignments for us, since money was beginning to be a problem.

In Calcutta, I found the camper just where we'd left it, in the parking lot behind the Lytton Hotel. The manager had guarded it faithfully, but he told me that when the war broke out just two days after we'd left for East Pakistan, he never thought he'd see us again. The camper was in pretty bad condition from being continuously outside in the pouring monsoon rains and high temperatures. I had to cut through the rusted locks to open it, and when I finally got inside, I discovered what monsoon dampness can do. Everything was rotted or mildewed. Papers, books, notes, manuals, maps were totally ruined; a movie camera was eaten away with corrosion; souvenirs fell apart at the touch; lanterns and stoves were jammed with rust; clothing was covered with mold. The only things that survived the penetrating dampness were the ones we'd stored in the insulated ice chest; fortunately, this included much of our color film.

With the help of a crew of boys I set to work cleaning and scrubbing and polishing. In three days what was salvageable had been salvaged and the camper was livable again. On the fourth day I received my export permit and made arrangements to ship the camper to Singapore. That same afternoon, at the American Consulate, I learned that

the blockade of Pakistan ports had eased, mostly because India didn't have enough ships to maintain it, and that Chittagong in East Pakistan was open to commercial shipping. It was good news. It meant that if I could find some way to get back to Dacca and then arrange to drive the Land Cruiser from there to Chittagong, I could ship it to Singapore and continue the expedition. I had earlier in the day received a letter giving us permission to take our equipment out of East Pakistan. One of our sponsors, Trade Winds, had written to their congressman, the Honorable Melvin Laird, who had contacted the State Department, who in turn had presented our case to the Pakistanis, and they had reluctantly agreed to take our car and equipment off the list of war contraband and permit us to ship it out of the country and resume our journey.

But the difficulty was getting back to Dacca. That had not changed. India and Pakistan were still at war, and their land borders were still closed. Commercial flight service to East Pakistan was still suspended, although there were rumors that Thai International might begin flights from Bangkok to Dacca if the hostilities moderated. It was a long shot, but I cabled Woodrow back in Bangkok and told him to put my name on the waiting list in case flights did resume.

At the cable office I met two missionaries who had just slipped across the border into India from East Pakistan. They had come by way of Shillong in Assam; they told me the frontier there was only lightly guarded. If they had come by that route, then why shouldn't I also use it—to slip out of India into East Pakistan? It was a long trip, but it offered hope. I checked my maps.

Assam is a wild and uncertain country occupying a strategic area between Tibet and Red China to the north and East Pakistan to the south. She is theoretically an independent country, but India handles all her foreign affairs and defense and has heavily fortified her against attacks from China. The maps do show a road running from the capital at Shillong into East Pakistan and down to Dacca, but after inquiring at Assam House in Calcutta I learned that foreigners are not permitted to enter or cross Assam——with one exception. The exception was a visit to the game sanctuary and wildlife refuge at Kaziranga.

For the next three days I filled out forms and wrote letters detailing my lifelong desire to see the one-horned white rhino, a rare creature found only in Kaziranga and a few isolated spots around the Himalayas. On the fourth day the Indian government granted me a permit to travel north to Darjeeling by rail and from there eastward into Kaziranga in Assam.

I was hurrying through the crowded streets of Calcutta with my permit, anxious to get packed and underway, when I saw a somewhat familiar figure ahead of me. For a moment I thought it was Manu, but when I studied him more closely I was certain this could not be the Spanish gentleman I had met in Madrid eight months before. The man ahead of me was thin and muscular. His trousers and shirt were threadbare. His hair was in need of cutting. His neck and arms were deeply tanned. As I came closer and began to pass him I noticed he had several days' growth of beard. At that instant he turned. It was Manu —Manuel Angel Leguineche Bolar, Spanish gentleman turned adventurer. He recognized me at once and threw out his arms. "Señor Stephens. What you do Calcutta?" he said, embracing me like a lost brother.

"Come to find you," I joked.

"Ahah, itz been dee-ficult," he said, shaking his fingers as if he had burned them. "And you, *jefe*, what about you?"

We went to a shop, and over a cup of tea I told him briefly what had happened since we parted in Calcutta almost three months before. When I finished he sat silently, nodding his head, and then, in his much improved English, now studded with Indian words, he told his own tale of war and adventure.

A few days after the war broke out Manu had received a cable from his news agency in Spain asking him to cover the fighting in Kashmir. He was the only Spanish journalist in India at the time. He flew immediately to New Delhi, was accredited as a correspondent, and went north to Kashmir. He was among the first foreign journalists to reach the front lines. As Manu spoke, his voice became agitated and his words confused. He would wave his arms and stand up—while all eyes in the tea shop were on us—and then sit down, covered with perspiration. "They crazy, everybody crazy," he said. "I run. Indian soldiers tell me stop or he shoot. I take my press card—" he held his press card above his head—"and I say, 'Itz me. Manu. Numero 14,' and I hold my card for him to see. Many times I think maybe Manu finish."

He told me about the suffering and misery and the senseless killings, and then, in a lighter tone, he told me how he met a Spaniard on a houseboat in Kashmir. The Spaniard had rented the boat and was waiting for his American fiancée to arrive so they could be married. Incredible, but the girl arrived, and in the midst of war, in the only Catholic church in the sector, they were married. Afterwards there was a celebration in true Spanish fashion with wine and music, and even the fighting stopped for a while. An Indian officer found a guitar, and Manu played and sang beautiful Spanish love songs for the couple on their wedding night.

From New Delhi, Manu had cabled his stories to Spain, and in between trips to the front lines he had interviewed such noted personalities as Premier Shastri and Krishna Menon. When the fighting had slacked off he returned to Calcutta, and when I met him there he was on his way to Darjeeling from which he hoped to enter Sikkim to do a story for a Spanish newspaper. When I told him that I, too, was going north, we decided to journey together to Darjeeling.

Manu helped me pack the camper and turn it over to a shipping agent, and at 7:30 the next morning we boarded the *Darjeeling Mail*. At noon the following day we reached the junction at Silgohuri where Manu and I were to part company. At the station, we learned that all the trains to Assam were being used by the Indian Army, and that there would be a delay of four or five days. Manu asked me to accompany him to Darjeeling, and I agreed.

When I looked at the train that waited for us I thought it was a joke, or a reject from Disneyland. It was four incredibly small coaches pulled by an incredibly small narrow-gauge coal-burning locomotive that blasted off puffs of steam like a teakettle about to blow its lid. But it was no joke; it was the famous Himalayan Toy Train.

We squeezed into an undersized compartment as the train started off across the lowlands at a shattering 25 miles an hour, picking up speed en route. At the first hills the tracks twisted into S-curves, and the toy engine chugged and groaned and spit out steam worse than ever. For 60 miles we continued upwards, never stopping for fear of never starting again. In the villages passengers had to run after the moving train to board.

After five hours we rounded a bend and suddenly found ourselves in Darjeeling, a breathtaking town built on the summit of a hill with the rugged, snow-capped Kanchenjunga Range looming up behind it.

We quickly found the District Commissioner's office, and Manu was quickly denied permission to enter Sikkim. It was heavily militarized because of the recent threats from China, and no foreigners could enter for any reason. We were walking away from the Commissioner's office, Manu cursing and I trying to persuade him to join me in my attempt to sneak into East Pakistan from Assam, when a young Tibetan boy came up to us with a cheery smile. "Good afternoon, sirs. Would you like to ride horse?"

"No, boy, we don't have time."

"Maybe you like to see Tibet refugee center at Kalimpong."

"No, some other time."

"Maybe you like ride over mountains."

Manu stopped short. "What he say, *jefe?*"

"Master's horses very good. Take you many places. Over mountains. Sikkim. Even Tibet, but Tibet not very good now."

We asked to see the horses. The boy led us through the town to an open shed on a street called Tenzing Norkay Road where he showed us several sturdy Mongolian ponies. He pointed to a gray one and said, "Meet Tenzing." Manu and I chuckled.

"Do not laugh, for my name is Tenzing also," the boy explained. "And, sirs, if you like, I take you see Sir Tenzing."

Manu hired a horse, and the boy was good as his word, for an hour later he took us to Tenzing Norkay, the first man to climb Mount Everest.

Tenzing is the field director of the Himalayan Mountaineering Institute in Darjeeling. To the people of the region he has become a legend and a man far more honored by them than Sir Edmund Hillary has been by the West. Streets have been named after him, his photograph hangs in all the shops, and his government-built home is prominent on the tourist map of the city.

Tenzing looked like what one would expect the conqueror of Everest to look like. He is tall, especially for a Nepalese, ruggedly built, deeply tanned, and when he smiles—which is almost always—he shows strong white teeth. When we met him, he was wearing a heavy knit pull-over and a rakishly tilted beret with the Mountaineering Institute emblem pinned on one side. He spoke English without error, but he was shy and not overly talkative. When I explained Manu's problem and his desire to cross into Sikkim, Tenzing was silent. I knew he could never consent to guide him, but I had hoped that from his vast storehouse of information about the Himalayan mountains he might be able to suggest the best or safest route for Manu to take. Instead he only shook his head sadly and said he could not help him. I appreciated his delicate position and pressed him no further on the matter. I hoped Manu could rely on the knowledge of the other Tenzing, the pony boy, to get him through, but I felt too much responsibility for this jovial Spanish gentleman, and I decided that East Pakistan could wait another day and that I would see Manu safely to the border of Sikkim.

Before dawn the next day, Manu and I set out with the pony boy as our guide for the border of Sikkim. The ponies were undersized —my feet almost dragged the ground—but they had the stamina of mountain goats. Not once did they falter, no matter how hard or how high we drove them.

We stopped to watch the sunrise, which came in red and orange streaks, casting purple shadows along the entire Himalayan range. The pony boy pointed out the famous peaks, and as the sun reached it, the mighty and distant Everest turned from a shadow to an awesome pyramid of glistening ice.

We camped that night halfway to the border and, fearful that a campfire might give us away, slept in freezing cold. The next afternoon we reached the frontier with Sikkim by a mountain river. The border was heavily patrolled by the military, but our guide knew a trail that paralleled the river and cut into Sikkim farther north near Gangkok. But even there the line was thickly posted with troops, and there was no way through. We turned our ponies around and headed back to Darjeeling.

Manu still strongly wished to get his Sikkim story, and he decided to wait in Darjeeling until Delhi considered his application. We talked about the expedition, but Manu felt the outlook was dim. We had lost months, and he could not foresee our ever completing it. Besides, he said, he had become intrigued with India and wanted to stay on and continue reporting the war news and other events to the Spanish press. As he explained this, I looked at him for the last time. How he had changed since that evening we met him in the caves of Madrid. How the ivory tower thinker and man of leisure from the Basque country had changed into a doer and a seeker. How by chance, how by whim, he had joined our expedition and embarked on a venture that had altered his way of life completely—and possibly permanently. We said good-bye, our last good-bye, and I turned eastward toward Kaziranga in Assam, traveling two days by train and then several hours by bus to reach the game sanctuary.

I arrived in the afternoon, saw a comfortable government lodge, and decided to spend the night before trying to head south into East Pakistan. A reserve officer greeted me and I presented him my papers. He noticed the occupation—journalist.

"We had no idea you were coming. Someone should have notified us," he said.

"It was rather sudden," I said, hoping I could let it go at that.

"Yes, it was. We found their trail just yesterday. They are moving south, and unless we find them soon they may move into Pakistan."

"Move into Pakistan? Who will?"

"The elephants. You came because of the elephants—"

"Yes, the elephants."

"There are a few dozen, we estimate. They may turn north again but who can tell. Elephants are migratory, you know, not like rhinos or buffalo. It's difficult for us to keep track of them." He went on to tell me all about elephant habits, but I only half listened. Only one thing interested me: they were heading into Pakistan. Then I heard him say, "We'll try to pick up their trail in the morning."

That evening I was introduced to a French zoologist and his wife who were studying the wild elephants in Assam. They had been in the reserve for weeks waiting for this chance. I sat with them on the veranda, and we listened to the reserve officer and two rangers tell stories about the jungle, about an old woman who had been run down by a rhino just outside the boundary of the sanctuary three days before, about tigers devouring lone workers in the fields, about rogue elephants laying waste entire villages. As we sat there, strange animal sounds came from the forest, frightening and thrilling, sounds that penetrated into the heart of the night, and often our conversation halted between phrases as we stopped to listen. As night pressed on, people drifted off to their rooms, and one by one I could hear the heavy wooden shutters on the windows fall closed.

Three tame female elephants bearing wooden benches were waiting for us at the gate the next morning. We took off, lobbing down the hill into the sanctuary. As the first light of dawn penetrated the thick forests and marshes, heavy mist and fog lay close to the ground, and in the stillness uncertain forms took shape.

By the time the sun was fully up we were deep in the sanctuary. Wild buffalo were everywhere, and deer, some with great racks. We entered a marsh where many thick-rooted trees and giant lilies grew so densely that they covered the surface of the water and made it look as though a man could walk across with ease. But it was certainly not so, for the water beneath was six and eight feet deep in places. Yet the elephants effortlessly slushed through the mire, uprooting the lilies with their trunks. After they had firmly grasped a clump they would swing their trunks from side to side to shake off the mud from the roots before stuffing the whole mass into their mouths. The process would never end; they ate constantly.

I quickly developed a great admiration for these beasts. No other animal could have carried us through the swamps and marshes, and certainly no vehicle. I realized how futile it would have been for me to have struck out from Kaziranga toward East Pakistan on my own. Even if there weren't the marshes, the fields of tall strong grass would have made walking impossible. I was seated ten feet off the ground, and the grass towered another six feet over me, but the elephants merely pushed through, knocking down everything in their path. The noise of the breaking reeds sounded like a raging fire. And when we came near wild animals the elephants signaled us immediately. If the game was threatening, they stopped short on their own and turned to face the menace. If the danger was really great, the three elephants would sidle together and face whatever was there.

The first rhino that saw us charged my elephant at full speed, but veered off a few yards away, taking her calf with her deeper into the swamp. Other rhinos seemed accustomed to the presence of men on elephants and were less wary.

We crossed the Diphlu River shortly before noon and turned south. Water came up to the side boards and swirled past. When we reached the opposite bank I realized that our elephants were becoming uneasy. The ranger explained that the herd of wild elephants we were tracking had passed that morning and were perhaps only a short distance ahead. We continued on, moving more cautiously now. There was good feeding along the river, but the elephants had stopped eating. Suddenly, above the tops of reeds a hundred yards away, we saw the head of a great bull elephant. He was motionless. From behind him came the sound of cracking brush and reeds. He was standing guard over his herd.

We turned back toward the river in hope of coming in upwind from him, but he caught our scent and moved his herd deeper into the thicket. We turned again and followed after them, moving ever more cautiously. We had gone a hundred yards without seeing them and had reached a small clearing. Suddenly, the brush splintered and the earth trembled. I looked up to find the largest elephant I had ever seen, or ever imagined, bearing down on us. His ears were spread out like sails in the wind and his great white tusks were so long they plowed the earth before him as he charged.

I had felt reasonably safe aboard my elephant when other beasts of the jungle were about, but with a big bull charging at me I was no longer so certain. The rangers and elephant boys were almost in a panic. They were shouting and waving their iron spikes, and when that didn't work, they beat the spikes on the wooden saddles. Our elephants stepped back in a jagged line, bumping into each other, their trunks raised high, giving out shrill cries. I was in the act too, shouting and screaming. The racket we made was enough to put fright into anyone, and the bull veered and returned to the bush.

There was no more tracking that day, for the rains moved in heavily, and I was told it might be several more days before the rangers picked up the trail again. And by then the herd might be in East Pakistan, and my permits would have expired and I'd have to return to Calcutta. So after we returned to the lodge I slipped out to the road and hitched a ride on a truck going into Gauhati, the railroad terminal north of Shillong.

I reached Gauhati at ten that night and roused a clerk who told me that a train left at midnight for Shillong. I knew that if I could make it to Shillong, the capital of Assam, I would be able to slip across into East Pakistan by the same route the missionaries had used. But my papers did not authorize me to go to Shillong. They were valid for a visit to Kaziranga and nothing farther. Rather than purchase my ticket in advance, I decided to buy it on the train so that if I was stopped by the authorities I could simply say I'd gotten on the wrong train. I never got the chance. I was pretending to be asleep on a bench, trying to make myself inconspicuous until the train arrived, when a patrol of soldiers marched up to me. The officer asked for my papers and passport, and I handed them to him.

"What are you doing in Gauhati?" he asked.

"Came back from Kaziranga. On my way back."

"Back where?"

"Calcutta."

"Then why did you ask about the train schedule to Shillong?" The information clerk had reported me. "Just curious," I said.

"You had better come with me," he said.

In the morning I was escorted by armed guard and put aboard the westbound express to Silgohuri. Two days later I was back in Calcutta.

In Calcutta I learned that Thai International had begun air service from Bangkok to Dacca. I caught the next plane back to Bangkok and went directly to the Thai International office. But Woodrow had not made reservations for me. There was a month's waiting list.

I was sitting in the Bamboo Lounge at the Oriental Hotel, contemplating my next move over a beer and listening to a pretty Australian singer, when an Englishman sitting on the stool next to me said, "Great town, this Bangkok." I wasn't in the mood for any conversation about how nice it was to be in Bangkok. "You live here?" he asked, not taking the hint.

"Yeah," I answered, thinking of the irony of it.

"Is there any action around here?" he continued. "I'm flying on to Dacca in the morning, but I hear this town has everything, and I'd like to get some of it before I go."

Dacca, I thought, and bought him a drink. At midnight we went to the Starlight, a bar which is stocked with more than a hundred of Thailand's prettiest and most accommodating hostesses. "Whatever you do," I said when I left him sitting with a particularly accommodating one to whom I'd slipped a 100 *baht* note and some special instructions, "go to the Playboy. You have never seen Bangkok until you see the Playboy." The Playboy is an all-night dive on New Road.

The next morning I was at the airport. There was one vacant seat. At noon our flight landed in Dacca. I was back, after three months. I checked with the American Consulate and found our Land Cruiser. It lay under a thick cover of dirt and grime, after months of idleness, but that was no matter. What was important was that it was there, and that it ran, and that nothing now could stop the expedition. I spent several hours cleaning and servicing it, filled the tank and spare cans, and then drove to the USIS to gather the rest of our equipment. Early the next morning I left Dacca for Chittagong. No one knew for certain if the road was open yet. There was only one way to find out: try it.

I arrived at the first ferry landing and held my breath. I handed the guard my passport, car documents, and the four-month old letter from the Tourist Minister. The guard checked the papers, handed them back, and waved me on. For the first time in many months I sang. I sang out loud.

There were three ferries in all, with army guards at each. At the second ferry, the guards motioned me past without checking papers, but at the last ferry, a guard threw up his hand and stopped me. He sauntered over to the Land Cruiser, looked it up and down for a minute, and leaned halfway into the window. He asked if I had a cigarette. I gave him the pack and drove onto the ferry.

A few cargo boats with triangular sails moved slowly up the main rivers, but most of the smaller waterways and canals were dry, and the jute fields were bare. The monsoons had passed.

The road from the ferry landing ran east to Comilia and then turned south and followed close beside a railroad track. My map showed they ran parallel to the Assam border and less than a hundred yards from it. After a few miles I saw a slow-moving freight train that was heading the same way I was. Bit by bit I began to gain on it. Suddenly it stopped. The engineer and two firemen leaped down from the locomotive and ran into the field between the tracks and road. They reached a shallow ditch and dove in. From a thick forest inside Assam, Indian guns had opened fire on the train. I drove the Land Cruiser off the road into the ditch, grabbed my pistol from under the seat, and took cover. A few minutes later a platoon of Pakistan soldiers came racing down the road. They were dressed in white T-shirts and canvas hats and carried automatic rifles. After they had passed there was more shooting, but it grew distant. In twenty minutes it was over, and again I was headed south.

The next morning I located the port of Chittagong and began negotiations to have the Land Cruiser and equipment shipped to Singapore. To make certain that they would sail aboard the first available ship, I took the papers through customs myself. I expected the process would be complicated, so each time I had to go to a different shipping office or government bureau I made a mark in my notebook. When I had completed the processing and had the papers finally stamped it was three days later. I counted 27 marks in my book.

None of the freighters leaving Chittagong carried passengers, so I took the train back to Dacca and there caught the next Thai International flight to Bangkok. It had been one month to the day since I had first left Bangkok to rescue our equipment. In that month I had flown to Calcutta, found Manu, traveled to Darjeeling by train and met Tenzing, ridden through the Himalayas on horseback to the border of Sikkim, been forced back, crossed Assam by train and bus to Kaziranga, been nearly run down by a bull elephant in heat, been forced to retrace my route, had flown back to Bangkok, flown from Bangkok to Dacca, picked up the equipment, driven south to Chittagong via three ferries and a road that was under Indian fire, taken a train back to Dacca, and flown back to Bangkok. I cabled Al in Hong Kong to pick up the stuff in Singapore. He cabled back,

WHAT TOOK YOU SO LONG?

Chapter 19
Kung Hei Fat Choy

New Year's Eve.

In New York, the great Times Square neon globe was hurtling down on the old year as thousands cheered . . .

Should auld acquaintance be forgot . . .

In Paris, snow lay thick on the dark camp ground of the Bois de Boulogne . . .

And never brought to mind . . .

In London, three pretty nurses recalled their adventures in Africa and raised a sherry toast to departing 1965 . . .

Should auld acquaintance be forgot . . .

In Andorra, on a snow-closed mountain road, the lights gleamed faintly in a little restaurant, and it was business as usual in a tool shed nearby . . .

In days of auld lang syne. . . .

In Madrid Viejo, the cave of Luis Candela rang with wild flamenco guitars and spirited *buleria* as the good red wine gushed from the high-held *botas* . . .

For auld lang syne, my dear . . .

In Jerez de la Frontera, Blackie McManus invited a dozen friends to his house for a party and ran out of ice before 10:00 and bourbon before midnight . . .

For auld lang syne . . .

In Gibraltar, the Rock resounded with defiant British voices raised so loud in song they carried to the Spanish border post at La Linea . . .

Let's drink a cup of kindness yet, For auld lang syne.

How far away and long ago those friends and cities seemed.

In Singapore, Al worked through the night and into the morning getting the Land Cruiser into shape for the run north, and then celebrated by joining Mr. Oii Pen Sung and his family for a bowl of pig's brain soup.

In Bangkok, I was falling in love with a girl named Joyce.

When my Bangkok cable had reached Al in Hong Kong, he had immediately caught a *Messageries Maritimes* ship for Singapore. But when he arrived in Singapore it was the Christmas holidays, and he had to wait three days for the shipping offices to open. He then had to spend another four days filling out complicated forms and documents to get our car and camper released, and another day and night tuning up the Land Cruiser and getting some water condensate out of its gas line. By New Year's Day everything was ready.

New Year's Day was 282 days after we'd first sailed from New York —and 40 days after we were due back there. And we still had half the world to cross.

The war between India and Pakistan had completely ruined our schedule which called for us to drive through East Pakistan, Burma, Thailand, and Malaya to Singapore. It had stranded us in East Pakistan and then dumped us in Singapore. In order to follow that schedule and achieve our goal of driving around the world wherever there was land on which to drive, we now had to make a 6,000 mile rough-road round-trip from Singapore all the way to Burma and back. On New Year's Day Al left Singapore to pick me up in Bangkok for the run to Burma. The Trans World Record Expedition was back on the road.

Al's trip to Bangkok was, all things considered, a fairly routine run of 1,500 mostly muddy rainy-season miles which took five days. On the first day he met a big-chested brunette hitchhiker at the Sikh temple in Kuala Lumpur, an Australian actress named Carla Christofoletti; on the second day they got chased by a small band of Communist guerrillas just inside the Thai border; on the third day Al fell off an elephant while showing off to Carla; on the fourth day he got chased by a shark when he and Carla went for a swim off the Beach of Passionate Love on the Gulf of Siam; and on the fifth day, he arrived in Bangkok with Carla, looking weary but happy. It was all, as I've said, and knowing Al, a fairly routine trip.

Bangkok had been my operating base since our evacuation, and one could hardly have asked for a more delightful city. It's a wild, sprawling, modern, ancient, frantic, exciting, glowing, happy city. It is, on the one hand, a beautiful Oriental city with *sampan*-filled *klongs;* huge Buddhist temples whose walls are covered with multicolored ceramics and whose roofs are sheathed with gold and atop which are beautiful bronze bells which tinkle in the breeze; a teeming Chinese section that throbs with life; and a unique floating market to which farmers from all the nearby villages pole their flat-bottomed boats loaded with strange fruits and squawking chickens. It is, on its other hand, a modern metropolis of some three million energetic Thais, a prosperous city adorned with broad boulevards, luxurious hotels, spacious parks, tall buildings, and traffic jams.

Partly because they have never been ruled by a foreign power or conquered in a war (Thailand means "land of the free"), and partly because of their Buddhist beliefs, the Thais are a carefree, fun-loving people. They believe that if something is pleasurable, it is also good; and they reason that since love is highly pleasurable, it must be very good, something created by their happy gods for their enjoyment. In Thailand, the only sin for a man is not to know how to enjoy life, and the only sin for a woman is not to know how to help her man enjoy it.

It is perhaps not surprising that under this influence, I surrendered to that most intoxicating of human emotions. The girl was an Australian singer and her name was Joyce. She was a blue-eyed, fair-skinned blonde, a warm and beautiful woman.

Our first meeting had been casual, back in October, after Al and I had just been evacuated from East Pakistan. It was only an introduction then, but after I returned from Singapore our romance began. She was singing at the Bamboo Room of the Oriental Hotel, billed as "The Down Under Girl with the Come On Over Voice," and I invited her for a drink after one of her shows. She accepted, and we enjoyed ourselves, and I asked if I could see her again. She suggested we have lunch at the hotel pool the next afternoon. It was a pleasant afternoon, and then came another, and another. Then there were dinners on the roof garden overlooking the lovely Chao Phraya River, afternoon strolls through the fairytale atmosphere of the golden temples, Sunday picnics on river boats gliding through the *klongs*, and retreats to beach resorts on the coast. There were many things—the smell of perfume, the sound of a soft voice, a hand that held mine when we talked.

Joyce and I decided to get married.

"Married? You can't get married," Al exclaimed when I told him. We were driving north from Bangkok toward the Burma border. "That's an institution for other people. You're not marriage material. You must be kidding."

I paused before answering. I looked for a moment out of the car windows at the dense jungles and the thick forests of teak, past the endless water-covered fields of rice on which the sun glimmered between the green shoots. "Joyce and I have it all arranged," I said. "We're going to be married when you and I get back to Singapore from Burma. It's too bad you didn't get to meet her, but she's singing in Penang for two weeks. You'll like her when you meet her, Al."

"How can I like someone who's crazy? Doesn't this girl realize that you're a roamer, a dreamer, a wanderer? You're the wild goose, man, footloose and fancy free. You're an adventurer. You're not a husband."

"That's what I've always thought, Al, but I'm serious this time. And anyway, isn't marriage a kind of exciting adventure?"

"Maybe for some people, but it's not your scene. How can you settle down to one woman and one place for the rest of your life? You change women like other men change their sheets, and you move from country to country like The Man from UNCLE. How can you get married?"

"I'm in love."

Also, I explained to Al, Joyce was an exceptional woman, a remarkable woman who understood my wandering soul and was willing to follow it wherever it led. In fact, one of the things that first drew her to me was my adventurous spirit.

"She's one in a billion if what you say is true," Al answered. "But where does that leave the expedition?"

"Just where it's always been," I said. I explained that Joyce realized how important it was for us to finish the expedition and had agreed that after we were married she would remain in Singapore until the expedition was over and I came back for her.

Al and I remained lost in private thoughts for the rest of the day. Two days later we reached the Burmese border.

The border was a river, the Mae Nam, broad and deep and rushing in the height of the northeast monsoon. It was spanned by a sturdy concrete bridge on the south end of which a Thai border guard explained to us that no automobiles and no foreigners were allowed into Burma. We in turn explained our mission and our need to cross Burma. He explained again; we explained again. He shook his head slowly, in resignation, and raised the barrier leading to the bridge. He wished us luck. As I glanced back I noticed that he hadn't lowered the barrier; he seemed certain we'd be sent right back.

The bridge was a busy microcosm of the country we were attempting to enter, teeming with Burmese trudging into Thailand to barter with handicrafts and vegetables. Most interesting were seven Indian girls from a remote tribe, dressed in black shorts and black jackets with purple decorations. They had obviously never seen an Occidental or an automobile before, and looked as frightened as if Al and I were extra-terrestials emerging from a flying saucer. When we tried to take their pictures, they took flight in terror, dropping their vegetables on the bridge; one of them climbed over the railing and seemed about to leap off until we put the cameras back in the car.

As we did, two men from the Naga tribe came by, heading back to their village in the hills after a shopping trip in Thailand. On their right shoulders they supported a long pole on which four dogs were hanging upside down, their feet tied together. They were scrawny mongrels, no more than eight pounds apiece, with less meat on their bones than a good chicken, but a delicacy to the Nagas. Another tribesman trudged behind the pair carrying six little puppies crammed into a wicker basket slung over his back.

There were women on the bridge also, beautiful brown-skinned girls with innocent eyes, their breasts barely covered by the sheerest of veils, a concession to the Thais who decreed a few years back that women could no longer go about the countryside bare-chested.

As we neared the border post, four shaven-headed Buddhist priests came toward us in single file, wearing brilliant saffron robes and leather sandals and carrying black umbrellas against the tropical sun. They were friendly, as were all the Buddhist priests we met in Asia, and stopped to talk to us; but since their English was limited to the word "Good-bye" and our Burmese to the phrase *"Yangon ko bel lan ga thwar ya tha le?"* ("Which way is Rangoon?") we were prevented from discussing the merits of their Himayanama branch of Buddhism compared to the Manayahana.

The officers at the Burmese border post, on the other hand, spoke perfect English, but a discussion of the Buddhist sects was the farthest thing from their minds.

"No one can drive into Burma," one of the guards said as he stopped us.

"You must return to Thailand," another declared as he pointed back the way we'd come.

We showed them our passports which contained visas for Burma, visas we had gotten the only way it was possible for anyone to get them, by buying plane tickets on a flight from Bangkok to Calcutta via Rangoon and then presenting these to the Burmese Embassy as proof that we required visas, and then cashing in the tickets after we got the visas.

"These visas are not valid here," the first guard snapped.

"No one can cross Burma by land," the second added.

"These are good only for Rangoon," the first continued.

"And only for 24 hours," a third threw in.

Pretending innocence about the Burmese border regulations and the inapplicability of our visas—which were rather clearly stamped "Stay Restricted to 24 Hours Only" and "Land Route Not Permissible"—we explained that we had decided at the last minute to drive to Rangoon rather than fly, and that if we had to do it in 24 hours we would. But the guards refused, pointing out that no tourists in Burma were ever allowed outside of Rangoon, that it was impossible to cross the country in less than ten days, that any foreigner who stayed in Burma more than 24 hours was immediately arrested, and that, in any case and all over again, no one was allowed to drive into Burma for any reason.

With a flourish, Al whipped out the letter from the American
Museum of Natural History authorizing him to collect Burmese termites. The guards were perplexed; this was a new one. After a lengthy
debate among themselves, one of the guards beckoned Al to follow
him, and they disappeared down the road and into Burma, evidently
going to pass the request on to the chief. I kept my fingers crossed,
realizing that Operation Termite had put us on the brink of doing what
nobody had been able to do in years.

In fifteen minutes the officer and Al were back, and I quickly pulled
Al aside and asked if he'd been able to get us special permission to
enter.

"Special permission, hell," he answered. "The guy took me over to
a dead tree in the woods with a lot of cow dung around it and
told me I could dig up all the termites I wanted."

The Thai border guard had a wave and a smile waiting for us as we
came back over the bridge.

On the way back from Burma to Bangkok we got detoured onto a
back road between Chungrai and Chungmai, Thailand's second largest
city. It turned out to be the roughest short stretch of our entire expedition, a dirt track hemmed in by thick jungles and roofed over with a
tight canopy of branches and leaves. The road must have been laid out
by a roller coaster designer, for every thirty yards or so it would dip
down ten feet and then zoom up twenty until our car felt like a cork
being tossed by a heavy sea. The dust we threw up was choking and
blinding, and the thick jungle so blocked the sun that by late afternoon
we had to drive with our lights. In six hours we made nineteen miles,
our slowest traveling of the trip.

There were small villages every few miles along the dirt road, and
their inhabitants came running out to stare in wonder at what was
possibly the first automobile and probably the first white-skinned foreigners they had ever seen. The small villages of Thailand, like those
throughout Southeast Asia, are far more cut off from the big cities and
central governments than those anywhere else in the world because of
the dense jungles, poor roads, non-navigable rivers, monsoon climate,
and—until recently—lack of interest on the part of the central government, secure in its comfortable capital. This isolation, this lack of

association and identification with the central government, is one of the main reasons why Communist rebel groups like the Vietcong and the Thai Patriotic Front have been able to make so much headway in these areas. The rebel groups show an interest in the villages that the central government has never shown and promise the villagers things the central government has never dreamed of offering.

The next morning, after a leisurely breakfast with some friendly villagers, we set out for Chungmai, again on the roller coaster of a road, again averaging no better than three or four miles an hour, barely passing the few cow-drawn carts which constituted the road's principal traffic.

It was late evening before we reached Chungmai. It had taken us two days to travel 40 miles. We were so famished that when we got to a small restaurant we held a steak-eating contest, with the loser picking up the tab. Al ate four steaks. I managed five. Al tried to pay with his Diner's Club card. It didn't work.

When we returned to Bangkok, en route to Singapore, we went to get Woodrow, but, as we had feared, he was no longer interested in conquering the world, no longer interested in the rough grind of the open road. He'd gotten a proofreader's job on a local English-language newspaper, and there he preferred to remain. Only Al and I were left of the five who had started. I phoned Joyce in Penang to tell her we were on our way to Singapore. Then Al and I climbed into the Land Cruiser for the run down the Malay Peninsula.

It took us five days to make the trip, along mud roads and through dense Thai forests where elephants hauled logs; past Buddhist shrines carved into the sides of hills; through mountain jungles so dense that any car that went off the road would be lost for years; past the range of purple mountains off to the right that marked the eastern boundary of Burma; then into Malaya along paved highways; past endless plantations of evenly spaced rubber trees, many being tapped, their sheets of white rubber hung on poles along the road to dry; past the great open-pit tin mines that scarred the jungle.

The trip was a quiet one until the last day, when we picked up two Indian students hitchhiking from Kuala Lumpur to Singapore. They spent the first three hours of the ride loudly bemoaning the wretched fate of the Indians in Malaya, criticizing first the native Malays, who are Moslem and who discriminate strongly against the Hindu Indians who were brought to their country by the British 50 years before to work on the rubber plantations, and then criticizing the Chinese, who were brought there for the same purpose but who endured and multiplied and prospered so much more than the Indians that they now comprise 43 per cent of the population of their adopted country and own or control almost every major industry and business in it.

Then, for the next endless hours, until we reached Singapore, the students bombarded us with arguments about the United States—about capitalism, spiritualism, divorce, Vietnam, suicide, race riots, drugs, LSD. For example:

Students: You have the highest divorce rate in the world.

Us: Divorce is not a sin. In a democracy, freedom of choice is the most important thing, the essence of the society, and divorce is a form of freedom of choice, a means of rectifying a previous choice if it turns out to be wrong, of freeing the individual to make a new choice that may lead to his greater happiness.

Students: We believe that once people are married they must remain married.

Us: And we believe that it is wrong to compel them to remain married if they are both unhappy. The ideal of democracy is to enable every man and woman to develop to the full limit of their abilities, and if a bad marriage prevents them from doing so, then it is best it is ended.

Students: If your people are so happy in America, then why do so many of them commit suicide? Why do you have so many crazy people, people in mental hospitals, people going to psychiatrists? It is because you are not a spiritual people, is it not?

Us: What you say has some truth. But understand the reasons. In other countries—in dictatorships, where there is no choice, or very poor countries, where there is no opportunity—people tend to expect less of life and are not as disturbed as many of our countrymen who expect so much. We have the freedom and the opportunity to do anything we want with our lives, and this places a great strain on many of our countrymen.

Students: Does that also explain why so many Americans take drugs? And why you have so many young people on LSD? And all your women on tranquilizers. Is it not better to be spiritual and . . .

By the time we got to Singapore and got rid of our hitchhikers, I had a roaring headache and wouldn't have minded a Miltown myself.

In Singapore we learned that it was still impossible to drive across Indonesia; she was still wracked by the aftermath of the attempted revolution of September 30, and would be for months. The army leaders and Sukarno were still struggling for control. The Communist Party was being broken up and its leading members killed or imprisoned. Overseas Chinese throughout the islands were being rounded up and put in special compounds. And mass murder was still the order of the day, with upwards of 300,000 people reportedly slaughtered. All our applications for permission to drive across were unconditionally rejected. It was a blow to our hopes to drive the land bridge from Asia to Australia, but given the conditions, there was nothing we could do about it other than lament, just as there was nothing we could do about Sinai or Burma or the many other places where politics played havoc with our plans.

We'd have to ship directly on to Australia, and even that was more easily decided than done. Because of Australia's large assisted immigration program, thousands of families from all over the world were migrating to the Land Down Under, and shipping facilities out of Singapore were booked to capacity. We would have to wait three months to get our car and camper and ourselves aboard a ship bound for Sydney. But, again, there was nothing else to do, unless we skipped Australia, and if we did that we'd lose all chance of setting our record. We booked passage on a ship sailing in April.

Then came our toughest problem: the lack of funds. The lengthy delays and the unexpected expense of retrieving our equipment from the war zone had consumed almost all the money we'd set out with. Al had just gotten us two magazine story assignments in Hong Kong, but other than that there was no other income. If we were to finish our trip, and get our car and camper the rest of the way around the world, one of us would have to return to New York to raise the money. There was no other way, sad as it was. Since I was familiar with the driving conditions in Australia, and since Al was familiar with the financial conditions in New York, we both knew who would have to go. Al assured me he'd somehow manage to raise the money from our sponsors or his publishing contacts, and that he'd rejoin me in Panama after I'd completed the Australian leg of the trip. In the meantime we'd both have to go to Hong Kong to work on the magazine assignments.

I phoned Joyce in Penang to tell her about the change in plans. I told her to meet us in Hong Kong when she finished her singing engagement and that we'd be married there instead of in Singapore.

Her voice broke over the phone: "Steve, I've missed you so very much. I don't want us to be separated ever again. I will come to Hong Kong to marry you, but you must promise me you won't leave me to continue this trip."

I tried to explain that I couldn't make that choice, but Joyce insisted. It was all or nothing. I had to choose between her and the expedition. I didn't know if I'd be able to keep my promise—but I promised.

Al and I caught the next plane to Hong Kong, but I couldn't bring myself to tell him what I'd promised Joyce. How could I tell him that the expedition was over? Maybe later.

In Hong Kong we went right to work on our magazine assignments. I did the one on the magic and mysteries of Oriental medicine, not because I was an expert, but because I was living proof that it worked. Al did the other, on the beauty secrets of Oriental women, not because he was an expert, but because he'd convinced the editors that he was.

After spending five dull days with smelly Chinese apothecaries discussing the therapeutic properties of frog intestines and the formula for Tiger Balm ointment—while Al spent his five days "interviewing" and "researching" the prettiest girls in Hong Kong—the cable that Joyce was arriving the next day made me singing happy. Al says I must have set some sort of a speed record as I drove us to the airport the next morning.

Joyce was even more beautiful and desirable than I remembered, and I immediately forgot all the dark confusions that had been plaguing me since I'd spoken to her from Singapore. The next morning we went to the American Consul to arrange the wedding.

When that was set, I went over to Al's room at the International Guest House to tell him I was getting married and would have to give up the expedition. I didn't know how to break it to him, so I began indirectly: "You know, Al, we were prepared to face just about everything on this trip. Snow storms. Disease. Deserts. And we overcame them all. Even survived a war. But there's one thing we never considered having to deal with, one thing there's no way to overcome, and that was one of us falling in love."

Al looked at me in astonishment for a minute that seemed forever. I had no idea what he was thinking. Then a smile came to his face. "But she's a great girl," he said.

I relaxed. He understood. "A great girl," I repeated. But I was still not sure he was prepared for what I had to tell him.

"She's wonderful. Truly wonderful," he went on. "She's beautiful, sweet, intelligent, affectionate, witty, understanding, and absolutely overpoweringly delightful."

I couldn't decide if he'd really discerned so much in that short a meeting with Joyce, or if he was pulling my leg. "Al, this is serious, now."

"I've never been more serious in my life. She's positively the finest girl I've ever met."

"I hope you realize that I'm talking about something far more than a mere romance."

"You mean marriage? Well, I don't know about marriage."

"And why not marriage?" I stormed back, prepared to defend my decision.

"For one thing it's the children. The States could be rough on them. And how would a Chinese girl fit in on Madison Avenue?"

"What?"

"She's so sensitive about things like that, and she's never been out of Hong Kong. I just don't know what to do."

I'd come to tell Al about Joyce, and instead he was telling me about Pamela Choy, an adorable Hong Kong girl he'd first met on his way back from Japan several months earlier. He'd mentioned her many times since, and I knew he wrote to her often when we were in Thailand, but I never thought it had gone so far and that Al, as I, had fallen in love.

Pamela was one of the most delightful girls I've ever met. She was wholly unique. When Al first introduced me to her she was chewing on watermelon seeds, nibbling away, to use Al's phrase, "like a beautiful little chipmunk." Under her arm she was carrying a book of philosophy by Bertrand Russell and another by Sartre. And she understood them. She was a joy and a delight. When she walked through the streets of Hong Kong, she half ran and half skipped, dragging her "darling Albert" by the hand behind her. Then she'd let go of his hand and run and hide in a building and jokingly tell a passerby she was being followed by a man with a big nose. Other times, as we were walking along, she might stop suddenly and, holding her thumb up at arm's length, view a distant building or temple with her head cocked to one side, like an artist studying a subject to be painted. Or she'd impulsively charge into a shop and come out with a bag of tasty Chinese delicacies for everyone to sample. Yet when she dressed up to go out with us in the evening, she was as genteel and poised as any woman could ever be. Such was the wonderful little Chinese girl with whom Al had fallen in love.

"What are you going to do?" I asked.

"Maybe we will get married, but not now. I explained to Pamela that the expedition comes first, and that if I don't raise the money there isn't any expedition. I couldn't let you down like that, Steve. By the way, what was it you were going to tell me before?"

"Nothing important."

Later that afternoon I told Joyce that, despite my promise, I had to continue with the expedition after we were married.

"How can you think of continuing this silly trip and in the same breath say you want to marry me?" she cried. "If you really loved me you'd forget this ridiculous expedition. What's so important about going around the world? How can you treat love so lightly?"

I didn't want to hurt her, but I had to tell the truth. She began crying. I tried desperately to explain, tried to make her realize that after all I'd gone through to keep the trip alive, after all the difficulties I'd overcome, that I couldn't possibly abandon it now, not even for love. I confessed to her that love was an obstacle I had not reckoned with and that until the trip was finished, I'd have to regard it as an obstacle if she insisted on making it such.

When her tears were dry, she agreed to marry me at the end of the week, as we'd planned, agreed that our love was indeed wonderful and rare and that she would not let it become an obstacle to the completion of my trip, agreed that, come April, she'd see me back on the road and wish me Godspeed for as long as it took me to finish. I loved her even more than before, if that were possible.

Two nights later, the night before Al was to fly back to the States, Pamela took us out to dinner in honor of our engagement. Pamela was subdued, and she told us why. She had tried to persuade Al to stay in Hong Kong a little longer so they could decide about their future, but he had told her he had to get back to New York to raise money so we could finish the trip.

"Why does Albert"—no one but Pamela ever called him Albert— "Why does he have to go? What is so important about this expedition?"

Why was a trip around the world more important than love? Joyce couldn't answer her question, and I couldn't even attempt to.

Pamela took us to an Oriental gourmet restaurant in the Wanchai district of Hong Kong where a stone-faced waiter seated us around a circular table that had a small round hole in the center. Pamela had promised us a dinner that would be long remembered, and it will be. The courses were varied, but all delicious. There was a steaming hot, tangy bird's nest soup; a bitter-sweet jelly made of shark's fins; succulent Beggar's Chicken; and exotic greens served baking hot in earthenware pots.

Near the conclusion of the meal the waiter brought out a live monkey in a basket. The monkey was still jabbering away happily as the waiter slipped him under the table and brought his head up through the hole in the center. Then, with a practiced chop of the cleaver, he cut off the top of the monkey's head, flipping it over to expose the brain, gray and moist and still pulsating inside. With Pamela demonstrating the proper technique for scooping out pieces of brain with a demitasse spoon and exhorting us to eat while it was still warm, we hesitantly complied. It was, as I said, a dinner we will not soon forget.

Since Al had to leave the next day and would miss the wedding, he had presents for us both. To Joyce he gave a beautiful gold watch with our wedding date engraved on the back. For me he had something special. That afternoon, he explained, while passing a Chinese shop, he'd seen the perfect gift for me—a big brown dog. I argued that I really didn't need a dog and that it would only cause problems, but Al persisted, explaining that the dog would take his place on the Australian part of the trip, and be a good companion for me, and stand guard over the equipment while I slept. He made it sound so good I began to wonder why I hadn't taken a dog in the first place and left Al home. In any case, I decided to humor him and told him I'd be glad to accept, realizing that I could always give the dog back to the shop after he left. When I gave my consent, Al telephoned the shop. "They'll hold him for us," he said. "I told them we'd be right over."

The shop was on a small alley off Tin Hua Temple Road. We waited outside as Al rushed into a little shop that had several dogs in the window and some Chinese lettering above the door. Pamela looked stunned. And so did Al, when he came out, carrying the dog he'd bought me, all neatly wrapped in a brown paper bag. The shop specialized in dog meat.

Al and Pamela stayed on the Victoria side of the city to share their last hours together before the morning plane came to wing him back to the States. Joyce and I left them to catch the late ferry back to our hotel on the Kowloon side.

The trouble began, perhaps, when I bought a second-class ticket. There are two classes on the Hong Kong ferries: the first class for tourists and businessmen, behind glass windows, which costs ten Hong Kong cents; the second, for peasants and workers, on an open deck, which costs five Hong Kong cents. The difference is an American penny, one U.S. cent, hardly economic justification for choosing second class; but I always preferred it because it seemed to me much more like the real world with real people. On the open deck that let the wind blow by I could feel Hong Kong to the very tips of my soul. I bought two second-class tickets without asking Joyce.

As the ship churned out of the Star Ferry Pier I felt the strong sea wind, damp with salt, blow cool across my brow. There was a junk beating up the channel, working hard on starboard tack, her broad wooden sails straining, and I saw a sailor, sure-footed on its bow, standing tall against the wind. I turned to Joyce and told her of my love for her and my desire to make her happy, my desire to share with her the world I had come to know so well and love so much.

"Joyce," I said, "after the expedition is over, I'm going to take you to Tahiti to live. We can spend a year there. Our honeymoon on Tahiti. I have always loved Tahiti, and you will, too, just wait. I want to show you the beauty of the islands, of all the South Seas. And then I want to take you to Spain, to Jerez, for the spring *feria*, and you'll meet Blackie and my bullfighting friends, and they'll love you as much as I do. And then, Joyce, then there are other places I want to show you. I want to go back to Colombia in South America for a year and we can spend the winter in Mexico City. And later, Paris. I like Paris in the winter. We can spend the winter in Paris, when we practically have the whole city to ourselves."

The ferry was halfway across now, heading for the Kowloon side, its lights twinkling like diamonds in the long beautiful necklace of Hong Kong harbor. Then Joyce asked, "But aren't we going to settle down and have a home, like other people? I thought maybe we could go to live in Sydney, near my family."

"Of course, darling, but not now. Later."

"When is later?" she asked, shivering slightly against the wind and looking off into the distance as a blast from the ferry horn cut deep into the wet night.

"After we've seen all there is to see and done all there is to do," I answered. "There's time for settling down, but first let me show you the world."

The ferry was almost at the pier, and the passengers were adjusting their bundles and moving toward the gangplank when Joyce turned to me. There were tears in her eyes as she kissed me softly and said, "Steve, Steve, my darling, I cannot marry you—because you're already married. You're married to an ideal, a dream—the world. If it were only another woman I wouldn't feel so badly because then I could take the competition. I can't compete with your world. But I'll always love you."

The next day Joyce left me in Hong Kong and flew off to sing for the troops in Vietnam. And sometime later, when I was down in Australia, I learned that while she was asleep in her hotel room in Danang, a Vietcong bomb exploded and the building collapsed.

Chapter 20
The Honeymoon Expedition

Few places are as empty and isolated as the center of Australia. Or as strange. The first man came a hundred years ago, to build a telegraph station. He settled on a dried river bed and named the settlement after the water hole—Alice Springs. The settlement had since grown to a town of 2,000, but it still remains a pioneer's town, an isolated outpost of the 20th century, surrounded by a land that remains in the Stone Age.

From the top of Anzac Hill I stood gazing out over the sprawling town. Alice Springs today is a distribution center. She stands at the terminus of the railroad line from Adelaide in the south, and at the beginning of a paved road that leads to the port of Darwin in the north. The buildings are all one- and two-story, neatly set off in square blocks. There are a few hotels and restaurants, a cinema, even a museum, and half a dozen pubs. There is little else, but for the people who live in the Northern Territory, many of whom can come to town only once a year, Alice Springs is everything.

To reach Alice I had driven north from Adelaide for a thousand miles along the eastern fringe of the Great Victoria Desert, and now my route was to carry me due west, across 1,200 miles of barren land called the Outback. And again people told me, as they had so often, "Impossible, it can't be done." As I stood on Anzac Hill, staring off into the west, I wondered if they might not be right this time, for as far as I could see, there was nothing but empty red earth.

Ten days before, I had unloaded the Land Cruiser in Sydney. Our original plan had been to unload in Perth on the west coast and drive eastward across the continent to Sydney, and from there ship across the Pacific to Panama. But the shipping difficulties in Singapore forced me to do exactly the opposite, so that now I was driving across Australia from east to west and would have to ship to Panama from Perth instead of from Sydney. That last leg, of course, depended on whether Al could raise the shipping money in New York. He'd raised enough from our sponsors to get me and the equipment down to Australia, and now he was negotiating for the rest from publishers who were interested in our story.

But regardless of direction or financial worries the whole continent of Australia faced me, a land as large as the United States, with fewer inhabitants than New York. And what is so amazing about Australia is that even the Australians don't know what they have, especially in the Outback, a wide open space where some ranches—called stations—are as large as the state of Rhode Island. In Sydney many tried to discourage me from making the trip. None of them had been in the Outback, but they spoke of trackless wastes with no water, of droughts that lasted seven years, of unfriendly aborigines, of experienced bushmen perishing on the deserts, never to be seen or heard of again. I knew that many of the stories were true, and that the Outback was wild and untamed, but I still felt there was no reason it couldn't be crossed.

Every adventure involves a certain risk or it wouldn't be a true adventure, and this certainly applied to crossing the Outback, but I couldn't regard it as any more risky or difficult than what we'd been through in the past fourteen months. I now had the added experience of having crossed four of the world's greatest deserts, and I was confident that the Land Cruiser and I could make it. The only difference now was that I was alone, and carried only the minimum essentials: Poptent, cameras, hunting equipment, sleeping bag, food chest, and ten jerry cans for fuel and water.

My first stop after leaving Sydney was Melbourne, and there something unexpected took place that changed my plans. Living in Melbourne were two old friends I wanted to visit, Nick and Ray, inseparable pals who had grown up in the Australian surf. In time, when they'd mastered the surf, they'd become lifeguards, those world-famed Aussies who swim through the breakers with a lifeline tied to their waists or crash through 40-foot waves in surf boats to rescue helpless swimmers.

I had met them for the first time five years before, in Tahiti, where they were looking for the perfect wave. They never found it, but Nick did find Leonie, a pretty Tahitian girl who was then one of the leading ladies in *Mutiny on the Bounty*. They fell hopelessly in love. It was one of those storybook romances, but unlike other South Sea affairs of its kind, it had a happy ending: Nick and Leonie got married, and they went to live in Melbourne.

After Nick and Leonie settled down to family life in Australia, Ray and I had roamed the South Pacific in a 47-foot schooner. But after I left the Pacific I didn't see him again until I arrived in Melbourne. It was an exciting reunion. He had recently returned from a sailing cruise around the world. While in San Francisco he had met a beautiful girl named Frieda. They'd become engaged. She had just flown in from the States, and they were to be married in two days.

Frieda, like Ray, was filled with enthusiasm and a passion for adventure; indeed she had to be, to come 9,000 miles to a strange land to marry the man she loved. So when I told them about my trip I wasn't too surprised when they asked if they could travel with me to Alice Springs. "That's where I've always wanted to have my honeymoon anyway," Ray said.

"We won't take up much room and we'll fly back from Alice," Frieda smiled. I had led the expedition through many trials, through many climes, but never did I expect it to become a honeymoon expedition. This certainly was a new twist. But why not? I was delighted to have them. I gave them the Poptent to use, and one of Ray's friends printed HONEYMOON COTTAGE on a sign to hang over the entrance.

The wedding went as scheduled: a small Presbyterian church, bridesmaids, flowers, tears, and then, in the true Aussie spirit of things, kegs of beer. The drinking began and continued. Then someone called for the bride and groom; Ray and Frieda appeared, but gone were the silk dress and navy blue tuxedo. They were dressed in khaki, with high boots and wide-brimmed hats. To loud cheers and a shower of rice we threw our bags into the Land Cruiser, and as the shouts grew louder we drove down the drive. Strings of tin cans and a fence post tied to the rear of the car clanged and banged behind us. Nick fired off a shotgun, and every kid and dog in the neighborhood chased after us

down the street. It was a far cry from escaping a revolution in Algeria
or dodging a war in Pakistan, but it had its own excitement.

We reached Adelaide the following evening, and the next morning
turned north to Port Augusta, the last outpost before the Great Victoria
Desert. We stopped long enough to buy supplies, for it was our last big
town for a thousand miles. Ray came out of a shop carrying two pots
with wire handles.

"They're not pots," he corrected me. "They're billies. I'll show you
how Aussie swaggies camp," he said and tied them to the rear bumper.

At the edge of Port Augusta the paved road ended. The wilderness
began. We turned north from civilization on the long trek to Alice
Springs.

The country became flat and arid, the earth dusty and red, the land
stippled with scattered scrub trees. The road was no more than a dirt
trail, deeply rutted and grooved, and often, when the wind blew dust
from across the Victoria, we lost it completely. There were no road
markers or billboards, not even telegraph posts to guide us. There was
nothing but 360 degrees of horizon.

Camping in the Outback is excellent. There's no need to search for a
site, for one spot is as good as the next. There is always a supply of dry
wood, so a roaring fire can be had in minutes. Ray would pitch the
Poptent and hang the sign, and I would open my sleeping bag in front
of the fire. He proved his skill with the billies and, as he sang "Waltzing Matilda," prepared great meals for three hungry travelers. The
evenings we spent talking, sitting around the fire. Ray spoke about
his years aboard the schooner *Fairweather,* about savage islands in the
Indian Ocean where spear-carrying head hunters paddled their out-
riggers after the schooner, racing the *Fairweather* to the opening in
the reef; about fighting the winds in the Red Sea where the force was
so great it knocked the paint from the spars; about anchoring in the
shining blue waters of the Greek isles where bikini-clad maidens came
swimming out to the ship. And like a ship at sea, we were alone on a
great desert, with billions of stars in cloudless skies above, surrounded
by clean silence.

On the second day in the Outback we removed the top from the
Land Cruiser so that we could stand and watch the country unroll

before us. We came to Mount Alba, a town that was big on the map. It had two houses, one store and four sheds. Later we spotted a herd of wild horses. We took up our cameras, drove off the trail and headed toward them. We stopped a hundred yards away. A magnificent black stallion put his head high and sniffed the air, his nostrils quivering. He stood guard over his harem of half a dozen mares. They were brumbies, no doubt sired by valuable stallions that had escaped from cattle stations. The mares backed away, but the stallion stood his ground, his head high, facing the menace. He pawed the earth with his front hoofs, a signal that sent the others galloping off. Then, with his black mane flying, he turned and followed them.

We next saw kangaroo, and took off after them. They were even more spectacular than the fleeing horses. In great bounds and leaps they sprang, effortlessly, first in one direction, then suddenly in another. Followed at close range, they appeared to be leaping in slow motion. They finally lost us when they jumped a ten-foot gully. We were far from our trail. To reach it again we had to navigate by the sun. "All we need is a sextant," Ray remarked. How right he was.

Thus we continued on to Alice. To capture the feeling, the mood of the land, I jotted down my impressions as rapidly as I could in my journal. This is what I wrote.

Wednesday. Cooper's Peddy. It sits on a shimmering plain. No trees, no grass, only shale earth as far as the eye can see. The street through the center of town is wide, very wide. Unpaved, of course. There are two stores. We went into each. Dust covers everything. The open bins, the counters. Put your hand down and it comes up dirty. Greeks run the stores. New Australians. Not as friendly as the Old Australians. All business, no time for chatting. They sell beer, but only by the gallon. Some law about the aborigines. Gasoline to these parts delivered in 50-gallon drums, pumped directly from drums into the cars. Bought 18 gallons, at 52 cents per gallon; also 10 gallons of water, at 10 cents per gallon. The area north of Cooper's Peddy is mining country. Opals. Piles of earth where the dredgers passed. 170 miles to the next gas station.

Haven't seen a car in two days. The road is wide. In fact, the whole country is one wide road. All gravel. Clumps of trees. The horizon is like the sea. The land is empty and dead, even the winter sun is dead. It shines but brings little warmth. We wear fur jackets but it is still cold. The tune 'Waltzing Matilda' keeps drumming through my mind.

Reached the turnoff to Oodnadatta. Met another car. When you

meet another car in the Outback you stop. We talked for five minutes, about driving and weather. Missed the last town. Didn't see
it, or else map is wrong. The sunset, the most glorious I have ever
seen. No clouds on the desert. The skies are clear. No reflections,
just a variation of shades, a continuum, from dark darks to light
lights. We drive toward the rim of the horizon where the sun has
set, like a moth drawn up to the flame, but our flame, like the
horizon, is unattainable. We set up camp. Roaring fire. We are
tired but the night is too great to sleep. We talk. We talk about
authors. Ray has never been to a university but he is well-read.
Five years at sea and good books. We talked ourselves dry. Voices
stopped. All things melt together and form the night.

Thursday. I awoke to realize the rifle slipped under my sleeping
bag. Push my head out. Others still asleep. The Land Cruiser picks
up the red of morning sun. The Land Cruiser. How that machine—
moving parts, wires, pistons, rubber wheels—how they have become
a part of me, an extension of myself. It stands there, absorbing the
morning rays of the sun, still cold and damp, but a turn of the
key and it grows warm and carries me off, wherever I want to go,
any place, every place. It becomes my life, and if it fails me, so
goes my life. Simple.

The coals are still warm. A few twigs, and fire sparks to life. Hot
coffee while we pack.

The track becomes worse. Washboard. Seldom more than 20
mph. There are a few cattle, but more sun-dried carcasses than
living steers. Sometimes wild horses. It breaks the monotony to
chase them, their manes flying, but they always lose us.

A Land Rover shot past. It annoyed me. I speeded up. A new
discovery. At 40 the tires don't sink into the ruts; they ride the tops
of them. But it is dangerous, for there is little control of the car
and we can roll sideways. But the effect is strange. Almost like
breaking the sound barrier. At a slow speed the car shakes and
pounds, and as I increase the speed it grows worse, until it feels
like we will shake apart. But faster, faster. The vibration becomes
greater, and then suddenly the sound disappears, the vibration
stops, and we seem to be gliding, almost as though there are no
more ruts. But the high speed plays on our nerves. One deep, unseen hole and we are finished. We slow down.

We cooked lunch under a gum tree. Sausages, toast, and tea in
the billy. Red parrots sing in the trees. No other sound for hundreds
of miles. But flies, stinging flies. We sit in the smoke and eat,
watching that magnificent billy boil——'Once a jolly swagman
. . . and waited till his billy boiled . . .'

We reached the turnoff to Ayer's Rock. The last 50 miles to
Alice is paved. Paved roads again. We arrived at dusk and found
a pub.

Alice was the end of the line for Ray and Frieda. I began to plot my
course across the west. I had in mind to strike out for Mount Olga,

cross the Petermann Ranges, and eventually reach Laveton in Western Australia. But to go this way, through a vast aboriginal reserve, I needed authorization which, I now learned, would take weeks to get. The alternative was to head westward to Mount Doreen and continue on to Gordon Downs in the state of Western Australia. I asked several people and was told that I could gas at Mount Doreen, 200 miles distant. This meant that if I could refuel there I should be able (since my jerry cans gave me the capacity to do 800 miles) to reach Gordon Downs with a hundred miles to spare. This is what I thought.

Ray and Frieda were heavy hearted as they went over the maps with me and then helped me pack. As I was filling the water jugs they went off to buy my food supply. I estimated that I could be across in less than two weeks, but I wanted enough food to last for a month. They returned with five boxes loaded with provisions. "I can't eat all that in three months," I said.

"Maybe not, but three of us can in one month," Ray said.

"What?"

"We want to go with you."

They wanted to go with me. I had no idea what exactly was ahead, but whatever it was, it would be too rough for a girl, and when I tried to explain this to her, Frieda countered with every argument in the book. She made some good points. I had to agree that during the past few weeks she had proved herself in the outdoors. And I had to agree that she never complained, even when she was tired and we pushed into the night. Nor did she mind sleeping on hard ground, in freezing nights, nor was she alarmed when dingos prowled a few yards from camp. "And besides," she said, "I want a kangaroo steak cooked over an open fire, and a roo hide to hang on the wall of our new house."

I finally agreed, and that morning we crossed the MacDonnell Ranges to the west. After the first hundred miles the road turned into a sand track and the land flattened out, and by the second day we came over the crest of a hill to see Mount Doreen ahead. We speeded up, excited that we had reached our first objective, only to meet with our first disappointment. The town was in ashes. I now knew what it was like in the Old West, to come across the plains in a stagecoach and find the fort burned down. All that remained in Mount Doreen were a few walls, a brass bed in one house, a teakettle, a bathtub and pipes, and several fifty-gallon drums near the ruins. We rushed to the drums. Empty. Frieda found one half full and we quickly pounded the cap off. Rusted water.

We slowly became aware of eyes watching us. Along the side of a hill was a lean-to, and peering out were an aborigine and his wife. We motioned to him, and he came, taking long strides, putting on a military-type leather jacket. He was tall, gray-bearded, and very black. He spoke pidgin English, and we were able to gather that the town had burned down six years before, but he said we could get petrol at the Vaughan Springs cattle station, some 50 miles to the south. I thanked him, gave him some cigarettes, and we turned south.

That night Frieda got her wish. We had kangaroo steaks cooked over an open fire, and a hide that measured almost nine feet when skinned out. For an old roo, the meat was remarkably tender, and I commended Ray on his fine shooting, and his ability to pick a tender roo.

The next morning we met Alan James, the foreman of Vaughan Springs. He stood by the corral and watched us come, with his hands in his pockets and a bored expression on his face, as though he were accustomed to having tourists stop to ask questions several times a day. Yet Alan hadn't seen a stranger in many months. He invited us to the house, and beneath his gruff exterior I could tell he was clearly delighted to have visitors.

The house was incongruous in the Outback. It was built of brick, painted pastel blue, and was immaculately clean inside. The kitchen was modern and had a gas range and refrigerator.

We asked Alan about life in the Outback. He wasn't talkative, so what we did learn came in bits and pieces. Alan, with the help of seventeen aborigines, ran the station, all 2,000 square miles of it. They grazed 8,000 head of cattle, and the previous year lost 4,000 of them in the drought. The first white man came to the territory in 1935, looking for gold. Abos killed him. Another prospector came a few years later and the Abos cut him up and stuffed him in a rabbit burrow. Then the law moved in. And civilization. "It ain't like it used to be," Alan said. "Now we have neighbors. Getting closed in."

"Where are your neighbors?" I asked.

"About 200 miles west of here."

With our tanks filled with gasoline, we returned to Mount Doreen and picked up the trail west again. But we had gone only a few miles when we saw the dust of a vehicle approaching. We stopped and waited, and soon a truck pulled up, driven by a half-caste who called himself Billy. He looked like a heavy out of a Western movie, but he was soft spoken and offered us assistance. I asked if we were on the right track to Gordon Downs. He pushed back his hat and scratched his head. "I don't think so. Maybe not—" he hesitated—"hasn't been anybody gone this way in years. Last week two blokes almost died. Car broke down. No water for six days. We found them; maybe one day more they had. The coppers in Alice told them the road was good. Crazy. Nobody knows what goes on out here—but everybody tells everybody else about it. Crazy."

He then suggested another route. "Much better," he said. He tried to explain the route, but I couldn't understand him. He squatted and began scratching a map in the red dust. The best I could make out was that if we followed the trail another 100 miles we would come to a water bore, and here we had to turn left and continue for another 50 miles until we came to a cattle station. There we were to ask for Joe. Joe would fix us up with a map of the territory to the west. The station was called Mongrel Downs.

Six hours later we came to the bore and turned left. The country had changed sharply. We could have been on the moon or on the planet Mars. The earth was cracked and split. There were ant hills everywhere, millions of ant hills that looked like tombstones, some higher than a man can reach, all the same color as the red earth. Golden patches of spinifex grass seen from a distance seemed like craters, and as the sun dropped low on the horizon, long shadows stole across the plains and added more mystery. The land seemed to try to speak to us, to want to tell us something; but the voice was mystic and unfathomable.

Each day this land, the fabulous never-never land, became more and more of a fascination to me. Maybe the voice was beginning to take on meaning. I had been driving across a country—an island continent, actually—that has for eons been isolated, and because of this isolation it was the home for plants and animals found nowhere else in the world. Each day offered something new and strange. We had, of course, seen and hunted kangaroo, some of which stood six feet tall, yet which at birth were no larger than a thumb nail. More than once we had been awakened in the still of night by the kookaburra, a bird which laughs like a human. We had watched the brolga, a bird which dances like a drunken sailor, and we had driven in chase of seven-foot high, flightless emus, only to have them outrun us. We had seen hundreds of varieties of eucalyptus trees, photographed others which looked like gigantic wine bottles, and pitched camp beneath blackboys, trees which grow only one foot every hundred years. But most fascinating of all life we saw on the Outback were the aborigines.

We watched them come out of the desert, naked as Greek statues, walking straight as gods. And the lone hunters, silhouetted against the blank sky, standing on one leg like cranes, a javelin in one hand, the other shielding their eyes from the glare of the sun. These were the more primitive ones, the ones who still gouge their bodies with flaming sticks, hunt with boomerang and spear, and shun the ways of white men. Some tribes have never learned to build even the crudest of shelters; still others have yet to develop speech.

To survive in the harsh environment, which provides little food and often no water, the aborigine has learned to expend little energy. He can sit idly for hours, even days. He will not lift an arm to brush away a fly or knock an ant from his torso; I've seen some of their children so covered with swarming bush flies that I could not see their faces. And when an aborigine runs, which he seldom does, he does not swing his arms, for that takes extra energy. Even the boomerang was developed to return to the hunter so that he would not need to tire himself retrieving it.

Since he had neither clothing nor shelter, the Australian aborigine has developed, through evolution, certain physical characteristics that set him apart from all other humans. During the freezing nights in the Outback, his metabolism drops. His pulse slows down, his body temperature falls off, and his blood circulation reaches only the vital inner organs. His outer skin becomes, in effect, an insulation against the extreme cold.

It was dark when we reached Mongrel Downs. We pulled up to the darkened house, blew the horn, shouted and whistled, but there was no response. We walked around the grounds. Nothing stirred. It was so strange and eerie that we decided to push on without meeting Joe or getting a map. A few miles beyond the station we camped for the night.

The next morning we found Joe asleep in his truck ten miles down the trail. He awoke with a start when he heard us pull up beside him, and I saw a rifle cradled across his lap. "Which way to Western Australia?" I asked, and he pointed ahead. He didn't seem overly friendly, especially with the rifle pointed in my direction, so I decided not to ask about a map of the territory. But half an hour later I saw his truck coming up behind us. I pulled over to wait for him.

"You scared me out of my wits," he said. "It isn't often you crap out in your ruddy truck and some Yankee comes up and asks you the way across the continent. Anyway, you took the wrong turn. This way you'll go around in a circle for a week, or until your petrol runs out, and then we'd find you, your white bones."

He then introduced himself. Joe Mahood was the name, part owner of Mongrel Downs. For the next hour he drew us a map, with mileage down to the fraction, landmarks we couldn't miss, and the name of every water bore from Mongrel Downs to a Catholic mission deep within Western Australia. When he finished he invited us to tea. "Have some drovers ahead," he said. "Was on my way to see them."

An hour later we reached the camp. Three drovers squatted around a smoldering fire. Their sleeping rolls were spread out on the ground a few yards away, and beyond them were a thousand or more head of cattle, tended by a few aborigines on horseback. The three men made a seedy group. They were long-haired and unshaven, and each wore odd bits and pieces of clothing, from military discards to double-breasted suit coats. They poured us tea from the billy and pulled up logs for us to sit on. "Had your tucker yet?" one of them asked me.

"He means are you hungry," Ray translated.

"We've got some kangaroo," I said.

"Roo meat," he spit. "That's no food for a man. You want a steak?"

"I wouldn't mind."

He grabbed his rifle, walked over to the nearest steer, and shot it through the brain. The second drover cut the steer into steaks which he tossed directly into the ashes. When the first drover saw Frieda looking amazed he said, "Ashes don't hurt nobody."

Frieda tried to be helpful. "Would you like some eggs?" she asked.

"We don't eat any of that city stuff," the first drover said.

We ate our steaks and thanked Joe and his men. As we were leaving they gave us half a leg of beef. It was enough meat to last us the entire trip.

We followed Joe's map, from bore to bore, with their interesting names: Wild Potato, Pommey's Head, Bloodwood, Pussycat. They averaged 25 to 30 miles apart, or about a day's ride by horseback. Many were dried up, but they made excellent markers across the flat land.

Two days later we entered Western Australia through a pass Joe had marked on the map. On both sides of the pass the rocks rose about 700 feet. We stopped in the pass, out of the wind, so Ray and I could change oil and grease the Land Cruiser. Frieda went off to explore. Suddenly we heard her screaming. We found her standing at the entrance of a cave pointing inside. We didn't know whether to be annoyed with her sudden outburst or to be pleased with her find. She had discovered a cave filled with aboriginal wall paintings. There were drawings of kangaroo and stick-figures with bows, and there were other designs we didn't understand. I returned for my cameras and photographed what I could with the available light.

Joe's map was precise. When he said we would drive twenty-seven and a quarter miles and come to a ridge, and then looked northwest from it we would see three rocks on the horizon, there were certain to be three rocks on the horizon. I hoped he was as good a rancher as he was a cartographer. We relied so fully on his map that several evenings later, when we saw what appeared to be lights of a town in the distance, we knew it was the Catholic mission at Bogda, buried in the Australian Outback, 500 miles from the nearest town. We drove toward it and came to a sign:

BOGDA ABORIGINE RESERVATION: DO NOT ENTER

Joe's map only went as far as the mission, and how far beyond it we had to travel to reach civilization we didn't know. We had gasoline for a few hundred miles more, but we didn't want to take the chance. Perhaps we could buy fuel from the mission, or at least get directions; but Joe had warned us about Father McGuire, the priest in charge. "He doesn't like trespassers. Other than that he isn't a bad bloke, considering what he's trying to do with those black ones." We were trespassers, but we decided to try our luck with Father McGuire anyway.

We came to a gate in the barbed wire fence, opened it, and passed through. We met a nun and asked her where we could find Father McGuire. She held back her surprise and pointed to a building with a single light burning in the window. We parked in front and I went and knocked on the door. The shaded lamp only threw light into the lower half of the room, and when a figure came to answer my knock I couldn't see his face. "What do you want?" he said, in a tone that was anything but welcoming.

"I want to know if we can buy some petrol."

"Buy petrol?" he shouted, coming out of the building into the light of the street lamp. "This is a house of the Lord, not a Shell station."

He was a man in his early forties, tall, with red hair. I could see an exasperated look on his Irish face. "And who might you be?" he asked.

"I am an American."

"Then what are you doing here?"

"Driving around the world."

His eyes showed fire. "Don't be smart with me, boy. Now what are you doing here?"

I explained again, that I was an American, that I was driving around the world, and that I had only learned a few miles back that we needed permission to enter the reservation. "And we've already driven over 800 miles from Alice," I said.

He continued with his fury. "You all come here looking for gins.* That's my problem now, half-breed children running around, and nobody wants them."

"Okay, Father, it doesn't matter," I said, and turned to walk away.

* Aborigine girls.

Frieda came out of the Land Cruiser to show Father McGuire that we
had a woman with us. She introduced herself. They began talking, and
there was mention of a new chapel, and I heard Frieda asking if she
could see it. The way of women. We not only got our petrol, but we
were also invited to dinner. After dinner, Father McGuire insisted that
we stay for the night. "Hot showers and clean white sheets," he said to
Frieda. It sounded tempting, but we knew what one night of luxury
can do; it takes two nights to get accustomed to the outdoors again.
We accepted the showers but, as Frieda explained to Father McGuire,
we rather enjoyed sleeping in red dust, with our sleeping bag in front
of the campfire.

That night we camped a few miles beyond the mission, in red dust,
in front of the campfire, dreaming of soft beds and clean white sheets.

For three days we continued driving westward. We hunted more
now, and brought down a few roo that weighed close to 200 pounds
each. I had learned a few tricks from the aborigines for hunting kangaroo. In the beginning Ray and I tried to outrun them, but we always
lost. Nor was it possible to hit them on the move, but I discovered that
kangaroo are curious beasts, and if you don't alarm them in the beginning, they stand their ground to see what you will do. Not only that,
but they imitate you. The procedure at that point is quite simple. You
hop a few steps; they hop a few steps. You scratch yourself; they
scratch themselves. And gradually you hop yourself up to within hand-
shaking distance. The only problem is you feel awfully damn silly, even
in front of the kangaroo.

We finally crossed the last range of hills, the Kimberleys, and came
upon a much traveled track which we followed to Broome on the Indian
Ocean. We had made it, across the continent.

In Broome I rechecked the shipping schedule which I had been
given in Sydney, and found that I had five days to drive the 1,500 miles
to Perth where I was to catch the ship to Panama; but the roads
turned out to be some of the worst I had been on in 35,000 miles
of driving around the world. The ruts were so deep we often had to
inch our way through. When we speeded up we were shaken apart.
The battery split open. Our food spilled over the car. The miles became endless, and we grew more weary by the hour, but we couldn't

stop. We had to make the ship. It was the only one from Perth to Panama in months. We took shifts at the wheel, never stopping.

We finally made Perth on schedule, but the ship hadn't. I learned that it was being held in the turmoil in Indonesia. There was no other ship from Perth to Panama for months; but the *Tahitien,* a French ship, would sail from Sydney in two weeks. I would have to recross the continent to get it. Ray and Freida abandoned their plans to fly back to Melbourne and insisted on going with me to share the driving. "After all, our honeymoon isn't over yet," they said.

Before we left Perth I collected my mail at the American Consulate. There was a big bank draft from Al, money he'd raised in New York, enough for us to finish the expedition, and a cable from Krinski:

NO FAIR. WITHOUT PODELL YOU MIGHT MAKE IT.

Day and night we drove, across the Nullarbor Plains, where bull dust lay a foot deep in unseen potholes. We finally reached Port Augusta and from there had all good road to Melbourne.

"Hurry back, Steve," Ray said as we shook hands.

"It may be a long time."

"Then you'll take our children on the next trip," Frieda said and kissed me on the cheek.

Two more days and I was in Sydney. I had recrossed the continent in four days and nineteen hours.

I discovered that I was a celebrity. The newspapers had been reporting the progress of my trip. Strangers greeted me on the street. The day before I was to sail to Panama and meet Al, I was invited by my friend Jack Mathews, the Chief Steward at the Sydney Speedway, to come out to see the races. But when I got there I saw that I had been tricked: a battery of TV cameras and interviewers were waiting for me. I also found out I was scheduled to drive the Land Cruiser as the pace vehicle for the feature race. I couldn't refuse, not after the heroic treatment the press gave me. Jack gave me instructions: "Drive at 50 miles an hour. Keep a steady pace. Keep an eye on me. I will have a board in my hand. When I turn it around, get off the track immediately, for the next time around I will bring the flag down and the race begins."

Despite what Al and I had been through, I knew he would never believe this one. I had to get photographs. I grabbed a driver from another event and asked him to drive while I took the pictures. He agreed, and we got into position on the starting line.

The twenty cars lined up behind us in two's. The drivers, with their faces half covered with goggles, looked like men from Mars. I adjusted my camera. We were off. I snapped away. Their engines sounded like a squadron of jet bombers. I kept my eye to the camera. Three laps, four laps—sliding on the turns as we went around—five laps, then suddenly I saw Jack bring the flag down. We were in the race. Good Lord, *we were in the race*. I had forgotten to tell the driver to leave the track when Jack turned the board. Dirt was flying and the smell of fumes and smoke filled the air. Race cars crowded to pass, and we were up to 75, still gaining speed, looking desperately for an opening to clear the track. We did two more laps before we found that opening.

Jack Mathews is one of the few Aussies I know who doesn't drink, but when the race was over he tied one on. We both did.

The next morning the press, which the day before had been so lavish in its praise, really blasted me. "The Yank who drove across the Outback almost ruined the feature race at Sydney Speedway yesterday when he. . . ."

Another paper headlined: JEEPERS, WHAT A WAY TO GO.

Chapter 21

The Last Chapter

And jeepers, what a way to arrive.

My ship across the Pacific reached Panama on August 15. It was the height of the season——the rainy season. And there was Al, who'd flown down from New York, bearded and exuberant, waving to me from the edge of Miraflores Lock as the *Tahitien* entered the Panama Canal. For the first time in six months the Trans World Record Expedition was back together. Al and I sat up late into the night drinking quarts of Balboa beer in a crowded Panama City cafe and exchanging stories about the women in Tahiti and the girls in New York as the incessant rain beat down on the corrugated metal roof.

By the end of the next day we had serviced our Land Cruiser and equipment and were ready to leave on the last leg home. There was only one problem——or, rather, there were eight problems. To take our vehicle and camper out of the country we needed special permits and papers from the dock officials, the chief of customs, the passport controller, the police, the secret police, the local treasury department, the mayor of Panama City, and the Panamanian Foreign Office. The Panamanians, it seemed, had picked up a few customs from their former Spanish rulers. They consumed two days.

The road north was bordered by thick tropical jungles and littered with the run-over carcasses of dozens of snakes, but it was paved and fast. Halfway up through Panama the cement ended, and we entered the worst stretch on the Inter-American Highway, more than 200 miles of jolting corrugations, loose gravel, razor-sharp rocks, and spring-busting potholes. And ahead loomed the highest mountain pass of our trip, the 11,400 foot summit of Cerro del Muerto, the notorious Peak of Death.

We didn't make it.

Fifteen hundred yards below the high pass, on a blind curve, we felt a sharp jolt and heard the shriek of tortured metal scraping on stone.

I jerked the Land Cruiser to a halt and leaped out to see our camper twenty yards behind us, its nose dug into the road, its A-frame still hitched to the car, snapped completely through at both joints. It was our worst possible breakdown. We had spare parts for fixing almost any other malfunction, but only a heavy-duty welding shop could fix this, and there just didn't happen to be any of those on the Peak of Death. Further, it was senseless to bring the A-frame to a welder unless we brought the camper to which it had to be reattached; and it was impossible to bring the camper more than five feet with its A-frame detached. We were broken down on a treacherous mountain road, in the middle of a dangerous blind curve, with heavy trucks charging down on us and no shoulder onto which to pull off, far from the nearest city, on the fog-shrouded summit of the highest peak on the Inter-American highway at the height of the rainy season. We might have been back on our home continent, but our difficulties were far from over.

After assessing the damage, we realized that there was only one way to get our trailer back on the road: we'd have to build an entirely new frame. We chopped down two young trees and——behind a protective barricade of warning boulders and reflectors——labored for three days with crude tools, trimming and shaping and fitting and binding them into place.

We hoped this log frame would enable us to haul the camper as far as a welding shop in San Jose. If it broke anywhere on Cerro del Muerto, the camper would probably roll out of control and be dashed on the rocks below. But we had no alternative. We headed for San Jose at a speed reduced from the slow fifteen miles an hour we'd been doing to an excruciating five miles an hour to avoid straining the unseasoned timbers. We figured it would take us two days to make the sixty-mile trip.

It took four. Under the impact of the tree-braced trailer springing up and down on the jagged road, the right tire went flat in an hour. We put on the spare, and it lasted 90 minutes before it was slashed

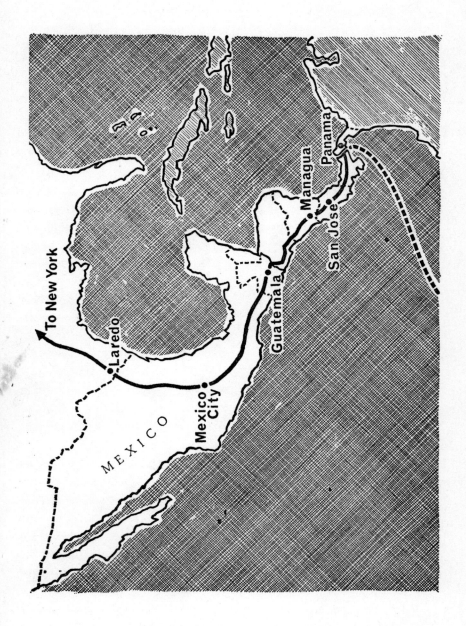

through. Our trailer, unfortunately, had tubeless tires when it had been pulled off the production line in Manawa; and tubeless tires, once they go flat, are impossible to re-inflate without special equipment—special equipment that service stations just don't have outside of Europe and the United States. We had the material for patching any leaks, but no equipment for putting pressure around the airless tire to seat its bead so it could be pumped up. We tried everything—ropes, chains, the winch cable, glue, tire irons—but nothing worked. Silly as it may seem for a fully equipped, travel-taught, supposedly self-sufficient globe-circling expedition to be thwarted by a flat tire, that was exactly our situation.

The next morning we took the tire to a mountainside gas station where we worked all day trying to seat the bead, but to no avail, for when we'd apply pressure at one point the tire would bulge in another. Toward evening Al noticed a huge truck tire lying on the ground and realized that the opening in its center was just large enough to accommodate our small tubeless tire. It proved to be a perfect fit, providing enough equal pressure all around to enable us to reinflate our problem tire and get back on the road.

Two hours later, when checking the frame, we heard a slow hiss of air from the tire we'd just repaired. It wasn't flat yet, but to prevent it from getting that way meant we'd have to stop periodically to pump it full to keep the seal from breaking, unless we wanted to go through the miserable bead-seating bit all over again. We found ourselves stopping every fifteen minutes to spend five minutes manning our hand pump, and occasionally an additional minute to contemplate the rather comical spectacle of two supposedly hardened and world-wise travelers, finally back on their continent, poking along at four miles an hour and slogging out of the car dead tired into the pouring rain every few yards to pamper a leaking tire.

After a day and a half without sleep, we were still far from San Jose but pretty close to complete exhaustion. But what could we do about the tire if we slept? Should we position it so the leak would be against the roadbed when we stopped, hoping this would plug it up? Or, exactly opposite, should we jack the camper completely off the ground so there'd be no weight on the tire that could break the seal? Or should we take turns waking up every few minutes to pump it up? In the spirit of true adventurers we said the hell with it and went to sleep— and woke up the next morning with a very flat tire and the necessity of going through the bead-seating routine all over again.

By the time we reached San Jose it had taken us nine days to cover the five hundred and ten miles between the capital of Panama and the capital of Costa Rica; but at least we'd pioneered two indispensable techniques for other world travelers who find themselves stuck atop Cerro del Muerto with a broken trailer frame and a leaking tubeless tire.

After we had the broken trailer frame welded and the chewed-up trailer tire replaced in San Jose, our spirits brightened. Al got back into his playful mood and was soon up to his old tricks.

In San Jose he told me to drive the Land Cruiser to a press conference early one morning. When I got there it turned out to be a drag race into which Al——taking a page from Jack Mathews, and with the connivance of the local Toyota distributor——had entered me. I finished last.

Two days later, as we rolled along a splendidly paved section of the Inter-American Highway that crossed several dozen rain-swollen rivers in northern Costa Rica, Al bet that I couldn't swim across one of them. I accepted the challenge and dove in——and got swept so far downstream I was on my way into the Pacific Ocean until two boys hauled me out.

The next day, after Al had taken a shower under a 60-foot waterfall near the Nicaraguan border, he talked me into doing the same thing——and I missed by two inches getting clobbered by a big dead tree trunk that came dropping over the rim.

But on the day we entered Nicaragua I got even. Telling Al that we needed some adventurous footage for our movie, I persuaded him to grab a jungle vine that hung from the top of a hundred-foot high tree by the roadside. As I focused the camera, Al climbed onto the roof of the Land Cruiser and, clutching the vine, leaped high into the air and went swinging off into the jungle like Tarzan. When the vine broke, as I knew it would, Tarzan dropped like a rock into a jungly thicket of prickly bushes and red ants with a hundred feet of vine on top of him, and peace returned to the Trans World Record Expedition.

We camped that night by the estuary of San Juan del Sur on the Pacific coast of Nicaragua. It was a calm and beautiful night, the night of the full August moon.

It was nearly midnight when we heard strange sounds down by the water and rushed out of our camper to see dozens of immense turtles crawling painfully up the beach. They stopped when they were a hundred yards above the high-tide line, near our camper. There, with their cumbersome flippers, they scooped out holes in the sand, deep holes into which, panting from the strain of the digging and the pangs of labor, they laid their eggs—80, 100, sometimes as many as 150. Although nearly exhausted, the turtles arduously filled in their nests and smoothed the surface sand to conceal them, then struggled their way—gasping and groaning in an almost human manner—back to the breakers, back to the depths, never to see their young born, never to know that their young would never be born.

A hundred boys from the nearby town had been waiting on the beach that night of the full August moon, waiting for the annual return of the turtles. When they sighted one emerging from the ocean they'd stealthily follow her to where she dug her hole and dig one themselves behind her, a few inches away and several feet deep, then tunnel through into her nest and pull out the white, soft-shelled eggs as quickly as she laid them. The mother turtles, struggling with single-minded determination to preserve their race, never knew what was happening, never suspected the fate of their eggs, even when greedy fingers grabbed them a hand's breadth away from the painful openings of their wombs.

Al was so upset that he ran up and down the beach all night lecturing the boys, in his incomprehensible version of Spanish, on the principles of conservation and fair play, imploring them to leave a half or a third of the eggs in the ground so that there might be turtles and eggs for future generations. But none of them listened. They were all too busy counting the eggs into sacks to be sold at the market, or piercing the shells on the beach and sucking the eggs down as they were, raw and still warm from the womb.

Two boys who had borrowed my flashlight returned it to me with thanks and a dozen of the eggs they'd gathered. They were the size of ping-pong balls and rubbery to the touch. I didn't fancy eating them raw, so I went to collect some wood for a fire, and when I got back to the camper there were only six eggs left. I looked for Al to tell him that someone had raided our camp and stolen half the eggs, but he wasn't around. I found him down on the beach, about a hundred yards above the high-tide line, gently burying the little turtle eggs back in one of the empty holes.

The next morning we drove from San Juan del Sur to Lake Nicaragua, a vast body of water 100 miles long, dominated by several volcanos along its shore and two perpetually cloud-capped volcanos that rise 7,000 feet above it from an island in its center. It is not an especially attractive lake up close, with its slate gray water and a shoreline rimmed with refuse, but after a hard, hot drive through humid Nicaragua in late summer, any lake would look inviting.

In the sweltering heat of mid-afternoon we reached its north end, passing through the charming city of Granada, one of the first Spanish settlements in the New World, a carefully preserved town with centuries-old churches and ancient homes; its only contemporary architectural feature was an impressionistic piscine monument that looked strangely out of place in the midst of all that mellow antiquity.

We drove down to the lake shore where, since we'd gotten so little sleep because of the turtle hunters the night before, we decided to make an early camp. It was Al's turn to shop for food, and while he drove back into town I dove in for a swim. I swam so hard to get away from the debris around the shore that I was soon a good quarter of a mile out, but the water was neither as cooling nor as comforting as I'd hoped; there was something ominous about the ugly volcano looking down on me from behind Granada, and something definitely spooky about the lake itself.

As I was about to head back, I saw something cutting the water about 30 feet from me, something black and sleek as a spear. My heart jumped. It was a shark, I was sure, but then I remembered that sharks live only in the oceans. As the thing sped away I saw it was only a swordfish. Swordfish! Now there *was* something wrong, for unless I'd completely forgotten my most rudimentary ichthyology, the sword was also strictly a salt-water fish.

I swam back toward our campsite with the eerie feeling that I was being followed. As I waded through the debris near the shore, I looked back. There were three gray fins circling the spot I'd just left. An ugly gray head rose slightly above the water and a vicious set of shark jaws snapped shut on an empty piece of Lake Nicaragua.

I'd been back at our campsite only a few minutes when Al returned from his shopping expedition with the strangest looking collection of vegetables I'd ever seen. A few I recognized—a small Central American potato, a thick chunk of taro root, a bunch of green soup bananas—but the rest could just as well have been grown on another planet. There were things that looked like pieces of cactus and others like pieces of bark; one that looked like a bowling ball; one that resembled a pepper, with green thorns an inch long; and another item that from the outside looked like a brown grapefruit and from the inside like a jar of brushless shaving cream. When I asked Al what I was supposed to do with them, he said all the native women were buying the same things.

When I asked him which were fruit and which vegetables, he said the market had been very busy so he'd just picked out one of everything.

"Well, tell me then," I asked, pointing to a purple, alligator-skinned specimen, "do I peel this one?"

Al nodded hesitantly.

"Or do I leave the skin on until it's cooked?"

Al shrugged.

"Or do we eat it with the skin on?"

Al suggested we save it for a souvenir.

"Then, what about this one?" I asked, holding up another winner, the ugly green giant with the jolly sharp spikes. "Do we boil it?"

Al looked a bit green himself.

"Or do we bake it and put chocolate sauce on top?"

Al looked as though he were going to change the subject.

"Or do we just eat it raw?"

Al changed the subject. "Guess what I found out in town," he began. "You know that funny looking statue with the fins we were wondering about? Well——"

"And what about this thing? All it needs is three finger holes. You sure you didn't end up in a sporting goods store by mistake?"

"——they told me it's a monument to the fresh-water sharks. They told me Lake Nicaragua is the only fresh-water lake in the world with man-eating sharks. Isn't that interesting?"

It was. But I wasn't going to let Al off that easily. I picked up the pepper-shaped thornball as gingerly as I might a hand grenade and regarded it with about as much affection, pretending to be more interested in it than in Al's news. In the meantime, Al had shifted into the pedantic tone he always used for lectures: "You see, Steve, Lake Nicaragua was once, many, many eons ago, a part of the ocean, but then a volcanic eruption sealed it off and transformed it into a lake." I clipped the spikes off the pepper-shaped thing, though even then it wasn't transformed into anything that looked edible. "The lake became ever less salty with the passing centuries, until it was eventually all fresh water. Many of the salt-water fish trapped by the eruption could not live in the altered environment, but the sharks and the swordfish and some others survived." I cut through the tough skin of the bowling ball to see if we could survive. It was a fruit. "They were able to acclimate themselves to its gradually diminishing salinity, and they thrive in the lake today. What do you think about that?"

First I told Al what I thought about his shopping ability. Then I told him about my own encounter with the fresh-water sharks and how I'd barely escaped.

As I turned back to my salvage operation, Al turned to me, full of understanding and sympathy and compassion. "God, that must have been an awful thing for you," he said as I knocked some awful fungus off the hard green bananas. "And to think I was away shopping while you were in trouble. I might have been able to do something."

He was obviously upset, so I decided to relent, and started washing the thick mud off the taro roots. After all, it was difficult to shop for some of these strange foods, and Al meant well, and he did deserve a good meal.

"I wish I'd been here," he continued, much distressed. "I'll bet I could have gotten some great pictures with those sharks all around you. What a shame!"

I looked up at Al. I stopped washing the mud off the taro root. I stopped pruning the spikes off the thornball. I dumped them, and all the other little bombs, just as they were, into a huge pot, and set it to boil. It was time for Al's stomach to have a little adventure.

It took an hour for the mess to melt down into something resembling a soup, and when I ladled a load into Al's bowl and invited him to begin, he nervously changed the subject, asking me what I was planning to do once the trip was finished. I told him I planned to go somewhere peaceful to work on my novel, and I told him to eat his soup.

"I had an idea for making another trip," he said, and it was the first time I'd heard about it, for all along he said he'd been planning to go back to editing magazines or to work for an advertising agency. "No, not an ordinary trip," he explained when he saw me looking at him and the soup suspiciously, "but a trip by automobile completely around the world, from north to south, over the poles. I did some research and found that nobody has ever driven that route in the whole history of the earth. We'd be the first. Just think of it." I closed my eyes and found myself thinking about it as Al continued. "From New York across Canada, then up the Alcan Highway into Alaska. Then by plane over the pole into Norway. Across Sweden. Stockholm. Copenhagen. Those great Scandinavian girls. You still with me?" I was, indeed, dreamily caught up in the plan; even Al's voice seemed to be growing more distant. "Then across the heart of Europe to Turkey, down to Africa, along the length of the Nile, the Sudan, Kenya, Mt. Kilimanjaro, Lake Victoria and Tanganyika, all the way to the Cape of Good Hope. You ever been there?" I hadn't, and when I opened my eyes I saw that Al wasn't where he should have been either. He was still talking. "By plane across Antarctica to Tierra del Fuego at the tip of South America." But he was several yards away, scooping out a hole in the beach. "Then up along the backbone of the Chilean Andes, into Peru, with its magnificent mountains and beautiful women." And I saw him deposit the soup into the hole, much less tenderly than he had the turtle eggs the night before. "Then through the jungles of Equador and Colombia, across the Darien Gap." He came edging innocently back to the camper. "Into Panama and through Central America up this way to New York. Wouldn't that be a great trip? What do you think, Steve?"

"I think you'd better have another bowl of soup."

Central Central America passed without major incident. We did camp atop a colony of biting red ants in Honduras, and our camper did come close to being blown off a fishing pier in La Libertad, El Salvador, when a freak windstorm struck one night, but there was nothing exceptional. The weather was still wet, with showers every afternoon, and the days hot, but the road was good, the language easy, and the people friendly and helpful. The worst was far behind us, and we seemed to have a clear run to New York and our record.

Until Guatemala. From the minute we entered this northernmost of the Central American republics, we sensed hostility. Whereas in all the other countries from Panama up, the people to whom we'd waved as we drove past had always waved back and smiled, in Guatemala our friendly gestures were greeted with cold stares. When we stopped the first evening to ask a woman for directions, she'd grabbed her children and run into the woods; when we'd walked into a roadside shop for dinner, the owner had told us he was out of food; and when we'd made camp in the jungle beside the road that first night, we felt we were being watched.

When we awoke the next morning we found our camper surrounded by six mean-looking Indians with mean-looking machetes. Wasting no time and offering no explanation, they formed a tight circle about us and forced us to go with them.

I couldn't understand what we'd done to upset them, and when I asked one of them, he rushed me. The Guatemalan Indians are peaceful people, unless they're drunk or someone interferes with their pagan religious rites, neither of which was here the case. Nor did robbery seem to be the motive, for although they had taken away our bows and arrows and machetes and my pistol, they were definitely more interested in us than in our possessions. We knew that some travelers had recently been held up in Guatemala, but they were mostly in the northern sections, along the highway from Guatemala City to Puerto Barrios, where the Castro-inspired rebels were active, and our captors looked more like simple local Indians than Communist guerrillas, so it just didn't make any sense.

For twenty minutes the Indians marched us beside the sweltering road at a fast pace, and when I asked them to stop to let us rest for a minute, I only got a machete point in the back for my efforts. When they did finally stop it was in the courtyard of an army building in a small village. The sloppily dressed soldiers who'd been lounging in the shade snapped into activity as we were brought in, four of them leveling rifles at our chests as their commander came out to interrogate us.

We showed him our passports, and Al pulled from his wallet some Spanish clippings about our trip from the newspapers in Panama and El Salvador. The captain studied them seriously, then broke into laughter, roaring and pulling our beards. His troops lowered their rifles and joined in, joking and shouting, *"Castroistas . . . ha, ha, Cuba . . . ha, ha . . . rojos."* When he stopped laughing, he tugged our beards again and explained that the Indians, having found us stalking through the jungle with so many weapons, and knowing that the only people in the country who wore beards were Communist guerrillas, had assumed we also were. Every loyal citizen in Guatemala, the captain told us, shaved every day so he wouldn't be mistaken for a rebel—and we might be well advised to do the same.

Since we liked our beards, and also the necks to which they were attached, we adopted a plan that would enable us to keep them both, we hoped. We unstrapped our machetes, put on our loudest, most touristy sports shirts, and unfurled our big American flag across the front of the Land Cruiser as we headed north.

For the next week, as we negotiated the rock-clogged rain-obscured cliff road through the notorious El Tapon landslide area out of Guatemala, as we drove north through the rugged mountains of

Chiapas, along the cow-crawling, donkey-detoured, burro-blocked roads of southern Mexico, through the pretty city of Oaxaca, festooned with colored lights for the celebration of Mexico's Independence Day, Al and I reviewed some of the hundreds of difficulties that had befallen us and turned our trip from an eight-month jaunt into an eighteen-month ordeal. We agreed on what they meant to us and what we wanted them to mean to those to whom we told our story.

We hoped we'd made it clear that our worst troubles had been the results of government policies and the personnel who enforced them, and that even where our difficulties were directly attributable to private citizens—like the Indians in Guatemala, or the robbers in Algiers, or the con-men in Alexandria, or the rioters in East Pakistan—those people were only reacting to a climate, whether of poverty or hatred or injustice, their governments had created.

Never on our trip did we meet people who disliked us or distrusted us as individuals; it was always because they had been taught to dislike or distrust members of different countries, different races, or different religions, or because we had blundered into disputes they were having with members of different countries, races, or religions. It was this universal intolerance that we found a far more forbidding barrier to world travel than the hottest desert or the roughest road.

Al and I also felt that, in view of all the disputes and hatreds boiling in all parts of the world, our expedition around it might be the last over land for many years. With Russia and China unwilling to permit land travel, there remains only a narrow corridor through which people can drive, and hostile conditions prevail in almost every country along that corridor. With fighting and hatred between India and Pakistan, guerrillas marauding in Thailand, the constant threat of war in the Middle East, the touchiness of Afghanistan, and the firm and absolute impossibility of driving across Burma, there is little hope, as we see it, of anyone being able, in the foreseeable future, to drive around the world.

And the situation is getting worse every year. Two months after we left Guatemala the newspapers reported that it was in a state of siege because of the conflict between the Communists and the military; and a month after that, Spain finally and fully lowered the boom on Gibraltar and put a complete stop to all traffic to the Rock; and a month after that the vital road between Jordan and Syria was cut and closed as they argued over policy against Israel; and the month after that it was announced that the situation in Thailand had become so serious that American helicopter crews were flying soldiers in to fight the guerrillas, and four months after that the hostility between the Arabs and Israel broke into a bloody war and the travel curtain fell across a quarter of the world from Morocco to the Great Syrian Desert.

No, it will be a long time before anyone else will be able to go in peace where we have gone and drive in safety where we have driven.

Finally we reached Mexico City and drove down Avenida Insurgentes toward the campgrounds in San Angel. Mexico City . . . with the snow-capped cone of 18,000 foot Popocatepetl volcano to the southeast . . . the magnificent Toltec pyramids of the Temple of the Sun and the Temple of the Moon to the north . . . the beautiful floating gardens of Xochimilco . . . the tree-lined Paseo de la Reforma, dominated by Maximilian's hilltop Chapultepec Castle . . . the Plaze de Toros, the largest bull ring in the world . . . the soaring Latino, the tallest building south of the Rio Grande . . . the Zocalo, a huge open square that can hold a million people. Mexico City. City of glass, concrete, mosaics, Aztec temples, Rivera murals. City of lights and color and gaiety.

We were getting organized at the camp when a black, chauffeur-driven Mercedes pulled in and two men jumped out. "Where have you boys been? We've been waiting for you for weeks." They introduced themselves: Ben Cooper, the manager, and Raul Tornell, the chairman of the board of directors of the Firestone Company of Mexico.

"We welcome you to our country," Raul said with a slight bow. "We have much planned, so let us get started. Mexico City awaits you."

It did, indeed. The newspapermen vied for exclusive interviews. The wire services filed stories on our trip which flashed around the world. Our Nielsen rating topped Jose Carson. Owners of taco stands besieged us for testimonials. Photographers dragged us to pose in front of every major building and monument in town. Firestone gave us a special decoration (based on the assumption that we'd make it back to New York) for being the first to ever drive around the world with one set of tires. One of Al's girlfriends flew down from Los Angeles to welcome him back. And one of mine came from Washington.

And then there were the parties. Endless parties, and feasts, and celebrations . . . my first dry martini in 18 months . . . wine . . . *paella* . . . Carta Blanca beer, the best in the world . . . *arroz con pollo* . . . tacos, tortas, tostadas, tamales . . . flamenco dancers . . . Spanish guitars . . . mariache bands . . . toasts and salutations . . . and everywhere the POP POP POP of exploding champagne corks as the celebrations went on and on.

After three days of this hero's welcome it was an effort to get back on the road. But we had to——we needed the rest.

We headed north toward the Rio Grande.

After we cleared the Mexican customs and immigration posts, we drove onto the long bridge that connects Nueva Laredo, Mexico, with Laredo, Texas, USA. Home at last. Home. The U.S.A. After 19 months.

Newsreel cameramen came racing down the bridge toward us. Chief Samuelson, the Toyota press agent, waved from the rail as he directed a photographer. And there was Asbury Nix from Trade Winds who'd flown down from Manawa (pop. 1,037) to welcome us back. And dozens of reporters. And a girlfriend of Al's from San Antonio.

The end of the bridge. The brick customs house with our flag flying proudly above it. The Stars and Stripes fluttered in the autumn breeze. I didn't think the sight would affect a seasoned old traveler, but I felt tears come to my eyes.

The gruff old guard looked at our car and camper, and I could see we'd be held up for hours with a customs inspection. But he broke into a smile and said, "Welcome home, boys," and waved us on.

As we drove out of Laredo, past a big Holiday Inn sign that said WELCOME HOME TRANS WORLD RECORD EXPEDITION, Chief Samuelson told us he'd arranged for us to go to the LBJ Ranch in Johnson City the next morning to present to the President the flag we had carried around the world.

When we reached San Antonio that night, I decided to phone my parents in California and tell them about our meeting with the President so they could watch it on TV. I'd last written them from Australia, and before that from Singapore, so my mother was sort of shocked to hear my voice.

"Where are you, Harold?" she said. She calls me Harold; that's why I ask everybody else to call me Steve.

"In Texas, mother. San Antonio."

"My goodness, Harold, what are you doing all the way out there? When are you coming to see us?"

"We're on our way to President Johnson's ranch, mother, to give him a flag we've carried with us around the world."

"That's nice. But you be careful, Harold, you hear? Don't go eating any of that rich barbecue they serve there. It'll give you an upset stomach. You hear?"

I heard, and so did Al who was holding his stomach laughing while trying to scribble notes on a piece of paper. "Great!" he said when I'd hung up. "Wait until I tell the newspapers. The world traveler returns after two years of living on fried baby mice and live monkey brains, and his mother tells him not to eat any charcoal broiled steak. My hero."

The States rolled by us in a blur of new interstate highways, the shoulders of which were better than most of the roads we'd driven on in other parts of the world. They zoomed by in a flash of Mustangs, miniskirts, mods and rockers, go-go girls, James Bond movie marquees, discotheques, Tijuana Brass and Rolling Stones and Herman's Hermits on the radio, LSD headlines and Great Society news, Head Start and heads up. How many, how vast, how amazing the changes had been in two years. No Marco Polo returning from twenty-three years abroad could have been more astounded than we were by the changes at home, for America, our once staid and complacent America, had, in two breathless years, become an alert, alive, aware, moving, modern, mind-expanding, turned on, tuned in, switched on, lit up teeny-bopper Go-Go Land.

Our trip across it passed in a blinding of flashbulbs and a hoarseness of interviews . . . Laredo, where we were welcomed home . . . San Antonio, where they posed us in front of the Alamo . . . Johnson City, where we missed LBJ by half an hour . . . Austin, where they photographed us in front of the Texas University tower . . . Dallas, where they put us on display at the Texas State Fair . . . Waco, where the cameramen invaded us at five in the morning because they wanted authentic footage of what it's like to wake up in a camper, and instead got some authentic footage on what it's like to be thrown out of a camper . . . Bartlesville . . . Durand, where the Oklahoma State Police radio operator tipped off the local news hawk that two characters with beards on their chins, and a set of Mexican bull horns on their car, and a map of the world on their trailer were camped behind the barracks . . . Tulsa, where the papers devoted most of the lengthy space they gave us to acclaiming the feats of our winch which had been manufactured right there in the "oil equipment capital of the world" . . . Chanute . . . Emporia . . . Kansas City, where we kept getting lost . . . St. Louis, where they photographed us beneath the magnificent new Arch, the gateway to the west . . . Independence, where we stopped to pay our respects to President Truman . . . Springfield, where the odometer passed 41,500 and Al lost a bet we'd made on our final mileage . . . Chicago, where Al introduced me to so many cute Playmates and bunnies he knew from when he'd been an editor of *Playboy* that I almost forgot we still had an expedition to finish . . . Toledo . . . Cleveland . . . Akron, where Raymond Firestone and half the Firestone board of directors were on hand to congratulate us . . . Bridgeville, where I was born and to which I hadn't been back in 18 years . . . Pittsburgh, which we passed one rainy night . . . the Pennsylvania Turnpike . . . and just 350 more miles to go . . . when disaster overtook us.

It began quietly and without warning. As we were driving along the turnpike the engine suddenly sputtered and conked out. We pulled off the turnpike and checked the gas gauge: EMPTY. We grabbed one of the spare gas cans we carried for just such emergencies, poured five gallons in, and took off.

We made about 50 yards before the engine died again, dead, right in the middle of the turnpike. With cars zooming by us at 70 miles an hour, we pushed the Land Cruiser to the side of the road and tried to get it started. For three hours we tried to get it started. The faithful Land Cruiser, which had carried us 99/100ths of the way around the world with no more trouble than a slight drip from the oil pan and a short in the electrical system, had given up on us a day's drive out of New York. We camped by the roadside and tried to get to sleep.

By morning's light, we found the trouble: flakes of red paint clogging the carburetor. They must have fallen into the gas tank when we'd poured in the spare can. We took the fuel filter and carb apart and cleaned them, and made another 50 yards before the engine died again. Again, thick red paint flakes in the carburetor. We cleaned it again, and it clogged again. Reluctant as I was to use it—for we were rather proud of having driven completely around the world with every piece of our original engine (except the points and plugs, of course) still in place and functioning—I unpacked our spare carburetor.

While I screwed it on, Al trotted off into the woods to answer a call of nature. When I thought I had the carburetor on tight, I pumped the accelerator and turned the key. A stream of gasoline shot out of the carburetor and ignited. In seconds the engine was in flames. Fire was pouring under the dashboard, crawling along the wires, leaping over the engine block, lapping at the hood, racing toward the gas tank.

I called to Al in the woods, and he shouted back that he was all right and had remembered to take paper.

I shouted and asked him where the hell our fire extinguisher had disappeared to, and he shouted back that he'd traded it to some Indians in Chichicastenango for a dozen fertility napkins.

Just then a truck pulled off the turnpike. The driver jumped down from the cab with a fire extinguisher and emptied it onto our engine, dousing the flame. He took a quick look to make sure the fire was completely out and drove away without saying a word just as Al came running out of the woods, hiking up his pants.

Two minutes later a Pennsylvania State Police car pulled up. The trooper got out, looked at us, and stopped short. He ducked back into his car and grabbed the radio mike. Maybe there were Castro guerrillas in Ohio?

He finished his message and came out after a minute. "Some fire you boys must've had. Motorist phoned it in." He took a look at the blackened engine, then came back to us. "I recognized you fellas from the TV last night. Come all around the world, haven't you? I meet all the celebrities when they have trouble. Shame this happened to you. I wonder if you'd let me have your autographs? For my kids, you know." It was the first time a state trooper had ever asked me to sign anything that cost less than fifteen dollars; I quickly obliged.

"I just radioed the tow truck and the stringer for United Press. They should be here in a few minutes. We work together on all the big ones. Same reporter did the story when I arrested that actress for drunken driving—you must have read about that—and he also did the story when——"

In fifteen minutes the news was clicking over the wires: TRANS WORLD RECORD EXPEDITION CATCHES FIRE ON PENNSYLVANIA TURN-PIKE . . ."

The tow truck pulled us four miles to the exit and a service station at Breezewood, Pa. They were four shame-faced miles for us, the first of 42,000 by land we hadn't driven under our own power, the first miles in 19 months through 32 countries that we hadn't done on our own.

"You know, Steve," Al was saying four days later, on October 25, 1966, as he drove our repaired Land Cruiser down Fifth Avenue behind a honking motorcade toward the finish line, "my computations show that, since we put in that new carb and gas line in Breezewood, we've been getting 16.3 miles to the gallon, which means we've increased gas consumption economy by a factor of 1.9 over 14.4, which is equivalent to 13.215 per cent which——" I barely heard him. I was lost in thought, reminiscing about all the things, good and bad, painful and wonderful, that had happened to us since the last time we'd driven down the same street. I thought of Fifth Avenue nineteen months before, and all the people who'd told us it couldn't be done.

"——means that, for 42,252 miles, at an average world price, assuming we'd bought all our SuperMexolina in Mexico at the D.F. price, and assuming——" I thought of our 581 days around the world, and the suns and moons and storms and heat of 581 days. "——currency conversion in India and Egypt at the fair market rate of exchange, of 12.6 cents a litre, and multiplying that by 3.85 litres per gallon——" The friends and foes and hopes and struggles and loves and labors of 581 days.

Al pulled to a halt in front of the library steps from which we'd started so many months before. We were lost in a jumble of TV trucks. Cameras. Newspaper cars. A mob of photographers. Reporters. Microphones. New York! Fifth Avenue! The library! The very spot! We were back! We had made it!! The crowd cheered. The policemen whistled. Friends threw confetti. Flashbulbs exploded. The reporters surged forward. And there, coming through the crowd, was Sandy Krinski, the Krinsk of the cables, smiling warmly, his hand extended.

"Congratulations," he said. "It's amazing. Absolutely amazing."

"You mean that we made it?"

"No, that you found a parking place in New York."

We were home.